COMPUTATION, DYNAMICS, *and* COGNITION

COMPUTATION, DYNAMICS, *and* COGNITION

MARCO GIUNTI

New York Oxford
Oxford University Press
1997

Oxford University Press

Oxford New York
Athens Auckland Bangkok Bogota Bombay Buenos Aires
Calcutta Cape Town Dar es Salaam Delhi Florence Hong Kong
Instanbul Karachi Kuala Lumpur Madras Madrid Melbourne
Mexico City Nairobi Paris Singapore Taipei Tokyo Toronto

and associated companies in
Berlin Ibadan

Published by Oxford University Press, Inc.
198 Madison Avenue, New York, New York 10016

Library of Congress Cataloging-in-Publication Data
Giunti, Marco.
Computation, dynamics, and cognition / Marco Giunti.
p. cm.
Includes bibliographical references and index.
ISBN 0-19-509009-8
1. Cognition—Mathematical models. 2. Cognition—Simulation methods.
3. Cognition—Data processing. 4. Human information processing. I. Title.
BF311.G535 1997
153—dc20 96-12616

9 8 7 6 5 4 3 2 1

Printed in the United States of America
on acid-free paper

For

Cilla, Massimo, Roberta, and Fabiana

Acknowledgments

This book grew out of my doctoral dissertation and my later work on dynamics and cognition. My greatest debt is to John Winnie, who provided suggestions, sharp criticisms, and continuous encouragement during the whole advancement of my dissertation project. Noretta Koertge supervised my earlier studies in the philosophy of science. What I learned from her about scientific problems, explanation, and discovery was the basis for many of the ideas of chapter 3. Michael Dunn introduced me to the mysteries of computation theory and provided valuable advice concerning chapter 2. Several discussions and exchanges with Tim van Gelder prompted me to give chapters 3 and 4 their present form. Finally, I also thank Linda Wessels and all the participants of the Blunderbuss group at Indiana University: Kevin Korb, Osvaldo Pessoa, Raymundo Morado, Yu-Houng Houng, David Chalmers, Gordon Beavers, Gary Curtis, and John Ritner.

Firenze, Italy M.G.
February 1996

Introduction

This book addresses a broad range of questions that belong to three different fields: computation theory, general philosophy of science, and philosophy of cognitive science. The first two chapters deal with foundational issues in computation theory. The third chapter analyzes a particular type of scientific explanation, which I call a Galilean explanation. The fourth chapter proposes a new view of the aims and methods of cognitive science. I will highlight the main ideas of each chapter and explain how the specific investigations are internally related to form an organized body.

From the methodological point of view, a single concept unifies the treatment of all specific problems. This basic concept is that of a mathematical dynamical system. Given the importance of this concept, it is useful to briefly introduce it here in an informal manner. A *real* dynamical system is any real system that changes over time. Therefore, since any real system can be thought to change in time (in some respect), *any* real system is a real dynamical system. A *mathematical* dynamical system, on the other hand, is an abstract mathematical structure that can be used to describe the change of a real system as an evolution through a series of states. If the evolution of the real system is deterministic, that is, if the state at any future time is determined by the state at the present time, then the abstract mathematical structure consists of three elements (see chapter 1, definition 1). The first element is a set T that represents time. T may be either the reals, the rationals, the integers, or the nonnegative portions of these structures. Depending on the choice of T, then, time is represented as continuous, dense, or discrete. The second element is a nonempty set M that represents all possible states through which the system can evolve; M is called the *state space* (or sometimes the *phase space*) of the system. The third element is a set of functions $\{g^t\}$ that tells us the state of the system at any instant t provided that we know the initial state; each function in $\{g^t\}$ is called a *state transition* (or a *t-advance*) of the system. For example, if the initial state is $x \in M$, the state at time t is given by $g^t(x)$, the state at time $u > t$ is given by $g^u(x)$, and so on. The functions in the set $\{g^t\}$ must only satisfy two conditions. First, the function g^0 must take each state to itself. For, if the initial state is x, the state $g^0(x)$ at time 0 obviously is x itself. Second, the composition of any two functions g^t and g^w must be equal to the function g^{t+w}. For, given an arbitrary initial state x, the state $g^{t+w}(x)$ reached at time $t + w$ can always be considered as the result of two successive state transitions, the first from state x to state $g^t(x)$, and the second from state $g^t(x)$ to state $g^w(g^t(x))$.

With regard to the content, each chapter can be considered as a separate work on a specific subject. However, the first three chapters also provide the conceptual framework for the methodological analysis of cognitive science that is developed in the last chapter.

The general thesis of chapter 1 is that a dynamical viewpoint allows us to better understand some important foundational issues of computation theory. Computation theory studies a family of abstract mechanisms that are typically used to compute or recognize numeric functions, sets of numbers, or numbers. These devices can be divided into two broad categories: automata (or machines) and systems of rules for symbol manipulation. I call any device studied by computation theory a *computational system*. The main goal of chapter 1 is to formulate a rigorous definition of this intuitive concept.

Dynamical systems theory provides the natural mathematical framework for carrying out this analytical task. Dynamical systems theory is traditionally concerned with those mathematical dynamical systems that arise from the study of differential (or difference) equations. As mentioned, it is, however, possible to define a mathematical dynamical system in such a way that it captures the idea of an arbitrary deterministic system. Once this definition is adopted, it is quite obvious that all known computational devices are mathematical dynamical systems, and looking at them in this light makes it possible to analyze the concept of computational system in a completely general and natural way.

The definition of a computational system that I propose in the first chapter employs the concept of *Turing computability*. In chapter 2, however, I will show that this concept is not absolute, but instead depends on the relational structure of the support on which Turing machines operate. Ordinary Turing machines operate on a linear tape divided into a countably infinite number of adjacent squares. But one can also think of Turing machines that operate on different supports. At the end of chapter 2, I will propose a new definition of a computational system that takes into account the relativity of the concept of Turing computability.

As mentioned, the main goal of chapter 3 is to analyze a particular type of scientific explanation, which I call a Galilean explanation. This analysis is based on a more general view of scientific explanation according to which *scientific* explanations are obtained by studying *models* of real systems. Galilean explanations are a particular type of scientific explanations, for they are based on the study of models of a special type. I call a model of this special type a *Galilean model of a real system*.

Galilean models are perhaps the most widespread in science. I have in mind here a traditional way of using mathematical dynamical systems to describe the change of real systems. Simple examples of this type of model can be found in many elementary books on differential or difference equations, and they cover such different fields as mechanics, electrodynamics, chemistry, population dynamics, and engineering. The first five sections of chapter 3 explain what I mean, exactly, by a Galilean model of a real system. The remaining sections analyze how one can in fact obtain explanations based on Galilean models.

I take a *cognitive system* to be any real system that has some cognitive property. Note that this definition includes both natural systems such as humans and other animals, and artificial devices such as robots, implementations of AI (artificial intelligence) programs, some implementations of neural networks, and so on. Focusing on what all cognitive systems have in common, we can state a very general but nonetheless interesting thesis: *all* cognitive systems are dynamical systems. Chapter 4 explains what this thesis means and why it is (relatively) uncontroversial. It will become clear that this thesis is a basic methodological assumption that underlies practically all current research in cognitive science.

Chapter 4 also contrasts two styles of scientific explanation of cognition: computational and dynamical. Computational explanations are characterized by the use of concepts drawn from computation theory, while dynamical explanations employ the conceptual apparatus of dynamical systems theory.

The last section of chapter 4 explores the possibility that scientific explanations of cognition might be based on Galilean models of cognitive systems. Most cognitive scientists have not yet considered this possibility. The goals of this section are (1) to contrast my proposal with the current modeling practice in cognitive science, (2) to make clear its potential benefits, and (3) to indicate possible ways to implement it.

Contents

COMPUTATION, DYNAMICS, *and* COGNITION

ONE

Mathematical Dynamical Systems and Computational Systems

1 Introduction

The main thesis of this chapter is that a dynamical viewpoint allows us to better understand some important foundational issues of computation theory. Effective procedures are traditionally studied from two different but complementary points of view. The first approach is concerned with individuating those numeric functions that are effectively calculable. This approach reached its systematization with the theory of the recursive functions (Gödel, Church, Kleene). This theory is not directly concerned with computing devices or computations. Rather, the effective calculability of a recursive function is guaranteed by the algorithmic nature of its definition.

In contrast, the second approach focuses on a family of abstract mechanisms, which are then typically used to compute or recognize numeric functions, sets of numbers, or numbers. These devices can be divided into two broad categories: automata or machines (Turing and Post), and systems of rules for symbol manipulation (Post). The mechanisms that have been studied include:

a. Automata or Machines

1. gate-nets and McCulloch-Pitts nets
2. finite automata (Mealy and Moore machines)

3. push-down automata
4. stack automata
5. Turing machines
6. register machines
7. Wang machines
8. cellular automata

b. Systems of Rules

9. monogenic production systems in general
10. monogenic Post canonical systems
11. monogenic Post normal systems
12. tag systems.

I call any device studied by computation theory a *computational system*. Computation theory is traditionally interested in studying the relations between each type of computational system and the others, and in establishing what class of numeric functions each type can compute. Accordingly, one proves two kinds of theorem: (1) that systems of a given type emulate systems of another type[1] (examples: Turing machines emulate register machines and cellular automata; cellular automata emulate Turing machines, etc.), and (2) that a certain type of system is complete relative to the class of the (partial) recursive functions or, in other words, that this type of system can compute all and only the (partial) recursive functions (examples of complete systems: Turing machines, register machines, cellular automata, tag systems, etc.).

All different types of computational systems have much in common. Nevertheless, it is not at all clear exactly which properties these mechanisms share. The accepted view is that a computational system is a deterministic system that evolves in discrete time steps and can always be described in an effective way. Intuitively, this means that the constitution and operations of the system are purely mechanical or that the system can always be identified with an idealized machine. While this informal characterization is certainly useful, for it conveys a concept that delimits the field of standard computation theory (see figure 1-1),[2] it is clear that this concept is not sufficiently rigorous. A precise definition of a computational system would give us a deeper, more unified insight into the whole field of computation theory and its applications.

As mentioned, one of the typical theorems of computation theory consists in showing that, for each device of a first type, there is a device of a second type that is able to emulate the first device. If we look at

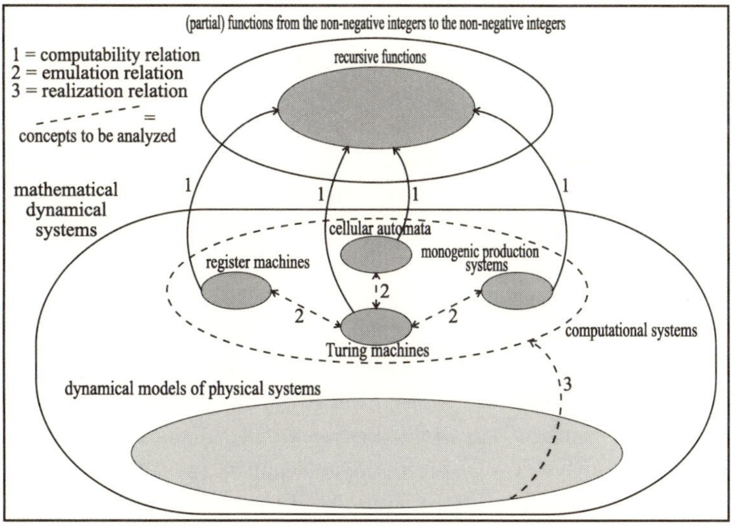

FIGURE 1-1 Standard computation theory.

several instances of these proofs, we discover two things. First, in many cases, the emulation relation is not formally defined. Second, it is not clear whether the relation which is proved to hold in different cases is in fact the same relation. For example, it can be proved that cellular automata emulate Turing machines and that, conversely, Turing machines emulate cellular automata. The emulation relation between cellular automata and Turing machines, however, has not been adequately defined,[3] and it turns out that cellular automata emulate Turing machines in a way that is prima facie different from the way Turing machines emulate cellular automata.[4] The emulation relation relation is also often invoked to introduce the concept of a *virtual system*, in which it is claimed that, whenever a computational system MDS_1 emulates a second computational system MDS_2, we can define a third system MDS_3 in terms of MDS_1 such that MDS_3 turns out to be essentially the same system as MDS_2. The system MDS_3 is called a virtual system, and this general example is usually given to explain how a machine with a certain computational architecture can implement a different architecture. However, since no general concept of emulation is defined, no theorem that ensures the existence of a virtual system can be proved.

We encounter a third foundational problem when we consider the relation between the abstract mechanisms studied by computation theory and the models of physical systems that supposedly realize them. This relation is never explicitly defined, but several facts about it are usually assumed. For example, it is generally believed that computational systems are in principle realizable by dynamical models of physical systems.[5] The informal account of how a dynamical model of a physical system would realize a computational system typically goes like this: We identify some of the states of the dynamical model of the physical system with the states of the computational system, so that each transition between computational states corresponds to a transition between physical states. This is a very plausible idea, but a simple observation shows that it needs some refinement. Many dynamical models of physical systems are reversible. In reversible dynamical models no state transition function can take two different states to the same state, while this is exactly what happens in most computational systems. Therefore, transitions between computational states cannot in general be identified with transitions between physical states. This observation thus suggests that a formal analysis of the realization relation is badly needed (unless we are willing to accept that most computational systems are not in principle realizable by reversible dynamical models of physical systems).

In this chapter, I will give an explication of the three concepts of *computational system*, *emulation*, and *realization*. Dynamical systems theory provides the natural mathematical framework for carrying out this analytical task. Cellular automata have already been fruitfully studied from this point of view (Wolfram 1983a, 1984c; Farmer, Toffoli, and Wolfram 1984; Wolfram, ed. 1986). However, since all computational systems are deterministic systems, they all fall under the scope of dynamical system theory. This discipline is traditionally concerned with those mathematical dynamical systems that arise from the study of differential (or difference) equations. It is, however, possible to define a mathematical dynamical system in such a way that it captures the idea of an arbitrary deterministic system. Once this definition is adopted, it is obvious that all known computational devices are mathematical dynamical systems, and looking at them in this light makes it possible to analyze the concepts of computational system, emulation, and realization in a general manner.

Section 2 states the definition of a *mathematical dynamical system* and introduces the concept of a *cascade*, that is, a mathematical dynamical system with discrete time. This is a crucial concept, for I will later define a computational system as a cascade that can be described in an effective way.

Section 3 carries out the analysis of the concept of a *computational system*. I introduce first the relation of *isomorphism* between mathematical dynamical systems, and I then define computational systems by means of this relation, of the concept of a cascade, and of the concept of Turing computability.

Section 4 analyzes the *emulation* relation and proves that this relation is a quasi-ordering (reflexive and transitive) on the set of all mathematical dynamical systems.

Section 5 introduces the distinction between reversible and irreversible systems and studies the possible types of orbits and state transitions in both kinds of system. I define three mutually exclusive and exhaustive classes of irreversible systems: *logically reversible*, *weakly irreversible*, and *strongly irreversible*. Strongly irreversible systems are the only systems with merging orbits, and many computational systems are in this class.

These results set the stage for two theorems found in section 6. The first theorem and the definition of the emulation relation entail the important consequence that all universal computational systems are strongly irreversible. An interesting consequence of the second theorem is that a universal computational system has at least four different types of orbits: periodic, eventually periodic, aperiodic, and merging. The second theorem also shows that the realization relation cannot be identified with the concept of emulation. I then turn to the formal analysis of the realization relation, and I prove that this relation is reflexive and transitive.

In section 7, I prove two general results. I first show that, whenever a mathematical dynamical system MDS_1 either emulates or realizes a second system MDS_2, it is possible to define a third system MDS_3 by means of the states and the state transitions of MDS_1, and that MDS_3 turns out to be isomorphic to MDS_2. For this reason, I propose to identify MDS_3 with the concept of a *virtual system*. Finally, I prove that, given an arbitrary irreversible system *MDS*, it is always possible to find a corresponding reversible system that realizes *MDS*. An immediate and important consequence of this theorem is the existence of reversible universal systems.[6]

2 Mathematical dynamical systems

A *real dynamical system* is any real system that changes over time. Therefore, since any real system can be thought to change in time (in some respect), *any* real system is a real dynamical system. A *mathematical* dynamical system, on the other hand, is an abstract mathematical structure that can be used to describe the change of a real system as an evolution through a series of states. If the evolution of the real system is deterministic, that is, if the state at any future time is determined by the state at the present time, then the abstract mathematical structure consists of three elements. The first element is a set T that represents time. T may be either the reals, the rationals, the integers, or the nonnegative portions of these structures. Depending on the choice of T, then, time will be represented as continuous, dense, or discrete. The second element is a nonempty set M that represents all possible states through which the system can evolve; M is called the *state space* (or sometimes the *phase space*) of the system. The third element is a set of functions $\{g^t\}$ that tells us the state of the system at any instant t provided we know the initial state; each function in $\{g^t\}$ is called a *state transition* (or a *t-advance*) of the system. For example, if the initial state is $x \in M$, then the state at time t is given by $g^t(x)$, the state at time $u > t$ is given by $g^u(x)$, etc. The functions in the set $\{g^t\}$ must only satisfy two conditions. First, the function g^0 must be reflexive; that is, if the initial state is x, the state $g^0(x)$ at time 0 is x itself. Second, the composition of any two functions g^t and g^w must be equal to the function g^{t+w}; that is, given an arbitrary initial state x, the state $g^{t+w}(x)$ reached at time $t + w$ can always be considered as the result of two successive state transitions, the first from state x to state $g^t(x)$, and the second from state $g^t(x)$ to state $g^w(g^t(x))$ (see figure 1-2). All these properties are expressed by definition 1.

DEFINITION 1 *(mathematical dynamical systems)*
MDS = $\langle$T, M, $\{g^t\}\rangle$ *is a mathematical dynamical system if and only if:*

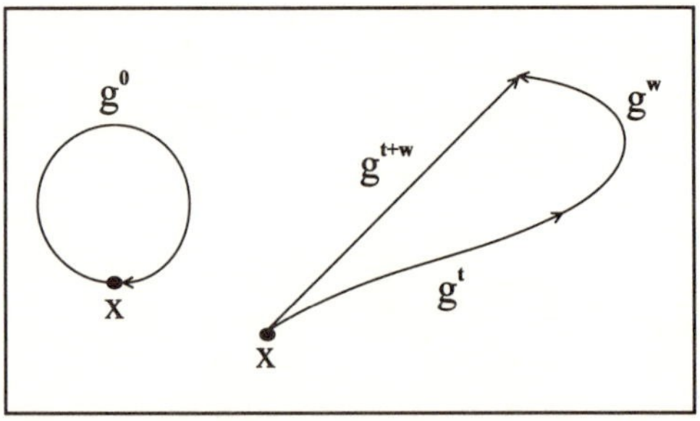

FIGURE 1-2 Mathematical dynamical systems. MDS = $\langle T, M, \{g^t\}\rangle$. For any t, g^t is a function from M to M. If, at time 0, MDS is in state x, then, at time t, MDS is in state $g^t(x)$.

1. T *is either* Z, Z^+, Q, Q^+, R, *or* R^+, *where* Z, Q, *and* R *are, respectively, the integers, the rationals, and the reals, and* Z^+, Q^+, *and* R^+, *are the nonnegative integers, rationals, and reals;*
2. M *is a nonempty set;*
3. *for any* $t \in T$, g^t *is a function from* M *to* M, *and the set* $\{g^t\}$ *satisfies:*
   a. g^0 *is the identity function on* M*;*
   b. $g^{t+w} = g^t \circ g^w$ *(*$\circ$ *is the composition operation and* g^t *is applied first).*

This definition is, essentially, the one given by Arnold (1977, p. 4); see also Szlensk (1984). The only difference between my definition and Arnold's is that I allow time (T) to be either R, R^+, Q, Q^+, Z, or Z^+, while Arnold considers only the case $T = R$. Traditionally, dynamical system theory is concerned with those mathematical dynamical systems that arise from the study of differential (or difference) equations. As a consequence, the state space of these systems is not a bare set, but has a richer structure (a differentiable manifold or, at least, a metric space). As Arnold makes clear, however, this further structure is not relevant if we are interested in a formal characterization of *any* possible deterministic system.

An important subclass of the mathematical dynamical systems is that of all systems with discrete time. Any such system is called a *cascade* (figure 1-3). More precisely, a mathematical dynamical system $\langle T, M, \{g^t\}\rangle$ is a cascade if and only if T is equal to the nonnegative integers (or to the integers).

$$\text{if } T = Z^+, \text{ then } g^t(x) = \underbrace{g^1(g^1(\ldots g^1}_{\text{t times}}(x)\ldots))$$

$$\text{if } T = Z, \text{ then } g^t(x) = \underbrace{g^1(g^1(\ldots g^1}_{\text{t times}}(x)\ldots)) \text{ and}$$

$$g^{-t}(x) = \underbrace{g^{-1}(g^{-1}(\ldots g^{-1}}_{\text{t times}}(x)\ldots))$$

FIGURE 1-3 Cascades. MDS = $\langle T, M, \{g^t\}\rangle$. T = Z^+ or Z. For any t, g^t is a function from M to M.

To obtain a cascade, we may start from any nonempty set M and any function $g: M \to M$. We then set T equal to the nonnegative integers, and we define the state transitions $\{g^t\}$ as follows: g^0 = the identity function on M and, for any $x \in M$, $g^{t+1}(x) = g(g^t(x))$. In other words, we generate an arbitrary state transition g^t $(t > 0)$ by iterating t times the function g (note that $g^1 = g$).

If we decide to take T equal to the integers, we may instead start from any nonempty set M and any bijection $g: M \to M$. We then define the state transitions $\{g^t\}$ as follows: g^0 = the identity function on M; for any $x \in M$, $g^{t+1}(x) = g(g^t(x))$ and $g^t(x) = g^{-1}(g^{t+1}(x))$, where g^{-1} is the inverse of $g = g^1$. That is, we generate a positive state transition g^t $(t > 0)$ by iterating t times the function g, and we generate a negative state transition g^{-t} by iterating t times the inverse of g.

Conversely, if $\langle T, M, \{g^t\}\rangle$ is an arbitrary cascade, then each positive state transition g^t $(t > 0)$ is generated by iterating t times g^1, and a negative state transition g^{-t} is generated by iterating t times g^{-1}.

Given an arbitrary mathematical dynamical system $MDS = \langle T, M, \{g^t\}\rangle$ and an arbitrary state $x \in M$, let us consider the function $g^x: T \to M$ defined by $g^x(t) = g^t(x)$. This function represents the time evolution of the state of the system when the state at time 0 is x. For this reason, the function g^x is called a *state evolution* (or a *motion*) of the system. The image of g^x is called the *orbit* of x, which I abbreviate by $orb(x)$. The *phase portrait* of the system is the set of all orbits. It is easy to verify that definition 1 entails the following properties:

THEOREM 1 *(some basic properties of mathematical dynamical systems)*

If $\mathrm{T} = \mathrm{Z}$, Q, *or* R, *then:*

1. *$\{\mathrm{g}^\mathrm{t}\}$ is a commutative group*[7] *with respect to the composition operation* $\circ$. *The unity is* g^0 *and, for any* $\mathrm{t} \in \mathrm{T}$, *the inverse of* g^t *relative to* $\circ$ *is* $\mathrm{g}^{-\mathrm{t}}$;
2. *for any* $\mathrm{t} \in \mathrm{T}$, g^t *is a bijection; therefore,* $(\mathrm{g}^\mathrm{t})^{-1}: \mathrm{M} \to \mathrm{M}$ *(the inverse function of* g^t*) exists, and* $(\mathrm{g}^\mathrm{t})^{-1} = \mathrm{g}^{-\mathrm{t}}$;
3. *for any* $\mathrm{x} \in \mathrm{M}$, *there is exactly one orbit that passes through* x; *for any* $\mathrm{t} \in \mathrm{T}$, *and any* $\mathrm{x} \in \mathrm{M}$, *there is exactly one state evolution* g^z *such that* $\mathrm{g}^\mathrm{z}(\mathrm{t}) = \mathrm{x}$ *(where* $\mathrm{z} = \mathrm{g}^{-\mathrm{t}}(\mathrm{x})$*).*

If $\mathrm{T} = \mathrm{Z}^+$, Q^+, *or* R^+, *then:*

4. *$\{\mathrm{g}^\mathrm{t}\}$ is a commutative monoid*[8] *with respect to the composition operation* $\circ$, *and the unity is* g^0;
5. *for any* $\mathrm{x}, \mathrm{y}, \mathrm{z} \in \mathrm{M}$, *for any* $\mathrm{t}, \mathrm{w} \in \mathrm{T}$, *if* $\mathrm{g}^\mathrm{t}(\mathrm{x}) = \mathrm{g}^\mathrm{w}(\mathrm{y}) = \mathrm{z}$, *then* $\mathrm{orb}(\mathrm{z}) \subseteq \mathrm{orb}(\mathrm{x})$ *and* $\mathrm{orb}(\mathrm{z}) \subseteq \mathrm{orb}(\mathrm{y})$.[9]

PROOF. All these properties are straightforward consequences of definition 1.

q.e.d.

Before concluding this section let us briefly consider two classic examples of mathematical dynamical systems. The first is the system with continuous time specified by Galileo's laws for the vertical position and velocity of a free-falling body. The second is the family of cascades generated by the logistic function.

EXAMPLE 1 (a mathematical dynamical system with continuous time)

Let us consider Galileo's laws for the vertical position and velocity of a falling body: $S(t) = s + vt + (1/2)\mathbf{c}t^2$ and $V(t) = v + \mathbf{c}t$, where s and v are, respectively, the vertical position and velocity of the falling body at time 0, and $\mathbf{c}$ is a constant (the acceleration due to gravity). If we identify the state of a falling body with the values of its vertical position and velocity, these two laws specify a mathematical dynamical system: $MDS_1 = \langle T, S \times V, \{g^t\}\rangle$, where $T = S = V = R$, and each state transition g^t is defined by $g^t(s, v) = \langle s + vt + (1/2)\mathbf{c}t^2, v + \mathbf{c}t\rangle$.

Let us now verify that conditions (*3a*) and (*3b*) of definition 1 hold. We must prove (a) $g^0(s, v) = \langle s, v\rangle$, and (b) $g^{t+w}(s, v) = g^w(g^t(s, v))$. By the definition of g^0, $g^0(s, v) = \langle s + v0 + (1/2)\mathbf{c}0, v + \mathbf{c}0\rangle = \langle s, v\rangle$. Therefore, (*a*) holds. By the definition of the set of state transitions $\{g^t\}$, $g^{t+w}(s, v) = \langle s + v(t + w) + (1/2)\mathbf{c}(t + w)^2, v + \mathbf{c}(t + w)\rangle = \langle s + v(t + w) + (1/2)\mathbf{c}(t^2 + 2tw + w^2), v + \mathbf{c}(t + w)\rangle = \langle s + vt + (1/2)\mathbf{c}t^2 + vw + \mathbf{c}tw + (1/2)\mathbf{c}w^2, v + \mathbf{c}(t + w)\rangle = \langle s + vt + (1/2)\mathbf{c}t^2 + (v + \mathbf{c}t)w + (1/2)\mathbf{c}w^2, v + \mathbf{c}t + \mathbf{c}w\rangle = g^w(s + vt + (1/2)\mathbf{c}t^2, v + \mathbf{c}t) = g^w(g^t(s, v))$. Therefore, (*b*) also holds.

EXAMPLE 2 (a family of mathematical dynamical systems with discrete time)

A family of simple cascades on R that leads to an extremely complex dynamical behavior is the one generated by the logistic function. Here $T = Z^+$, $M = R$, and $g: M \to M$ is defined by $g(x) = \mathbf{a}x(1 - x)$, where $\mathbf{a}$ is an arbitrary constant. For example, the cascade determined by the value $\mathbf{a} = 4$ displays chaotic behavior. If $0 < x < 0.5$ or $0.5 < x < 1$, the orbit of x almost completely fills up the unit interval.[10]

3 Computational systems

An important problem concerning mathematical dynamical systems consists in determining whether two systems are equivalent from the point of view of their dynamical behavior. Intuitively, this will be the case if there is a one-to-one mapping between the states of the two systems so that each state transition of one system will correspond, through this mapping, to a state transition of the other (and conversely). We can make this idea precise as follows:

DEFINITION 2 *(isomorphic mathematical dynamical systems)*
MDS_1 *is isomorphic to* MDS_2 *if and only if:*

1. $MDS_1 = \langle T, M_1, \{h^t\}\rangle$ *and* $MDS_2 = \langle T, M_2, \{g^t\}\rangle$ *are mathematical dynamical systems;*
2. *there is* $f: M_2 \rightarrow M_1$ *such that* f *is a bijection and, for any* $t \in T$, *for any* $x \in M_2$, $f(g^t(x)) = h^t(f(x))$.

It is easy to verify that the isomorphism just defined is an equivalence relation on the set of all mathematical dynamical systems (theorem 2). This set is thus divided into equivalence classes, and any two systems in each of these classes can be taken to be the same system as far as their dynamical behavior is concerned (see figure 1-4).

THEOREM 2
The relation of isomorphism is an equivalence relation on the set of all mathematical dynamical systems.

PROOF. See the appendix.

Each computational system is a special type of mathematical dynamical system, and recognizing this fact allows us to better under-

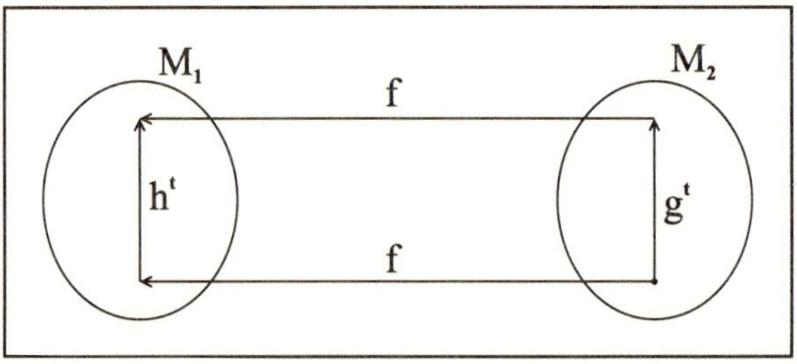

FIGURE 1-4 Isomorphic systems. $MDS_1 = \langle T, M_1, \{h^t\}\rangle$. $MDS_2 = \langle T, M_2, \{g^t\}\rangle$. f is a bijection from M_2 to M_1.

stand many important properties of computational systems. As a first confirmation of this thesis, I will show that any Turing machine can be naturally identified with two different cascades which, however, turn out to be isomorphic.

A Turing machine is an ideal mechanism that evolves in discrete time steps. This mechanism is usually pictured as having three parts. First, a *tape* divided into a countably infinite number of adjacent squares. Each square contains exactly one symbol taken from a finite alphabet $\{a_j\}$. The first symbol of the alphabet a_0 is usually identified with a special symbol, the *blank*, also indicated by b. Only a *finite number* of squares may contain nonblank symbols. All the other squares must contain the blank. Second, a *head* which is located on a square of the tape and can perform three different operations: write a symbol on that square, move to the adjacent square to the right, or move to the adjacent square to the left. Third, a *control unit* which, at any time step, is in exactly one of a finite number of internal states $\{q_i\}$. The behavior of the machine is specified by a *set of instructions*, which are conditionals of the form: if the internal state is q_i, and the symbol on the square where the head is located is a_j, write symbol a_k on this square (move one square to the right, move one square to the left) and change internal state to q_l. Each instruction can thus be written as a *quadruple* of one of the three types: $q_i a_j a_k q_l$, $q_i a_j R q_l$, $q_i a_j L q_l$, where R and L stand, respectively, for "move to the right" and "move to the left." The only requirement that the set of quadruples must satisfy is that it be consistent, in the sense that this set cannot contain any two conflicting instructions, that is, two different quadruples that begin with the same ⟨*internal state, symbol*⟩ pair.

Given this standard description of an arbitrary Turing machine, we see that this ideal mechanism can in fact be identified with a mathematical dynamical system $MDS_1 = \langle T, M_1, \{h^t\}\rangle$. Since a Turing machine evolves in discrete time steps, we may take the time set T to be the set of nonnegative integers. Since the future behavior of the machine is determined when the content of the tape, the position of the head, and the internal state of the control unit are fixed, we may take the state space M_1 to be the set of all triples ⟨*tape content, head position, internal state*⟩. And, finally, the set of state transitions $\{h^t\}$ is determined by the set of quadruples of the machine. To see this point, first note that the set of quadruples tells us how the state of the machine changes after *one* time step. That is, the set of quadruples defines the state transition h^1. We then obtain any other state transition h^t ($t > 1$) by iterating h^1 t times, and we simply take the state transition h^0 to be the identity function on M_1. We may thus conclude that any Turing machine is in fact a mathematical dynamical system $MDS_1 = \langle T, M_1, \{h^t\}\rangle$ with discrete time, that is, a cascade.

To show that a Turing machine is a cascade, I have identified the *state of the machine* with the triple ⟨*tape content, head position, internal state*⟩. For technical reasons, however, it is often convenient to take the state to be a finite string of symbols. Let x_0 be a fixed square of the tape, and suppose that the machine head is located on square x_0, or on a square to its left. The state can then be identified with the finite string of symbols uq_ia_jv/z, where q_i is the internal state of the control unit, a_j is the symbol on the square where the head is located, u is the string of symbols to the left of a_j up to the leftmost nonblank symbol (included), v is the string of symbols to the right of a_j up to the symbol on square x_0 (included), and z is the string of symbols to the right of square x_0 up to the rightmost nonblank symbol (included). On the other hand, if the machine head is located on a square to the right of square x_0, the state can be identified with the finite string of symbols u/vq_ia_jz, where q_i is the internal state of the control unit, a_j is the symbol on the square where the head is located, z is the string of symbols to the right of a_j up to the rightmost nonblank symbol (included), v is the string of symbols to the left of a_j up to the symbol on square x_0 (excluded), and u is the string that includes the symbol on square x_0 and all the symbols to its left up to the leftmost nonblank symbol (if the symbol on square x_0 and all the symbols to its left are blank, the string u is empty).

Therefore, an arbitrary state of a Turing machine can be represented in two different ways. First, by a triple ⟨*tape content, head position, internal state*⟩ and, second, by a finite string of symbols of the form uq_ia_jv/z or u/vq_ia_jz. However, these two representations of the state of a Turing machine are in fact equivalent. This means that the two different cascades that correspond to these two representations are isomorphic mathematical dynamical systems (see example 3).

EXAMPLE 3 (two isomorphic cascades that individuate the same Turing machine)

An arbitrary Turing machine can be naturally identified with at least two different cascades which are, intuitively, the same system. The two cascades that correspond to the same Turing machine turn out to be isomorphic in the sense of definition 2.

Let C be an arbitrary Turing machine. Let $\{a_j\}$ be the alphabet of C, where $\{a_j\}$ contains n symbols ($0 < n \in Z^+$). One of these symbols (say a_0) is called the *blank* and is indicated by b. Let $\{q_i\}$

be the set of all internal states of the control unit, where $\{q_i\}$ has m elements ($0 < m \in Z^+$). A quadruple is any string of the form $q_i a_j D q_l$, where $D = a_k$, L, or R (L stands for "move to the left", and R stands for "move to the right"). An arbitrary Turing machine C is specified by a consistent set G of mn quadruples, where two different quadruples are consistent if and only if they do not begin with the same pair ⟨*internal state, symbol*⟩.[11] Consider now M_2 = the set of all finite strings of the form uq_ia_jv/z or u/vq_ia_jz, where the symbol / is not member of the alphabet of C, a_j is an arbitrary symbol of the alphabet, q_i is an arbitrary internal state, and u, v, and z are finite strings of symbols of the alphabet (u, v, or z may be empty and, if u (or z) is not empty, its leftmost (or rightmost) symbol is not the blank). The Turing machine C is supposed to be in internal state q_i and read the symbol a_j immediately to the right of q_i. We can thus take each string member of M_2 to be a state of the Turing machine C because, given the set of quadruples G, and a finite string of symbols $x \in M_2$, the future behavior of C is determined.

In fact, G determines a function[12] $g[G]: M_2 \rightarrow M_2$ which is defined as follows. Let $q_ia_jDq_l$ be the quadruple member of G that begins with q_ia_j. If $D = a_k$ and $x = uq_ia_jv/z$, then $g[G](x) = uq_la_kv/z$; if $D = a_k$ and $x = u/vq_ia_jz$, then $g[G](x) = u/vq_la_kz$; if $D = L$, $x = uq_ia_jv/z$, and u is empty, then $g[G](x) = uq_lbv'/z$, where $v' = a_jv$; if $D = L$, $x = uq_ia_jv/z$, and $u = u'a_k$, then $g[G](x) = u'q_la_kv'/z$, where $v' = a_jv$; if $D = L$, $x = u/vq_ia_jz$, v is empty, u is empty, $a_j = b$, and z is empty, then $g[G](x) = uq_lbv/z$; if $D = L$, $x = u/vq_ia_jz$, v is empty, u is empty, and $a_j \neq b$ or z is not empty, then $g[G](x) = uq_lbv/z'$, where $z' = a_jz$; if $D = L$, $x = u/vq_ia_jz$, v is empty, $u = u'a_k$, $a_j = b$, and z is empty, then $g[G](x) = u'q_la_kv/z$; if $D = L$, $x = u/vq_ia_jz$, v is empty, $u = u'a_k$, and $a_j \neq b$ or z is not empty, then $g[G](x) = u'q_la_kv/z'$, where $z' = a_jz$; if $D = L$, $x = u/vq_ia_jz$, $v = v'a_k$, $a_j = b$, and z is empty, then $g[G](x) = u/v'q_ia_kz$; if $D = L$, $x = u/vq_ia_jz$, $v = v'a_k$, and $a_j \neq b$ or z is not empty, then $g[G](x) = u/v'q_la_kz'$, where $z' = a_jz$; if $D = R$, $x = uq_ia_jv/z$, v is empty, z is empty, $a_j = b$, and u is empty, then $g[G](x) = u/vq_lbz$; if $D = R$, $x = uq_ia_jv/z$, v is empty, z is empty, and $a_j \neq b$ or u is not empty, then $g[G](x) = u'/vq_lbz$, where $u' = ua_j$; if $D = R$, $x = uq_ia_jv/z$, v is empty, $z = a_kz'$, $a_j = b$, and u is empty, then $g[G](x) = u/vq_la_kz'$; if $D = R$, $x = uq_ia_jv/z$, v is empty, $z = a_kz'$, and $a_j \neq b$ or u is not empty, then $g[G](x) = u'/vq_la_kz'$, where $u' = ua_j$; if $D = R$, $x = uq_ia_jv/z$, $v = a_kv'$, $a_j = b$, and u is empty, then $g[G](x) = uq_la_kv'/z$; if $D = R$, $x = uq_ia_jv/z$, $v = a_kv'$, and $a_j \neq b$ or u is not empty, then $g[G](x) = u'q_la_kv'/z$, where $u' = ua_j$; if $D = R$, $x = u/vq_ia_jz$, and z is empty, then $g[G](x) = u/v'q_lbz$, where $v' = va_j$; if $D = R$, $x = u/vq_ia_jz$, and $z = a_kz'$, then $g[G](x) = u/v'q_l a_k z'$, where $v' = va_j$. We can thus identify C with the cascade $MDS_2 = \langle T, M_2, \{g^t\}\rangle$, where $T = Z^+$, g^0 is the identity function on M_2 and, for any $t > 0$, the state transition g^t is obtained by iterating t times the function $g[G]$.

On the other hand, it is also clear that we could identify an arbitrary state of C with a triple $\langle p, s, q_i\rangle$, where p is a finite string of symbols of the alphabet surrounded by an infinite number of blanks (that is, p is the content of an arbitrary tape), s is a position of the machine's head, and q_i is an internal state of the control unit. Let M_1 be the set of all such triples. G then determines a function $h[G]$: $M_1 \to M_1$, and C can also be identified with the cascade $MDS_1 = \langle T, M_1, \{h^t\}\rangle$, where $T = Z^+$, h^0 is the identity function on M_1 and, for any $t > 0$, the state transition h^t is obtained by iterating t times the function $h[G]$.

The two cascades MDS_1 and MDS_2, however, turn out to be isomorphic in the sense of definition 2. This is clear when the obvious one-to-one correspondence between M_2 and M_1 is considered.

A second fact about Turing machines usually accepted without proof is that changing the alphabet, and switching the direction of motion, does not matter. More precisely, suppose that we are given a Turing machine C. We then construct a second machine C^* by relabeling the symbols and the internal states of C, and by switching *left* and *right*. It is intuitively clear that C^* and C are essentially the same machine. We can give a formal proof of this fact by considering the two cascades that correspond to C and C^*, for these two cascades turn out to be isomorphic in the sense of definition 2.

EXAMPLE 4 (changing the alphabet of a Turing machine and switching *left* and *right* produces an isomorphic system)

If C is an arbitrary Turing machine, let C^* be a second Turing machine obtained by relabeling the symbols and the internal states of C, and by switching L and R. It is intuitively clear that C and C^* are essentially the same machine. This can be formally proved once the two cascades that correspond to C and C^* are considered. These two cascades turn out to be isomorphic in the sense of definition 2.

Let A and A^* be, respectively, the alphabets of C and C^*, and let h: $A \to A^*$ be a bijection. Let Q and Q^* be, respectively, the sets of internal states of the control units of C and C^*, and let f: $Q \to Q^*$ be a bijection. Then, if $q_i a_j a_k q_l$ is a quadruple of C, $f(q_i)h(a_j)h(a_k)f(q_l)$ is a quadruple of C^*; if $q_i a_j R q_l$ is a quadruple of C, $f(q_i)h(a_j)Lf(q_l)$ is a quadruple of C^*; if $q_i a_j R q_l$ is a quadruple of

$C, f(q_i)h(a_j)Lf(q_l)$ is a quadruple of C^*; nothing else is a quadruple of C^*. We already know that we can identify C with the cascade $MDS_2 = \langle T, M_2, \{g^t\}\rangle$ (see example 3), where M_2 = the set of all finite strings of the form uq_ia_jv/z or u/vq_ia_jz. Given an arbitrary state $x \in M_2$, the Turing machine C is supposed to be in internal state q_i and read the symbol a_j immediately to the right of q_i. Let $\boldsymbol{u}$, $\boldsymbol{v}$, and $\boldsymbol{z}$ be the finite strings of symbols of A obtained by reversing the order of the strings u, v, and z. Let $h(\boldsymbol{u})$, $h(\boldsymbol{v})$, and $h(\boldsymbol{z})$ be the finite strings of symbols of A^* obtained by applying h to each symbol in $\boldsymbol{u}$, $\boldsymbol{v}$, and $\boldsymbol{z}$, and by then concatenating the results. We can thus identify C^* with the cascade $MDS^* = \langle T, M^*, \{g^{t*}\}\rangle$, where M^* = the set of all finite strings of the form $h(\boldsymbol{z})\backslash h(\boldsymbol{v})h(a_j)f(q_i)h(\boldsymbol{u})$ or $h(\boldsymbol{z})h(a_j)f(q_i)h(\boldsymbol{v})\backslash h(\boldsymbol{u})$. Given an arbitrary state $x^* \in M^*$, the Turing machine C^* is supposed to be in internal state $f(q_i)$ and read the symbol $h(a_j)$ immediately to the left of $f(q_i)$. For any $t > 0$, the state transition g^{t*} is obtained by iterating t times the function $g[G]^*: M^* \rightarrow M^*$. This is the function determined by the set of quadruples of C^*, and its definition is similar to the definition of $g[G]: M_2 \rightarrow M_2$ (see example 3). Let $\rho: M_2 \rightarrow M^*$ be defined as follows: for any $x \in M_2$, if $x = uq_ia_jv/z$, $\rho(x) = h(\boldsymbol{z})\backslash h(\boldsymbol{v})h(a_j)f(q_i)h(\boldsymbol{u})$; if $x = u/vq_ia_jz$, $\rho(x) = h(\boldsymbol{z})h(a_j)f(q_i)h(\boldsymbol{v})\backslash h(\boldsymbol{u})$. By its definition, ρ is a bijection between M_2 and M^*, and it is immediately verifiable that ρ satisfies definition 2. MDS_2 and MDS^* are thus isomorphic cascades.

In order to formulate a formal definition of a computational system, let us consider the mechanisms studied by computation theory and ask first what type of systems they are, and second what specific feature distinguishes these mechanisms from other systems of the same type.

As mentioned in section 1, computation theory studies many different kinds of abstract systems. A basic property shared by all these mechanisms is that they are mathematical dynamical systems with discrete time, that is, cascades. I have just shown that this is true of Turing machines, and it is not difficult to give a similar argument for any other kind of mechanism that has been actually studied by computation theory. Therefore, on the basis of this evidence, we may reasonably conclude that all computational systems are cascades.

However, computation theory does not study all cascades. The specific feature that distinguishes computational systems from other mathematical dynamical systems with discrete time is that a computational system can always be described in an effective way. Intuitively, this means that the constitution and operations of the system are purely mechanical or that the system can always be identified with an idealized machine. However, since we want to arrive at a formal definition of a computational system, we cannot limit ourselves to this intuitive characterization. Rather, we must try to express it in a precise form.

Since I have informally characterized a computational system as a cascade that can be effectively described, let us ask first what a *description* of a cascade is. If we take a structuralist viewpoint, this question has a precise answer. A description (or a representation) of a cascade consists of a second cascade isomorphic to it where, by definition 2, a cascade $MDS_1 = \langle T, M_1, \{h^t\}\rangle$ is isomorphic to a given cascade $MDS = \langle T, M, \{g^t\}\rangle$ if and only if there is a bijection $f: M \to M_1$ such that, for any $t \in T$ and any $x \in M, f(g^t(x)) = h^t(f(x))$.

Second, let us ask what an *effective* description of a cascade is. Since I have identified a description of a cascade $MDS = \langle T, M, \{g^t\}\rangle$ with a second cascade $MDS_1 = \langle T, M_1, \{h^t\}\rangle$ isomorphic to MDS, an effective description of MDS will be an *effective cascade* MDS_1 isomorphic to MDS. The problem thus reduces to an analysis of the concept of an effective cascade. It is natural to analyze this concept in terms of two conditions: (1) there is an effective procedure for recognizing the states of the system or, in other words, the state space M_1 is a *decidable* set; (2) each state transition function h^t is *effective* or computable. These two conditions can be made precise in several ways which turn out to be equivalent. The method I prefer utilizes the concept of Turing computability.[13] If we choose this approach, we will then require that an effective cascade satisfy these conditions:

1. The state space M_1 is a subset of the set $P(A)$ of all finite strings built out of some finite alphabet A, and there is a Turing machine that decides whether an arbitrary finite string is member of M_1.
2. For any state transition function h^t, there is a Turing machine that computes h^t.

We should also note that, since MDS_1 is a cascade, the second condition is equivalent to the Turing computability of h^1 (or, if $T = Z$, to the Turing computability of both h^1 and h^{-1}).

Finally, we are in the position to formally define a computational system. This definition expresses in a precise way the informal characterization of a computational system as a cascade that can be effectively described (see figure 1-5).

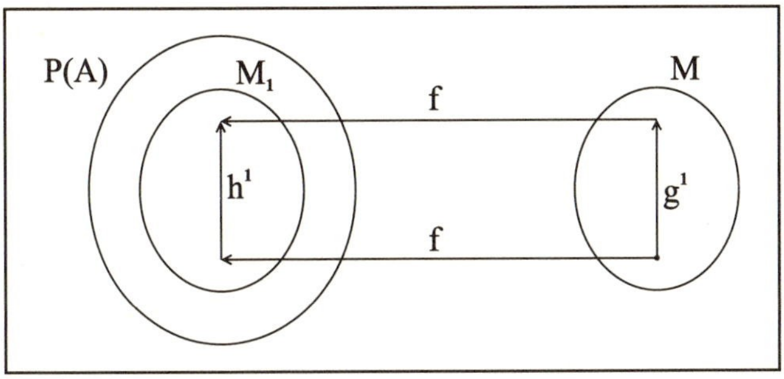

FIGURE 1-5 Computational systems. MDS = $\langle T, M, \{g^t\}\rangle$ and MDS_1 = $\langle T, M_1, \{h^t\}\rangle$ are cascades. MDS_1 is isomorphic to MDS. f is a bijection from M to M_1. $P(A)$ = set of all finite strings built out of finite alphabet A. M_1 is included in $P(A)$. The characteristic function of M_1 is computable by a Turing machine. The state transition h^1 is computable by a Turing machine.

DEFINITION 3 *(computational systems)*

MDS *is a computational system if and only if* MDS = $\langle T, M, \{g^t\}\rangle$ *is a cascade, and there is a second cascade* $MDS_1 = \langle T, M_1, \{h^t\}\rangle$ *such that* MDS_1 *is isomorphic to* MDS *and*

1. *if* P(A) *is the set of all finite strings built out of some finite alphabet* A, $M_1 \subseteq P(A)$ *and there is a Turing machine that computes the characteristic function*[14] *of* M_1*;*
2. *there is a Turing machine that computes* h^1 *and, if* T = Z, *there is also a Turing machine that computes* h^{-1}.

If definition 3 does indeed capture the intuitive concept of a computational system, any system that has been studied by computation theory must fall within its scope. In particular, the following example shows that Turing machines themselves turn out to be computational systems.

EXAMPLE 5 (all Turing machines are computational systems)

Let C be an arbitrary Turing machine with alphabet $\{a_j\}$, set of internal states $\{q_i\}$, and set of quadruples G. As we have seen in example 3, C can be identified with the cascade $MDS_2 = \langle T, M_2, \{g^t\}\rangle$, where $T = Z^+$, g^0 is the identity function on M_2, any state transition g^t $(t > 0)$ is obtained by iterating t times the function $g[G]$, and M_2 = the set of all finite strings of the form uq_ia_jv/z or u/vq_ia_jz, where the symbol / is not member of the alphabet of C, a_j is an arbitrary symbol of the alphabet, q_i is an arbitrary internal state, and u, v, and z are finite strings of symbols of the alphabet (u, v, or z may be empty and, if u (or z) is not empty, its leftmost (or rightmost) symbol is not the blank). This shows that an arbitrary Turing machine $C = MDS_2$ is a cascade. Let us then take $MDS_1 = MDS_2$. MDS_1 is thus isomorphic to MDS_2. Furthermore, condition (1) of definition 3 holds because M_2 is a proper subset of the set $P(\{a_j\} \cup \{q_i\} \cup \{/\})$ of all the finite strings built out of the alphabet $\{a_j\} \cup \{q_i\} \cup \{/\}$, and it is obvious that there is a Turing machine that computes the characteristic function of M_2. Finally, condition (2) is also satisfied because we can construct a Turing machine C' that computes the function $g[G] = g^1$. The alphabet of C' is $\{a_j\} \cup \{q_i\} \cup \{/, \$, \#\}$ and, in broad outline, C' operates as follows. Suppose that C' is started in internal state q_0, and on the left marker $\$$ of a tape whose content is $\ldots bb\$uq_ia_jv/z\#bb \ldots$ or $\ldots bb\$u/vq_ia_jz\#bb. \ldots$ First, C' goes to the right until it encounters q_i and, second, C' operates the transformation that corresponds to the quadruple of C that begins with q_ia_j, taking care of repositioning the left marker $\$$ or the right marker # (if needed). After this, C' positions itself on the left marker $\$$ and stops. Also note that this argument does not depend on the particular cascade MDS_2 I have chosen to represent C. If C were identified with any other cascade isomorphic to MDS_2, definition 3 would still be satisfied.

Example 5 also shows that there is nothing wrong with the apparent circularity of definition 3. I have defined the general concept of a computational system using the notion of a Turing machine, which obviously is a special kind of computational system. Therefore, in a certain sense, I have presupposed the concept of a computational system, and one might worry that this circularity invalidates definition 3. But this is not a real problem. First, the circularity of definition 3 is not complete, because I have defined the general concept of a computational system by means of one of its specifications, but I have not *directly* defined a computational system in terms of itself. Second, the partial circularity of definition 3 would be vicious if one could not prove that the specific concept I have used to define the general one is a special case of the defined concept. But example 5 does provide this proof.

A complete proof of the adequacy of definition 3 is out of the question, for this would involve showing that any *possible* formal specification of the concept of a computational system is a special case of definition 3. Obviously, one cannot know in advance all the possible specifications of this concept. Therefore, this proof cannot be produced. However, it is not difficult to show that all the *known* formal specifications of of this concept (register machines, cellular automata, monogenic production systems, etc.) satisfy definition 3. Intuitively this is to be expected, for we know that the behavior of each of these systems can be exactly reproduced by a suitably designed Turing machine. The next example outlines the proof for linear cellular automata. One can then give analogous arguments for all other cases.

EXAMPLE 6 (all linear cellular automata are computational systems)

A linear cellular automaton is constituted by a doubly infinite sequence of cells. At any time, each cell is in one of n possible states. The next state of each cell is determined by its present state and by the present state of m cells to its left and m cells to its right (that is, by its *neighborhood of radius m*). Updating is synchronous. Each cellular automaton C is thus specified by a rule ϕ: $A^{2m+1} \rightarrow A$, where A is the set of all possible cell states. One of the n cell states is called the blank state and is conventionally indicated by b. I also require that the function ϕ take the sequence of $2m + 1$ blank states to the blank state, and that, at any time, only a finite number of cells be in a nonblank state.[15] A cell is *quiescent* if and only if it is in the blank state, and all the cells in its neighborhood of radius m are in the blank state as well. I am now going to show that all linear cellular automata satisfy definition 3.

Let C be an arbitrary $\langle n, m\rangle$ linear cellular automaton,[16] and let ϕ be its rule. Let x_0 be an arbitrary cell. An arbitrary state of the cellular automaton C can thus be identified with a finite string of symbols of the form u/v, where (1) the symbol / is not member of A; (2) u is the sequence of cell states from cell x_0 (included) up to the leftmost nonquiescent cell (included) (if cell x_0 and all the cells to its left are quiescent, then u is empty); (3) v is the sequence of cell states from cell x_0 (excluded) up to the rightmost nonquiescent cell (included). If all the cells to the right of cell x_0 are quiescent, then v is empty. Let M be the set of all states of C. The rule ϕ determines a function Φ: $M \rightarrow M$, and C can thus be identified with $MDS = \langle T, M, \{g^t\}\rangle$, where $T = Z^+$, g^0 is the identity function on M, and any state transition g^t $(t > 0)$ is obtained by iterating t times the function Φ. This shows that C is a cascade. Let us then take $MDS_1 = MDS$. Obviously, MDS_1 is thus isomorphic to MDS. Furthermore, condition (1) of definition 3 holds, because $M \subseteq P(A \cup \{/\})$, and there is a Turing machine that computes the characteristic function of M. To verify this fact, let us consider all the strings of symbols members of the alphabet A of form $b \ldots ba_Lza_Rb \ldots b$ or $b \ldots$

$ba_Lb \ldots b$, where both a_L and a_R are nonblank symbols, z is an arbitrary string of symbols (z may be empty), and $b \ldots b$ is a string of m blanks. Let $\boldsymbol{b}$ be a string of k ($0 \leq k$) blanks. Then, a string of symbols members of the alphabet $A \cup \{/\}$ is a state of the cellular automaton C if and only if it is of the form u/v and one of the following cases holds: (1) both u and v are empty; (2) both u and v are not empty, and $uv = b \ldots ba_Lza_Rb \ldots b$ or $uv = b \ldots ba_Lb \ldots b$; (3) v is empty, and $u = b \ldots ba_Lza_Rb \ldots b\boldsymbol{b}$ or $u = b \ldots ba_Lb \ldots b\boldsymbol{b}$; (4) u is empty, and $v = \boldsymbol{b}b \ldots ba_Lza_Rb \ldots b$ or $v = \boldsymbol{b}b \ldots ba_Lb \ldots b$. It is thus clear that these conditions allow us to construct a Turing machine that computes the characteristic function of the state space M.

I finally show that also condition (2) of definition 3 is satisfied, because there is a Turing machine C_Φ that computes the function $\Phi = g^1$. The alphabet of C_Φ is $A \cup \{/, \#, \$\}$ (where $A \cap \{/, \#, \$\} = \phi$) and, in broad outline, C_Φ operates as follows. C_Φ starts in state q_0 on the left marker $\$$ of a tape ... $bb\$u/v\#bb$ ... whose content represents an arbitrary state $u/v \in M$ of the cellular automaton. Each square of the tape (except the ones where the symbols /, $\$$, and # are located) can thus be identified with a cell of the cellular automaton. The Turing machine C_Φ then goes to the right, sequentially updating all the cells up to the right marker #, according to rule ϕ. When the new state a_j of a cell is computed, C_Φ provisionally assigns to that cell the symbol a_ka_j that codes for both the present state a_k and the new state a_j. This allows for the correct updating of the next cell. When all the new states have been computed, C_Φ first repositions the right marker # (if needed) and then goes back, replacing each provisional symbol a_ka_j with the updated state a_j of each cell. The Turing machine C_Φ ends this routine as soon as it encounters the left marker $\$$. It then repositions this marker (if needed) and stops on it.

Let me finally raise one further point. The definition of a computational system that I have proposed in this section (definition 3) employs the concept of *Turing computability*. In particular, this formal concept has allowed me to make precise the requirement that the system $MDS_1 = \langle T, M_1, \{h^t\}\rangle$ is an *effective cascade* or, in other words, that its state space M_1 is a *decidable* set, and that each state transition function h^t is *effective* or computable. In chapter 2, however, I will show that the concept of Turing computability is not absolute, but instead depends on the relational structure of the support on which Turing machines operate. Ordinary Turing machines operate on a linear tape divided into a countably infinite number of adjacent squares. But one can also think of Turing machines that operate on different supports. For example, we can let a Turing machine work on an infinite checkerboard or, more generally, on some n-dimensional infinite array. I call an arbitrary support on which a Turing machine can operate a *pattern field*. Depending on the pattern field F we choose, we obtain different concepts of computability. At the end of chapter 2, I will thus propose a new definition of a computational system (a *computational system on pattern field* F) that takes into account the relativity of the concept of Turing computability. If F is a doubly infinite tape, however, computational systems on F reduce to computational systems.

4 The emulation relation

The fact that a certain system can be emulated by a different system is familiar to any student of computation theory. The relation that holds between any two such systems can be intuitively characterized as follows: Some state evolutions of the emulating system can be divided into consecutive parts so that the two states reached by this system at the end of two consecutive parts correspond to one step in the evolution of the emulated system (see figure 1-6). The emulation relation is not peculiar to computational systems, but it may in fact hold between two arbitrary mathematical dynamical systems.

We can make this concept precise by considering two functions, u and v, which relate the states and the state transitions of the two

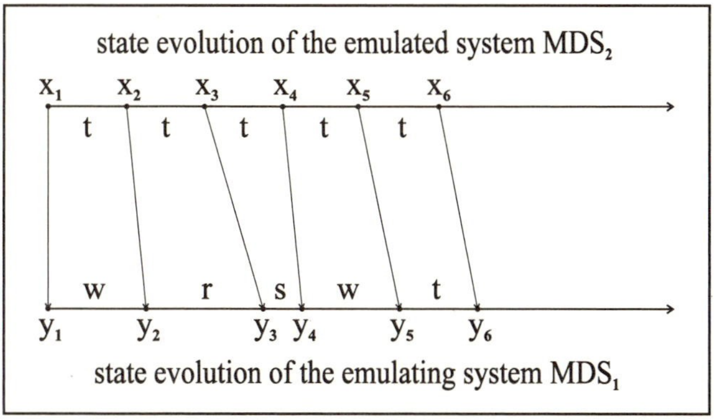

FIGURE 1-6 Two state evolutions of two systems in the emulation relation. $MDS_1 = \langle T_1, M_1, \{h^t\}\rangle$. $MDS_2 = \langle T_2, M_2, \{g^t\}\rangle$. MDS_1 emulates MDS_2.

systems. The function u injectively maps the states of the emulated system into the states of the emulating one. Therefore, by means of this mapping, each state of the emulated system can be identified with a corresponding state of the emulating one. The function v, instead, maps each step of the emulated system into a corresponding step of the emulating one. Each step is individuated by the state involved in that step and by the length of the step, that is, by the time necessary for transforming the state into another state. The function v tells us the length of the corresponding step of the emulating system. For example, suppose we consider state x and state transition g^t, that is, we consider the step $x \rightarrow g^t(x)$. The function v, when applied to x and t, gives us the time $v(x, t)$ that the emulating system will employ to transform the state $u(x)$ that corresponds to x into the state $u(g^t(x))$ that corresponds to $g^t(x)$. Thus, if $\{h^t\}$ is the set of state transitions of the emulating system, the functions u and v must satisfy $h^{v(x,t)}(u(x)) = u(g^t(x))$. Therefore, $u(x) \rightarrow h^{v(x,t)}(u(x))$ is the step of the emulating system that corresponds to step $x \rightarrow g^t(x)$. Obviously, we should also require that v assign longer times to longer steps, and that v assign time 0 to any step of length zero. Finally, since each state in the image of u can be identified with a state of the emulated system, we should also require that a step of the emulating system that takes state $u(x)$ to state $u(y)$ correspond to a step of the emulated system. That is, if $h^t(u(x)) = u(y)$, there must be a time w such that $g^w(x) = y$ and $v(x, w) = t$. I give below the formal definition of the emulation relation (see figure 1-7).

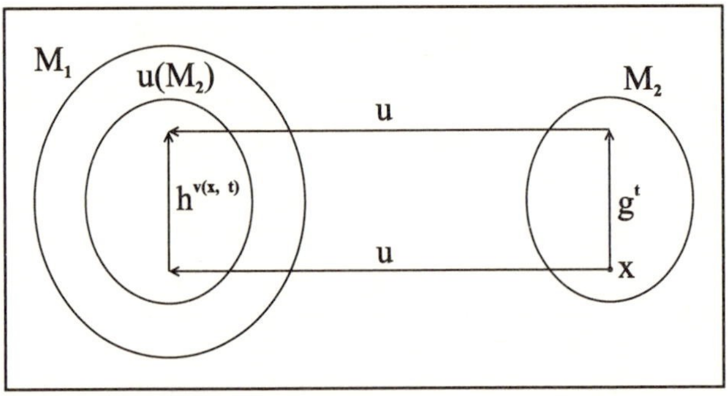

FIGURE 1-7 The emulation relation. $MDS_1 = \langle T_1, M_1, \{h^t\}\rangle$. $MDS_2 = \langle T_2, M_2, \{g^t\}\rangle$. u is an injective function from M_2 to M_1. v is a function from $M_2 \times T_2$ to T_1.

Definition 4 *(emulation)*

MDS_1 *emulates* MDS_2 *if and only if:*

1. $MDS_1 = \langle T_1, M_1, \{h^t\}\rangle$ *and* $MDS_2 = \langle T_2, M_2, \{g^t\}\rangle$ *are mathematical dynamical systems;*
2. *there are two functions* u *and* v *such that:*
   a. $u: M_2 \rightarrow M_1$ *and* u *is injective;*
   b. $v: M_2 \times T_2 \rightarrow T_1$, $v(x, 0) = 0$ *and, if* $w < t$, *then* $v(x, w) < v(x, t)$*;*
   c. *for any* $t \in T_2$, $h^{v(x, t)}(u(x)) = u(g^t(x))$*;*
   d. *for any* $t \in T_1^+$, *if* $h^t(u(x)) = u(y)$, *there is a time* $w \in T_2$ *such that* $g^w(x) = y$ *and* $v(x, w) = t$ *(where* T_1^+ *is the nonnegative portion of* T_1*).*

Condition (*2b*) of definition 4 entails that the function v also satisfy the following properties: $v(x, t) = 0$ if and only if $t = 0$, $v(x, t) > 0$ if and only if $t > 0$, and $v(x, t) < 0$ if and only if $t < 0$.

The function u injectively maps the states of the emulated system into states of the emulating system which thus represent them. Intuitively, the meaning of the function v is the following: $v(x, t)$ is the time that the emulating system employs to emulate the step from x to $g^t(x)$ of the emulated system. This time may depend on how long this step requires (that is, on t) and also on the particular state x that is transformed by this step. Condition (*2b*) ensures that the dependence of v on time is correct, in the sense that a "zero step" (x transformed into x) is emulated in zero time, and longer steps are emulated in longer times. Condition (*2c*) ensures that any step of the emulated system is emulated by the emulating system. Conversely, condition (*2d*) ensures that any step of the emulating system that links any two states which represent states of the emulated system does in fact emulate a corresponding step of this system.[17]

The reason for restricting condition (*2d*) to positive instants is that definition 4 applies to mixed cases, that is, cases in which system MDS_2 only evolves through positive times, while MDS_1 may also perform negative steps. If the restriction to positive instants were dropped, an arbitrary mixed case of this type would not satisfy the emulation relation. Note, however, that, because of conditions (*2b*) and (*2c*), definition 4 never applies to the converse mixed case, in which MDS_1 only evolves through positive times, while MDS_2 may also perform negative steps.[18]

As a partial confirmation of the material adequacy of definition 4, I give below two examples of systems that stand in the emulation relation. The first example concerns a linear cellular automaton with two cell states and neighborhood of radius one (Wolfram's rule 22) that exactly reproduces the behavior of a second cellular automaton with the same cell states and neighborhood (rule 146). The second example shows that, given an arbitrary Turing machine, we can construct an appropriate linear cellular automaton that emulates it.

EXAMPLE 7 (a simple cellular automaton that emulates another one)

Stephen Wolfram has noted that there are very simple cellular automata that emulate other cellular automata (Wolfram 1983a, 629–30). Let C_0 and C_1 be linear cellular automata with cell states {0, 1}. The next state of each cell depends on its present state and on the present states of its left and right neighbors. These two automata are individuated by the following rules (in binary):

rule 22

C_0	1 1 1	1 1 0	1 0 1	1 0 0	0 1 1	0 1 0	0 0 1	0 0 0
	0	0	0	1	0	1	1	0

rule 146

C_1	1 1 1	1 1 0	1 0 1	1 0 0	0 1 1	0 1 0	0 0 1	0 0 0
	1	0	0	1	0	0	1	0

It turns out that C_0 emulates C_1 in the sense of definition 4. Let M be the set of all doubly infinite sequences of 0*s* and 1*s* that contain a finite number of 1*s*. M can thus be identified with the state space of both C_0 and C_1. To see that C_0 emulates C_1, let $u: M \to M$ be the function which, for an arbitrary $x \in M$, replaces 0 with 00, and 1 with 01. Let $v: M \times Z^+ \to Z^+$ be defined by: $v(x, t) = t$, if x does not contain any 1; $2t$, otherwise. It is then easy to verify that u and v satisfy definition 4 (substitute 00 for 0 and 01 for 1 in each transformation of rule 146, and then apply rule 22).

EXAMPLE 8 (linear cellular automata emulate Turing machines)

For an arbitrary Turing machine C_1, there is a linear cellular automaton C_0 such that C_0 emulates C_1. C_0 is a linear cellular automaton with a neighborhood of radius 3, and C_0 is constructed as follows.[19]

If A and Q are, respectively, the alphabet and the set of internal states of the Turing machine C_1 (where $A \cap Q = \varnothing$), $A \cup Q$ is the set of cell states of the cellular automaton C_0. If b is the blank symbol of C_1, b is the blank cell state of C_0. If . . . $aaaq_iaaa$ . . . is an arbitrary state of the Turing machine C_1, . . . $bababaq_iababa$ . . . is the state of the cellular automaton C_0 that represents . . .

aaaq$_i$*aaa* . . . Given the quadruples of C_1, the rule of C_0 is obtained as follows. An arbitrary quadruple of C_1 has three possible forms: $q_ia_ja_kq_l$, $q_ia_jRq_l$, $q_ia_jLq_l$. Each of these quadruples can be rewritten as a matrix of two rows and eleven columns, where a is a place holder[20] for an arbitrary symbol of the alphabet A:

	1	2	3	4	5	6	7	8	9	10	11	
1	a	b	a	b	a	q_i	a_j	b	a	b	a	corresponds to $q_ia_ja_kq_l$
2						q_l	a_k					

	1	2	3	4	5	6	7	8	9	10	11	
1	a	b	a	b	a	q_i	a_j	b	a	b	a	corresponds to $q_ia_jRq_l$
2						b		q_l				

	1	2	3	4	5	6	7	8	9	10	11	
1	a	b	a	b	a	q_i	a_j	b	a	b	a	corresponds to $q_ia_jLq_l$
2				q_l		b						

Each of the quadruples may change the state of at most two cells: cells 6 and 7 for the first quadruple, cells 6 and 8 for the second, and cells 4 and 6 for the third. All other cells maintain their previous states. Each quadruple thus corresponds to two transformation forms of the cellular automaton:

a	b	a	q_i	a_j	b	a	
			q_l				correspond to $q_ia_ja_kq_l$
b	a	q_i	a_j	b	a	b	
			a_k				

a	b	a	q_i	a_j	b	a	
			b				correspond to $q_ia_jRq_l$
a	q_i	a_j	b	a	b	a	
			q_l				

a	b	a	b	a	q_i	a_j	
			q_l				correspond to $q_ia_jLq_l$
a	b	a	q_i	a_j	b	a	
			b				

The cellular automaton rule that individuates C_0 is obtained from these transformation forms by substituting all possible symbols of the alphabet A for each occurrence of a. Any sequence of seven cell states that cannot be obtained from these transformation forms is taken to the state of its central cell. Let u and v be defined by $u(\ldots aaaq_iaaa \ldots) = \ldots bababaq_iababa \ldots$; $v(\ldots aaq_iaaa \ldots, t) = t$. Then, by the construction of C_0, and by the definitions of u and v, C_0 emulates C_1.

The emulation relation is reflexive and transitive, but it is not symmetric. It is thus a quasi-ordering on the set of all mathematical dynamical systems (theorem 3). The proof that reflexivity holds is immediate, once u is taken to be the identity function and v the function that takes $\langle x, t\rangle$ to t. As for transitivity, suppose MDS_1 emulates MDS_2, MDS_2 emulates MDS_3, and that u_1: $M_2 \to M_1$, u_2: $M_3 \to M_2$, v_1: $M_2 \times T_2 \to T_1$, and v_2: $M_3 \times T_3 \to T_2$ satisfy definition 4. Then it is easy to verify that $u_3(z) = u_1(u_2(z))$ and $v_3(z, t) = v_1(u_2(z), v_2(z, t))$ satisfy definition 4.

THEOREM 3
The emulation relation is a quasi-ordering on the set of all mathematical dynamical systems.

PROOF. See the appendix.

Finally, theorem 3 implies that the emulation relation is also transitive with respect to the relation of isomorphism:

COROLLARY 3.1
If MDS_1 *emulates* MDS_2 *and* MDS_2 *is isomorphic to* MDS_3, *then* MDS_1 *emulates* MDS_3.

PROOF. Note that, if MDS_2 is isomorphic to MDS_3, then MDS_2 emulates MDS_3. From this and theorem 3 the thesis follows.

q.e.d.

5 Reversible versus irreversible systems

Let T be the reals, the rationals, or the integers, and let T^+ be the nonnegative reals, nonnegative rationals, or nonnegative integers. Then, a mathematical dynamical system MDS is *reversible* if and only if $MDS = \langle T, M, \{g^t\}\rangle$. On the other hand, MDS is *irreversible* if and only if $MDS = \langle T^+, M, \{g^t\}\rangle$. These two types of systems are described in figure 1-8.

We already know (see theorem 1) that, for any reversible system, an arbitrary negative state transition g^{-t} is equal to $(g^t)^{-1}$ = the inverse of g^t. Therefore, if x is the state of the system at the present time t_0,

Mathematical dynamical system MDS = <T, M, {g^t}>			
Reversible		Irreversible	
T = R, Q, or Z		T = R$^+$, Q$^+$, or Z$^+$	
Simply reversible	Time symmetric	Logically reversible	Logically irreversible
reversible and not time symmetric	reversible and there is $\sim: M \to M$ such that $\sim(g^t(\sim(x))) = g^{-t}(x)$	irreversible and, for any t, $x \xrightarrow{g^t}$ $y \xrightarrow{g^t}$	there is t such that $x \xrightarrow{g^t}$ $y \xrightarrow{g^t}$
		Weakly irreversible	Strongly irreversible
		logically irreversible and not strongly irreversible	$x \xrightarrow{g^t}$ $g^z \uparrow$ $y \xrightarrow{g^z}$

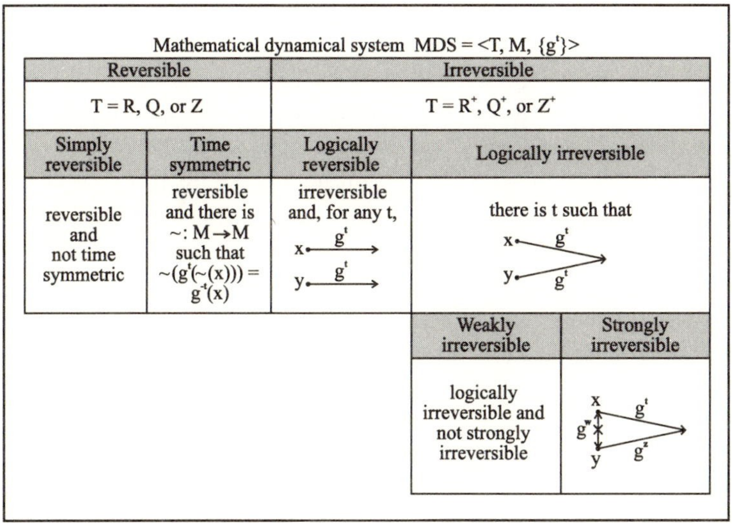

FIGURE 1-8 Types of mathematical dynamical systems.

we can always find the state of the system at any previous time $t_0 - t$ by applying the negative state transition g^{-t} to the present state x.

If a system is irreversible this is not possible, because no negative state transition belongs to {g^t}. Yet, one might consider whether an arbitrary nonnegative state transition g^t is injective. If this is the case, and x is the state of the system at the present time t_0, we can still find the state of the system at any previous time $t_0 - t \geq 0$ by considering the inverse of the state transition g^t, for this state is $(g^t)^{-1}(x)$. For this reason, I call any irreversible system $MDS = \langle T^+, M, \{g^t\}\rangle$ such that g^t is injective for any t *logically* (or *quasi*) *reversible* (see Bennett 1973). On the other hand, if a mathematical dynamical system MDS has some state transition g^t that is not injective, I call MDS *logically irreversible*. It follows from theorem 1 that any logically irreversible system is irreversible.

Let me now distinguish two more types of mathematical dynamical systems. MDS is *strongly irreversible* if and only if there are state transitions g^t and g^z and two different states x and y such that $g^t(x) = g^z(y)$ and, for any time w, $g^w(x) \neq y$ and $g^w(y) \neq x$; MDS is *weakly irreversible* if and only if MDS is logically irreversible and MDS is not strongly irreversible.

Many computational systems are strongly irreversible. By contrast, all dynamical models of mechanical systems are reversible, for the time set T of these mathematical dynamical systems is the set of the real numbers. In fact, these models typically satisfy an even stronger property: They are time symmetric, in the following sense. An arbitrary state x of a dynamical model of a mechanical system is specified when all the positions and velocities are given. If we consider the state $\sim(x)$, obtained from x by changing the sign of all velocities, it holds that $\sim(g^t(\sim(x))) = g^{-t}(x)$, for any t and x. That is, the "opposite" of the forward evolution from state $\sim(x)$ is equal to the backward evolution from state x. Obviously, if this property holds, then $\sim(\sim(x)) = x$ for any x, because $\sim(\sim(x)) = \sim(g^0(\sim(x))) = g^0(x) = x$. This motivates the following definitions. *MDS* is *time symmetric* if and only if *MDS* is reversible and there is a function $\sim: M \rightarrow M$ such that, for any x and t, $\sim(g^t(\sim(x))) = g^{-t}(x)$; *MDS* is *simply reversible* if and only if *MDS* is reversible and *MDS* is not time symmetric.

EXAMPLE 9 (a time symmetric mathematical dynamical system)
The mathematical dynamical system $MDS_1 = \langle T, S \times V, \{g^t\}\rangle$ specified by Galileo's laws for the vertical position and velocity of a falling body is time symmetric. Recall (see example 1) that $T = S = V = R$, and each state transition g^t is defined by $g^t(s, v) = \langle s + vt + (1/2)ct^2, v + ct\rangle$. Let $\sim: S \times V \rightarrow S \times V$ be defined by $\sim(s, v) = \langle s, -v\rangle$. Then, $\sim(g^t(\sim(s, v))) = \sim(g^t(s, -v)) = \sim(s - vt + (1/2)ct^2, -v + ct) = \langle s - vt + (1/2)ct^2, v - ct\rangle = g^{-t}(s, v)$. MDS_1 is thus time symmetric.

I will now prove two theorems that are direct consequences of the definition of a strongly irreversible system. The first theorem simply states that a strongly irreversible system is logically irreversible (that is, it has some state transition that is not injective). The second theorem gives a necessary and sufficient condition for a system to be strongly irreversible: A system is strongly irreversible if and only if there are two state evolutions whose images intersect but are not in the subset relation.

THEOREM 4
If MDS *is strongly irreversible,* MDS *is logically irreversible.*

PROOF. Suppose that *MDS* is strongly irreversible. Then, there are g^t, g^z, x, and y such that $x \neq y$, $g^t(x) = g^z(y)$, and, for any time w, $g^w(x) \neq y$ and $g^w(y) \neq x$. If $t = z$, g^t is not injective. Suppose $t > z$. Then, $g^z(g^{t-z}(x)) = g^{z+t-z}(x) = g^t(x) = g^z(y)$. But $g^{t-z}(x) \neq y$, hence g^z is not injective. Results are analogous if $t < z$. Therefore, for some t, g^t is not injective.

q.e.d.

THEOREM 5
MDS *is strongly irreversible if and only if there are two state evolutions* g^x *and* g^y *such that* $x \neq y$, $\mathrm{Im}(g^x) \not\subseteq \mathrm{Im}(g^y)$, $\mathrm{Im}(g^y) \not\subseteq \mathrm{Im}(g^x)$, *and* $\mathrm{Im}(g^x) \cap \mathrm{Im}(g^y) \neq \varnothing$.

PROOF. Assume that *MDS* is strongly irreversible. Then, there are x and y such that $x \neq y$ and $Im(g^x) \cap Im(g^y) \neq \varnothing$. If $Im(g^x) \subseteq Im(g^y)$ or $Im(g^y) \subseteq Im(g^x)$, there is w such that $g^w(x) = y$ or $g^w(y) = x$. But there is no such w because *MDS* is strongly irreversible. Conversely, by the hypotheses of the theorem, it follows that there are x, y, t, and z such that $g^t(x) = g^z(y)$ and $x \neq y$. If there are w such that $g^w(x) = y$ or $g^w(y) = x$, then $Im(g^x) \subseteq Im(g^y)$ or $Im(g^y) \subseteq Im(g^x)$, against the hypotheses.

q.e.d.

Recall that the orbit of a state x [indicated by $orb(x)$] is the image of the state evolution g^x whose initial state is x. Orbits are thus sets of states. I will now define four different types of orbit, and I will then study the relations between the classes of mathematical dynamical systems I have just introduced and these four types of orbit.

First, $orb(x)$ is *periodic* if and only if there is a time $t > 0$ such that $g^t(x) = x$; second, $orb(x)$ is *eventually periodic* if and only if $orb(x)$ is not periodic, but there is a state y and a time t such that $g^t(x) = y$ and $orb(y)$ is periodic; third, $orb(x)$ is *aperiodic* if and only if $orb(x)$ is neither periodic nor eventually periodic; fourth, $orb(x)$ is *merging* if and only if there is a state y such that $x \neq y$, $orb(x) \cap orb(y) \neq \varnothing$, $orb(x) \not\subseteq orb(y)$, and $orb(y) \not\subseteq orb(x)$.

Note that periodic, eventually periodic, and aperiodic orbits are three mutually exclusive and exhaustive classes. Furthermore, a merging orbit cannot be periodic.[21] Therefore, there are only two possible types of merging orbits: merging and aperiodic, or merging and eventually periodic.

We will see later (theorem 7) that a system with eventually periodic or merging orbits is logically irreversible. Therefore, a reversible system may only have two types of orbit: periodic, or aperiodic and not merging (see figure 1-9). By contrast, irreversible systems may have orbits of five types: periodic, aperiodic and not merging, eventually periodic and not merging, merging and aperiodic, or merging and eventually periodic (see figure 1-10). We know by theorem 1 that in reversible systems any state transition g^t is injective and surjective. Therefore, reversible systems may only have one type of state

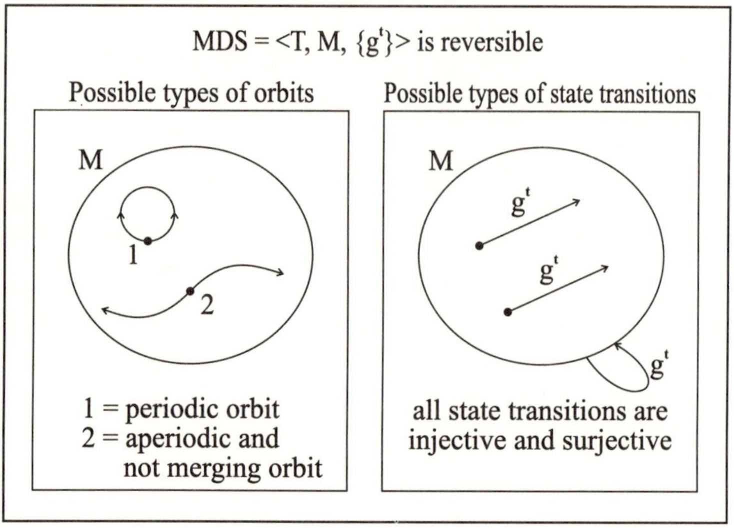

FIGURE 1-9 Possible types of orbits and state transitions in reversible systems.

transition (see figure 1-9). By contrast, irreversible systems may have state transitions of four types: injective and surjective, injective and not surjective, surjective and not injective, or neither injective nor surjective (see figure 1-10).

Since the orbit of state x is the image of the state evolution g^x, let us restate theorem 5 as follows:

COROLLARY 5.1
MDS *is strongly irreversible if and only if* MDS *has merging orbits.*

PROOF. By theorem 5 and the definition of merging orbit.

q.e.d.

Corollary 5.1 characterizes strongly irreversible systems in terms of a special type of orbit they possess. A similar characterization of weakly irreversible systems is possible, but we first need two lemmas. The first lemma states that any system that has eventually periodic orbits or merging orbits is logically irreversible. If there are merging orbits, the thesis follows immediately from corollary 5.1 and theorem 4. As for the case of eventually periodic orbits, the thesis follows from the definitions of eventually periodic orbit and periodic orbit.

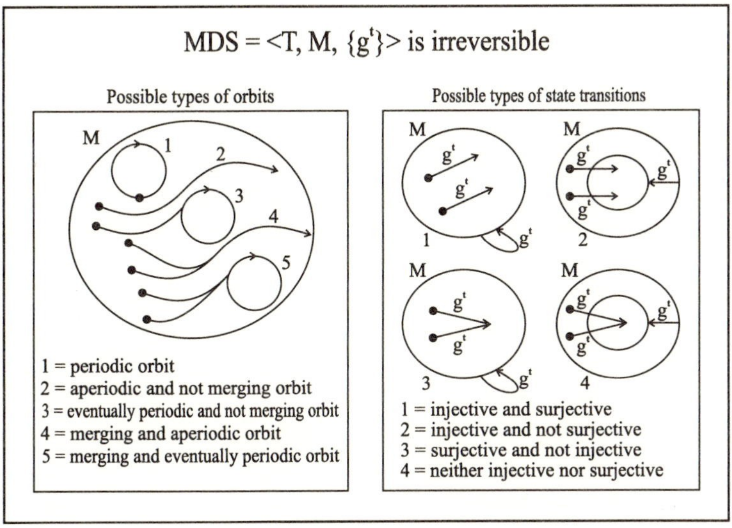

FIGURE 1-10 Possible types of orbits and state transitions in irreversible systems.

LEMMA 6.1
If MDS *has eventually periodic orbits or* MDS *has merging orbits,* MDS *is logically irreversible.*

PROOF. Suppose *MDS* has merging orbits. Then the thesis follows from corollary 5.1 and theorem 4.

Suppose *MDS* has eventually periodic orbits. Then, by the definition of eventually periodic orbit, there are x, y, and t such that $orb(x)$ is not periodic, $g^t(x) = y$, and $orb(y)$ is periodic. By the definition of periodic orbit, there is $w > 0$ such that $g^w(y) = y$. Therefore, $g^t(x) = y = g^w(y) = g^w(g^t(x)) = g^t(g^w(x))$, and $g^w(x) \neq x$. Hence, g^t is not injective.

q.e.d.

Before going on, let me mention an interesting consequence of lemma 6.1. It is well known that the *halting problem* for the class of *all* Turing machines is undecidable. More precisely, given an arbitrary Turing machine, there is no mechanical procedure to decide whether that machine will stop when started on an arbitrary input. However, it is obvious that the halting problem for *some specific* machine is instead decidable. For example, the machine specified by $\{q_0 0 0 q_0,$

$q_0 1 1 q_0\}$ immediately stops on any input. The problem which thus arises is to find nontrivial classes of Turing machines for which the halting problem is decidable. The interesting result is that lemma 6.1 allows us to find one such class.

First, we need to think of the halting condition of a Turing machine in dynamical terms. When a Turing machine stops, its tape content, head position, and internal state no longer change. Dynamically, this means that the Turing machine enters a cycle of period one in state space. More precisely, there are two possibilities. Either the Turing machine immediately enters the cycle, or it gets to it after one or more steps. Therefore, in the second case, the Turing machine has an eventually periodic orbit.

Let us now consider the class of all logically reversible Turing machines. It can be seen that the halting problem for this class of machines is decidable. By lemma 6.1, no such machine has eventually periodic orbits. But then, given *any input*, a logically reversible Turing machine either halts immediately or never halts. Therefore, to decide the halting problem for a logically reversible Turing machine, we may just check whether the machine halts on the first step.[22]

This result gives us a better understanding of the halting problem: We now know that the undecidability of the halting problem is limited to logically irreversible Turing machines. In other words, we have discovered an intriguing connection between one of the classic negative results of computation theory and the dynamical concept of logical irreversibility. We will see in section 6 that a second important property of Turing machines, universality, is necessarily associated with strong irreversibility.

Lemma 6.2 states that any system that does not have merging orbits, but has some state transition that is not injective, has eventually periodic orbits. The hypotheses of the lemma, together with the definition of merging orbit, corollary 5.1, and the definition of a strongly irreversible system, imply that there are t, w, x, y, and z such that $t > 0$, $w > 0$, $x \neq y$, $g^t(x) = g^t(y) = z$, and $g^w(x) = y$ or $g^w(y) = x$. Therefore, by the definition of eventually periodic orbit, the lemma will be proved if, in the case $g^w(x) = y$, we can show that $orb(x)$ is not periodic and $orb(z)$ is periodic. (In the case $g^w(y) = x$, we must instead show that $orb(y)$ is not periodic and $orb(z)$ is periodic.)

LEMMA 6.2

If there is t *such that* g^t *is not injective, and* MDS *has no merging orbits,* MDS *has eventually periodic orbits.*

PROOF. The hypotheses of the lemma, together with the definition of a merging orbit, corollary 5.1, and the definition of a strongly irreversible system, imply that there are t, w, x, y, and z such that $t > 0$, $w > 0$, $x \neq y$, $g^t(x) = g^t(y) = z$, and $g^w(x) = y$ or $g^w(y) = x$. Let us consider first the case $g^w(x) = y$, and show that $orb(z)$ is periodic and $orb(x)$ is not periodic.

First, $orb(z)$ is periodic, for $z = g^t(y) = g^t(g^w(x)) = g^w(g^t(x)) = g^w(z)$. Second, assume for *reductio* that $orb(x)$ is periodic. Since $z = g^t(x)$, $z \in orb(x)$. Thus, since $z = g^w(z)$ and $orb(x)$ is periodic, $g^w(x) = x$. Since $g^w(x) = y$ and $g^w(x) = x$, then $x = y$. But $x \neq y$. Therefore, $orb(x)$ is not periodic.

Results are analogous for the case $g^w(y) = x$.

q.e.d.

We can now characterize weakly irreversible systems as those systems that have eventually periodic orbits but do not have merging orbits.

THEOREM 6
MDS *is weakly irreversible if and only if* MDS *has eventually periodic orbits and* MDS *has no merging orbits.*

PROOF. By lemma 6.1, lemma 6.2, corollary 5.1, and the definitions of a logically irreversible system and of a weakly irreversible system.

q.e.d.

Lemmas 6.1 and 6.2 also allow us to characterize logically irreversible systems as those systems that have eventually periodic or merging orbits.

THEOREM 7
MDS *is logically irreversible if and only if* MDS *has eventually periodic orbits or* MDS *has merging orbits.*

PROOF. Right/left is lemma 6.1. As for left/right, suppose *MDS* is logically irreversible. Then, there is t such that g^t is not injective and, furthermore, either *MDS* has merging orbits, or *MDS* does not have merging orbits. From this and lemma 6.2 the thesis follows.

q.e.d.

We can summarize the previous results as follows (see figure 1-11). First, by theorem 7, a reversible system does not have eventually periodic or merging orbits. Therefore, a reversible system may only have two types of orbit: periodic, or aperiodic and not merging. Second, by theorem 7, the same conclusion also holds for logically reversible systems. Third, by theorem 6, a weakly irreversible system has eventually periodic orbits and does not have merging orbits. Therefore, a weakly reversible system may have only three types of orbits: periodic, aperiodic and not merging, or eventually periodic and not merging. Fourth, by corollary 5.1, a strongly irreversible system has merging orbits. Therefore, a strongly irreversible system may have five types of orbits: periodic, aperiodic and not merging, eventually periodic and not merging, merging and aperiodic, or merging and eventually periodic.

Since orbits are sets of states, it is also interesting to look at the set theoretical relationships that may hold between two arbitrary orbits in different types of mathematical dynamical systems (see figure 1-12). Given any two orbits $orb(x)$ and $orb(y)$, we must consider five cases: first, $orb(x) = orb(y)$; second, $orb(x) \cap orb(y) = \varnothing$; third, $orb(x) \subset orb(y)$; fourth, $orb(y) \subset orb(x)$; fifth, $orb(x) \not\subseteq orb(y)$, $orb(y) \not\subseteq orb(x)$, and $orb(x) \cap orb(y) \neq \varnothing$. If a system is reversible, only the first and second cases are possible. If a system is logically reversible or weakly irreversible, only the first four cases are possible, for the fifth

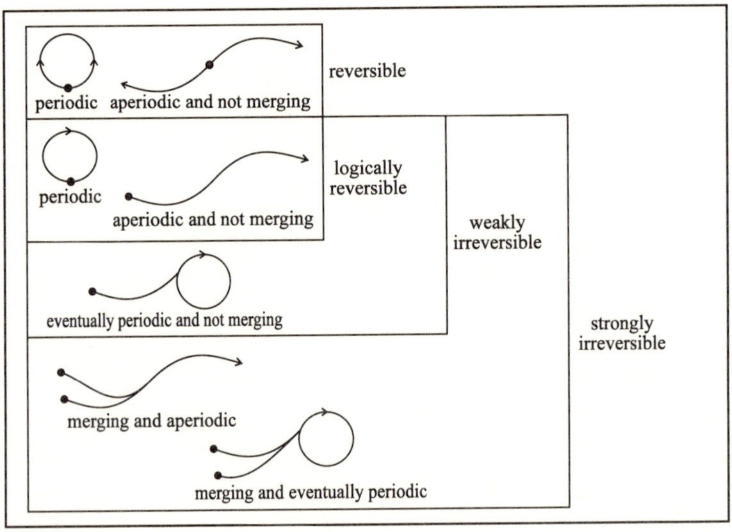

FIGURE 1-11 Possible types of orbits in different types of mathematical dynamical systems.

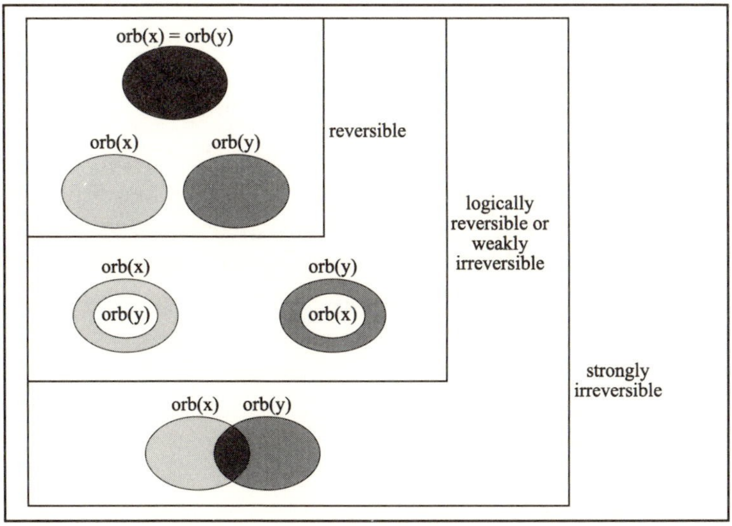

FIGURE 1-12 Possible set theoretical relationships between two orbits in different types of mathematical dynamical systems.

case implies that the system has merging orbits. Finally, if a system is strongly irreversible, all five cases are possible.

6 The realization relation

A *universal computational system* is a computational system that emulates all computational systems. This class is not empty, for there is a Turing machine that is universal in this sense. By the definition of a computational system (definition 3), if MDS is an arbitrary computational system, the state transition h^1 of a system MDS_1 isomorphic to MDS is computable by a Turing machine. We can thus modify this Turing machine to obtain a Turing machine that emulates[23] MDS_1. Also, there is a Turing machine C_U that emulates any other Turing machine.[24] Therefore, by the transitivity of the emulation relation (theorem 3), and since the emulation relation is transitive with respect to the relation of isomorphism (corollary 3.1), the Turing machine C_U emulates all computational systems.

It is interesting to note that the computational property of universality is necessarily associated with the dynamical property of strong irreversibility, for any universal computational system is strongly irreversible. This conclusion follows from three premises. First, by the definition of a universal computational system, any such system emulates all computational systems; second, some computational systems are strongly irreversible[25] and, third, any system that emulates a strongly irreversible system is strongly irreversible. We can prove this third premise by *reductio* (see theorem 8). We assume first that a strongly irreversible system MDS_2 is emulated by a system MDS_1 which is not strongly irreversible, and we then use the definition of a strongly irreversible system, and the definition of emulation, to deduce a contradiction.

THEOREM 8
If MDS$_2$ *is strongly irreversible and* MDS$_1$ *emulates* MDS$_2$, MDS$_1$ *is strongly irreversible.*

PROOF. Suppose MDS_2 is strongly irreversible, and MDS_1 emulates MDS_2; suppose for *reductio* that MDS_1 is not strongly irreversible. Since MDS_2 is strongly irreversible, there are x and y, $x \neq y$, such that, for some t and z, $g^t(x) = g^z(y)$ and, for any w, $g^w(x) \neq y$ and $g^w(y) \neq x$. Since MDS_1 emulates MDS_2, by condition (*2c*) of definition 4, $u(g^t(x)) = h^{v(x,t)}(u(x))$ and $u(g^z(y)) = h^{v(y,z)}(u(y))$. Therefore, since $g^t(x) = g^z(y)$, $h^{v(x,t)}(u(x)) = h^{v(y,z)}(u(y))$. Since MDS_1 is not strongly irreversible, MDS_1 has no merging orbits. Therefore, either $orb(u(x)) \subseteq orb(u(y))$ or $orb(u(y)) \subseteq orb(u(x))$. Thus, there is a time $s \geq 0$ such that $h^s(u(x)) = u(y)$ or $h^s(u(y)) = u(x)$. Hence, since MDS_1 emulates MDS_2, by condition (*2d*) of definition 4, there is a time w such that $g^w(x) = y$ or $g^w(y) = x$. But, for any w, $g^w(x) \neq y$ and $g^w(y) \neq x$. We have thus reached a contradiction. Therefore, MDS_1 is strongly irreversible.

q.e.d.

A second dynamical property of universal computational systems is that they have orbits of at least four different types: periodic, aperiodic, eventually periodic, and merging. If any of these four types is missing, the system cannot be universal. This is a consequence of the definition of a universal computational system, of the fact that, for each of these four types of orbit, there is a computational system with orbits of this type,[26] and of the following theorem:

THEOREM 9

1. *If* MDS$_2$ *has periodic orbits and* MDS$_1$ *emulates* MDS$_2$, *then* MDS$_1$ *has periodic orbits;*
2. *if* MDS$_2$ *has aperiodic orbits,* MDS$_1$ *emulates* MDS$_2$, *and* MDS$_1$ *is a cascade, then* MDS$_1$ *has aperiodic orbits;*

3. *if* MDS_2 *has eventually periodic orbits and* MDS_1 *emulates* MDS_2*, then* MDS_1 *has eventually periodic orbits;*
4. *if* MDS_2 *has merging orbits and* MDS_1 *emulates* MDS_2*, then* MDS_1 *has merging orbits.*

PROOF. See the appendix.

We have just seen that all universal computational systems are strongly irreversible. Yet other authors have proved that certain reversible systems are computationally universal (see Margolus 1984). At first glance, these two results seem to be inconsistent. This apparent paradox, however, only tells us that the emulation relation cannot be the relation that holds between a reversible universal system and an arbitrary computational system. I am now going to propose an explication of this second relation, and I will always refer to it as *realization*. The word *emulation*, instead, always refers to the relation defined in section 4.

I said in the introduction of this chapter that we need to give a precise meaning to the statement that computational systems are in principle realizable by dynamical models of physical systems. One might think that the emulation relation (definition 4) is sufficient to accomplish this goal. However, we should keep in mind two facts. First, many dynamical models of physical systems are reversible. Therefore, by theorem 7, these models do not have eventually periodic or merging orbits. Second, most computational systems are logically irreversible. Therefore, by theorem 7, these systems have eventually periodic or merging orbits. But then, by theorem 9, a reversible dynamical model of a physical system cannot emulate a logically irreversible computational system. We must thus conclude that we cannot identify the realization relation with the emulation relation (unless we are willing to accept that logically irreversible computational systems are not in principle realizable by reversible dynamical models of physical systems).

Even though we cannot *directly* use the emulation relation to produce an explication of the realization relation, it is nonetheless possible to accomplish this goal by means of a natural generalization of the emulation relation. If a system $MDS_1 = \langle T_1, M_1, \{h^t\}\rangle$ emulates a second system $MDS_2 = \langle T_2, M_2, \{g^t\}\rangle$, each state x of the emulated system can be identified with the corresponding state $u(x)$ of the emulating system. We can naturally generalize the emulation relation by instead taking $u(x)$ to be a *set* of states of the emulating system. If we choose this approach, we must first modify condition (*2a*) of definition 4 by requiring that u be a bijection between M_2 and a set D of mutually disjoint subsets of M_1. Second, we must also modify conditions (*2c*) and (*2d*). Since $u(x)$ and $u(g^t(x))$ are now sets of states, we can no longer require $h^{v(x,t)}(u(x)) = u(g^t(x))$. However, we can generalize condition (*2c*) by requiring that $h^{v(x,t)}$ take any state member of $u(x)$ to a state member of $u(g^t(x))$. As for condition (*2d*), we will now require that, for any state $\alpha \in u(x)$ and any state $\beta \in u(y)$, if $h^t(\alpha) = \beta$, there is a time w such that $g^w(x) = y$ and $v(x, w) = t$. With these generalizations we thus obtain definition 5 (see also figure 1-13).

DEFINITION 5 *(realization)*
MDS_1 *realizes* MDS_2 *if and only if:*

1. $\mathrm{MDS}_1 = \langle \mathrm{T}_1, \mathrm{M}_1, \{\mathrm{h}^t\}\rangle$ *and* $\mathrm{MDS}_2 = \langle \mathrm{T}_2, \mathrm{M}_2, \{\mathrm{g}^t\}\rangle$ *are mathematical dynamical systems;*
2. *there are two functions* u *and* v *such that:*
   a. $\mathrm{u}: \mathrm{M}_2 \rightarrow \mathrm{D}$, D *is a set of mutually disjoint subsets of* M_1, *and* u *is a bijection;*
   b. $\mathrm{v}: \mathrm{M}_2 \times \mathrm{T}_2 \rightarrow \mathrm{T}_1$, $\mathrm{v}(\mathrm{x}, 0) = 0$ *and, if* $\mathrm{w} < \mathrm{t}$, *then* $\mathrm{v}(\mathrm{x}, \mathrm{w}) < \mathrm{v}(\mathrm{x}, \mathrm{t})$*;*
   c. *for any* $\mathrm{t} \in \mathrm{T}_2$, *for any* $\alpha \in \mathrm{u}(\mathrm{x})$, *there is* $\beta \in \mathrm{u}(\mathrm{g}^t(\mathrm{x}))$ *such that* $\mathrm{h}^{\mathrm{v}(\mathrm{x},\mathrm{t})}(\alpha) = \beta$*;*
   d. *for any* $\mathrm{t} \in \mathrm{T}_1^+$, *for any* $\alpha \in \mathrm{u}(\mathrm{x})$, *for any* $\beta \in \mathrm{u}(\mathrm{y})$, *if* $\mathrm{h}^t(\alpha) = \beta$, *there is a time* $\mathrm{w} \in \mathrm{T}_2$ *such that* $\mathrm{g}^w(\mathrm{x}) = \mathrm{y}$ *and* $\mathrm{v}(\mathrm{x}, \mathrm{w}) = \mathrm{t}$ *(where* T_1^+ *is the nonnegative portion of* T_1*).*

Condition (*2b*) of definition 5 entails that the function v also satisfies the following properties: $v(x, t) = 0$ if and only if $t = 0$, $v(x, t) > 0$ if and only if $t > 0$, and $v(x, t) < 0$ if and only if $t < 0$. Because of the

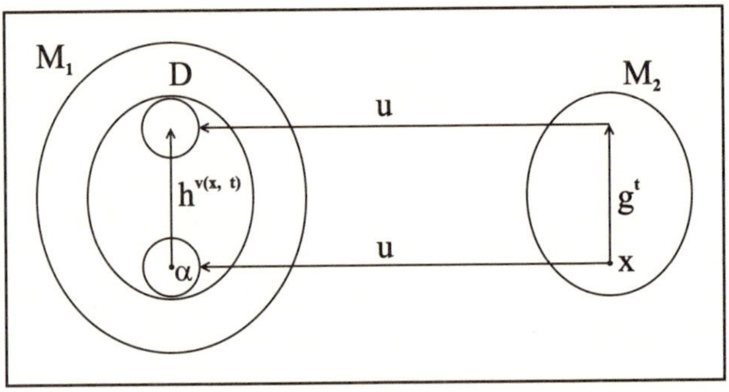

FIGURE 1-13 The realization relation. $\mathrm{MDS}_1 = \langle T_1, M_1, \{h^t\}\rangle$. $\mathrm{MDS}_2 = \langle T_2, M_2, \{g^t\}\rangle$. D = set of mutually disjoint subsets of M_1. u is a bijection from M_2 to D. v is a function from $M_2 \times T_2$ to T_1.

restriction of condition (*2d*) to positive instants, reversible systems may realize irreversible ones. However, because of conditions (*2b*) and (*2c*), the converse case is impossible.

Like the emulation relation, the realization relation is reflexive and transitive, that is, it is a quasi-ordering on the set of all mathematical dynamical systems (see theorem 10). The proof that reflexivity holds is immediate, for the realization relation reduces to the emulation relation once each state x of a system is identified with the set $\{x\}$ that only contains this state. The proof that transitivity holds is analogous to the corresponding proof for the emulation relation (see theorem 3 in the appendix). However, the functions u_3 and v_3 must now be defined in a somewhat different way. Suppose $MDS_1 = \langle T_1, M_1, \{g_1^t\}\rangle$, $MDS_2 = \langle T_2, M_2, \{g_2^t\}\rangle$, $MDS_3 = \langle T_3, M_3, \{g_3^t\}\rangle$, MDS_1 realizes MDS_2, and MDS_2 realizes MDS_3. Furthermore, let u_1: $M_2 \to D_1$, v_1: $M_2 \times T_2 \to T_1$, u_2: $M_3 \to D_2$, and v_2: $M_3 \times T_3 \to T_2$ satisfy definition 5. We then must show that there are two functions u_3: $M_3 \to D_1$ and v_3: $M_3 \times T_3 \to \mathrm{T}_1$ that also satisfy definition 5. Recall that, to prove transitivity for the emulation relation, we defined $u_3(z) = u_1(u_2(z))$ and $v_3(z, t) = v_1(u_2(z), v_2(z, t))$. The problem is that now $u_2(z)$ is not a state of MDS_2 but, rather, a set of states, so that the two compositions $u_1(u_2(z))$ and $v_1(u_2(z), v_2(z, t))$ do not make sense. However, we can solve this problem with a simple strategy. Instead of u_2: $M_3 \to D_2$, we use a function[27] f: $M_3 \to M_2$ that satisfies $f(z) \in u_2(z)$ and $f(g_3^t(z)) = g_2^{v_2(z,t)}(f(z))$, and we then define $u_3(z) = u_1(f(z))$ and $v_3(z, t) = v_1(f(z), v_2(z, t))$. It is then easy to prove that u_3 and v_3 satisfy definition 5.

THEOREM 10
The realization relation is a quasi-ordering on the set of all mathematical dynamical systems.

PROOF. See the appendix.

Finally, theorem 10 implies that the realization relation is also transitive with respect to the relations of emulation and of isomorphism, as described in corollary 10.1.

COROLLARY 10.1

1. *If* MDS$_1$ *realizes* MDS$_2$ *and* MDS$_2$ *emulates* MDS$_3$, *then* MDS$_1$ *realizes* MDS$_3$;
2. *if* MDS$_1$ *realizes* MDS$_2$ *and* MDS$_2$ *is isomorphic to* MDS$_3$, *then* MDS$_1$ *realizes* MDS$_3$.

PROOF OF (*1*). Note that, if MDS_2 emulates MDS_3, then MDS_2 realizes MDS_3. From this and theorem 10 the thesis follows.

q.e.d.

PROOF OF (2). Note that, if MDS_2 is isomorphic to MDS_3, then MDS_2 emulates MDS_3. From this and (1) the thesis follows.

q.e.d.

7 Virtual systems, the reversible realizability of irreversible systems, and the existence of reversible universal systems

In computation theory it is customary to talk of the virtual computational architectures implemented by a machine with a different computational architecture. These virtual architectures are supposedly defined in terms of the lower level workings of the implementing machine. The relations of emulation and realization allow us to make this idea precise. For, whenever a mathematical dynamical system MDS_1 either emulates or realizes a second system MDS_2, we can use the states and the state transitions $\{g_1^t\}$ of MDS_1, together with the functions u and v, to define a third system $MDS_2(MDS_1)$, which turns out to be isomorphic to MDS_2. I will call this system the *virtual* MDS_2 *implemented by* MDS_1.

The basic idea of this definition is that, first, we can identify each state y of MDS_2 with $u(y)$, where $u(y)$ is the state (or set of states) of MDS_1 that represents the state y of MDS_2. Second, we can then use $v(y, t)$ and g_1^t to define the state transition g_3^t of the virtual system that corresponds to $g_2^t(y)$, where g_2^t is an arbitrary state transition of MDS_2. If $u(y)$ is a state of MDS_1 (that is, if MDS_1 emulates MDS_2) we simply define $g_3^t(u(y)) = g_1^{v(y,t)}(u(y))$ (see figure 1-14). If, instead, $u(y)$ is a set of states of MDS_1 (that is, if MDS_1 realizes MDS_2), we first choose

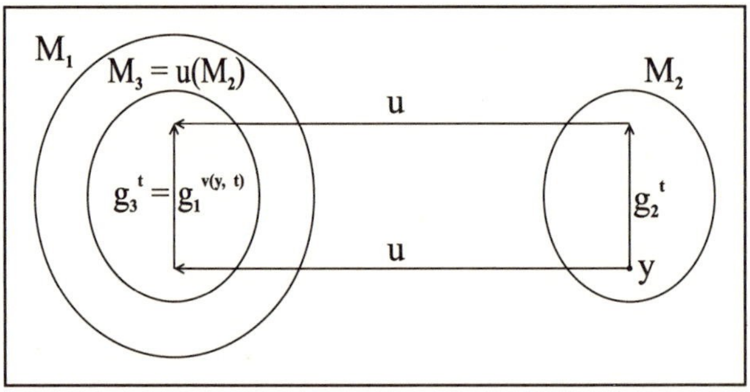

FIGURE 1-14 The virtual system $MDS_2(MDS_1)$ when MDS_1 emulates MDS_2. $MDS_1 = \langle T_1, M_1, \{g_1^t\}\rangle$. $MDS_2 = \langle T_2, M_2, \{g_2^t\}\rangle$. MDS_1 emulates MDS_2. u is an injective function from M_2 to M_1. v is a function from $M_2 \times T_2$ to T_1. $MDS_2(MDS_1) = \langle T_2, M_3, \{g_3^t\}\rangle$.

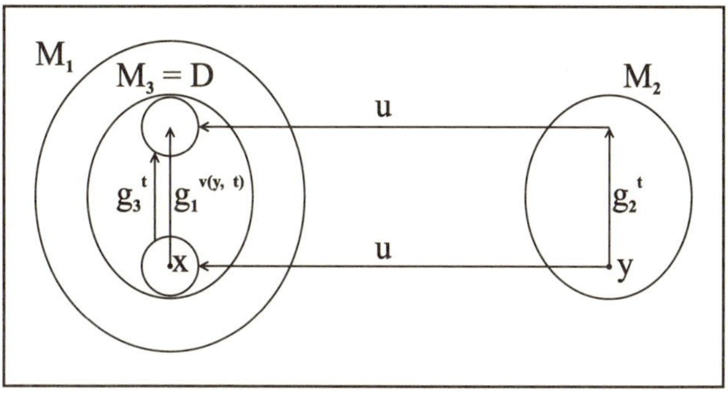

FIGURE 1-15 The virtual system $MDS_2(MDS_1)$ when MDS_1 realizes MDS_2. $MDS_1 = \langle T_1, M_1, \{g_1^t\}\rangle$. $MDS_2 = \langle T_2, M_2, \{g_2^t\}\rangle$. MDS_1 realizes MDS_2. D = set of mutually disjoint subsets of M_1. u is a bijection from M_2 to D. v is a function from $M_2 \times T_2$ to T_1. $g_3^t(u(y))$ = the set in D that contains $g_1^{v(y,t)}(x) = u(g_2^t(y))$. $MDS_2(MDS_1) = \langle T_2, M_3, \{g_3^t\}\rangle$.

an arbitrary $x \in u(y)$, and we then take $g_3^t(u(y))$ to be the set in the image of u that contains $g_1^{v(y,t)}(x)$ (see figure 1-15). Conditions (2c) and (2a) of definition 5 ensure the existence and uniqueness of this set ($= u(g_2^t(y))$), and that g_3^t does not depend on the particular x we choose to represent $u(y)$.

DEFINITION 6 *(virtual systems)*

$MDS_2(MDS_1)$ *is the virtual* MDS_2 *implemented by* MDS_1 *if and only if* $MDS_1 = \langle T_1, M_1, \{g_1^t\}\rangle$, $MDS_2 = \langle T_2, M_2, \{g_2^t\}\rangle$, *and* $MDS_2(MDS_1) = \langle T_2, M_3, \{g_3^t\}\rangle$ *satisfy these conditions*:

1. *either* MDS_1 *emulates* MDS_2 *or* MDS_1 *realizes* MDS_2*;*
2. *for some* u *and* v *that satisfy either definition 4 or definition 5,*
   a. $M_3 = \text{Im}(u)$*;*
   b. *for any* $y \in M_2$, *if* u *and* v *satisfy definition 4, let* $\chi(u(y)) = \sigma(u(y)) = u(y)$*; if* u *and* v *satisfy definition 5, let* $\chi(u(y)) \in u(y)$ *and, for any* $x \in u(y)$, *let* $\sigma(x) = u(y)$. *Then, for any* $t \in T_2$, $g_3^t(u(y)) = \sigma(g_1^{v(y,t)}(\chi(u(y))))$.

Theorem 11, presented below, is a straightforward consequence of the definitions of virtual system, mathematical dynamical system, isomorphism, emulation, and realization. In particular, the proof that $g_3^{t+w}(u(y)) = g_3^w(g_3^t(u(y)))$ employs the equality $\sigma(g_1^{v(y,t+w)}(\chi(u(y)))) = \sigma(g_1^{v(g_2^t(y),w)}(g_1^{v(y,t)}(\chi(u(y)))))$, which follows from the definitions of χ, σ and from condition (2c) of the definition of emulation (definition 4) or realization (definition 5).

THEOREM 11

1. MDS$_2$(MDS$_1$) *is a mathematical dynamical system;*

2. MDS$_2$(MDS$_1$) *is isomorphic to* MDS$_2$.

PROOF OF (*1*). Let us prove first that $g_3^0(u(y)) = u(y)$. By definition 6 and (*2b*) of definition 4 or 5, $g_3^0(u(y)) = \sigma(g_1^{v(y,0)}(\chi(u(y)))) = \sigma(g_1^0(\chi(u(y)))) = \sigma(\chi(u(y))) = u(y)$.

Second, we prove that $g_3^{t+w}(u(y)) = g_3^w(g_3^t(u(y)))$. By definition 6, $g_3^{t+w}(u(y)) = \sigma(g_1^{v(y,t+w)}(\chi(u(y)))) = \sigma(g_1^{v(g_2^t(y),w)}(g_1^{v(y,t)}(\chi(u(y)))))$ $= \sigma(g_1^{v(g_2^t(y),w)}(\chi(\sigma(g_1^{v(y,t)}(\chi(u(y))))))) = g_3^w(\sigma(g_1^{v(y,t)}(\chi(u(y))))) = g_3^w(g_3^t(u(y)))$.

q.e.d.

PROOF OF (2). First notice that u: $M_2 \rightarrow M_3$ is a bijection. Furthermore, by (*2b*) of definition 6 and (*2c*) of definition 4 or 5, $g_3^t(u(y)) = \sigma(g_1^{v(y,t)}(\chi(u(y)))) = u(g_2^t(y))$.

q.e.d.

We have seen in section 6 (theorem 8) that no strongly irreversible system can be emulated by a reversible one. Strongly irreversible systems, however, can be realized by reversible systems. This is an immediate consequence of an interesting general result. Given an arbitrary irreversible system *MDS*, it is always possible to define a reversible system *R*(*MDS*) that realizes *MDS*. Here is the basic idea of the definition: Suppose *MDS* is irreversible and that its state at the present time *s* is *y*. If the initial state is *x*, the state *y* has been reached by going through a series of previous states (the evolution up to time *s* of *x*) but, since *MDS* is irreversible, *y* could have been reached through an evolution that starts from a different initial state. Thus, if we want to recover the past of *y*, we must take into account the actual evolution that produced *y*, not only the present state *y*. This observation leads to the idea of considering, for any irreversible system *MDS*, a corresponding reversible system *R*(*MDS*) whose state space is the set of all η such that, for some time *s* and state *x*, η is the evolution up to time *s* of *x*. I will then prove that this system realizes *MDS*.

Let us see first the details of the definition of *R*(*MDS*) (figure 1-16). Let $MDS = \langle T^+, M, \{g^t\}\rangle$ be irreversible. Then, $R(MDS) = \langle T, E, \{h^\lambda\}\rangle$ satisfies the following conditions. If $T^+ = R^+$, Q^+, or Z^+, then $T = R$, Q, or Z, respectively. Let us define, for each $s \in T$ and $x \in M$, the evolution up to time *s* of state *x* . This is the state evolution that starts with *x*, up to time *s*. Furthermore, let us add the pair $\langle r, x\rangle$ for each time $r < 0$. Formally: $evol(s, x) = \{\langle r, y\rangle$: $r \in T, r \leq s, y \in M$ *and, if* $r < 0$, $y = x$; *if* $r \geq 0$, $y = g^r(x)\}$. Let us then take the state space *E* to be

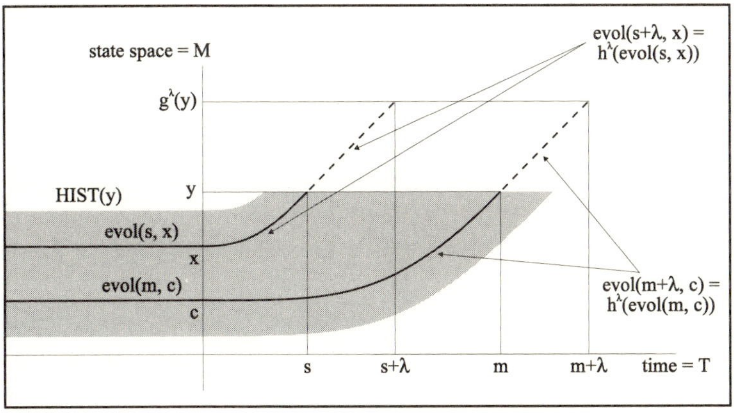

FIGURE 1-16 Definition of a reversible system R(MDS) that realizes an irreversible system MDS. MDS = $\langle T^+, M, \{g^t\}\rangle$ is irreversible. R(MDS) = $\langle T, E, \{h^1\}\rangle$ is reversible. $E = \{h\text{: } h = \text{evol}(s, x), \text{ for some } s \in T \text{ and } x \in M\}$. $h^1(\text{evol}(s, x)) = \text{evol}(s + 1, x)$.

the set $\{\eta\text{: } \eta = evol(s, x), \textit{ for some } s \in T \textit{ and } x \in M\}$. And, finally, let us define the set of state transitions $\{h^\lambda\}$ as follows: $h^\lambda(evol(s, x)) = evol(s + \lambda, x)$, for any $x \in M$ and $s, \lambda \in T$. Thus, $R(MDS)$ is a reversible dynamical system, because $T = R$, Q, or Z; $h^0(evol(s, x)) = evol(s + 0, x) = evol(s, x)$; and $h^w(h^\lambda(evol(s, x))) = h^w(evol(s + \lambda, x)) = evol(s + \lambda + w, x) = h^{\lambda+w}(evol(s, x))$.

It can be shown (theorem 12) that *R*(*MDS*) realizes *MDS*, and that the virtual *MDS* implemented by *R*(*MDS*) is isomorphic to *MDS*. The second part of the thesis follows from the first part and from theorem 11. The proof that *R*(*MDS*) realizes *MDS* is based on the following idea: If *y* is an arbitrary state of *MDS*, consider all the evolutions that might have produced *y* at some time *s*. I call this set the *history of y*, and I indicate it by *HIST*(*y*). Intuitively, since *HIST*(*y*) is the set of all evolutions that produce *y* at some *s*, we can identify *y* with *HIST*(*y*). To show that *R*(*MDS*) realizes *MDS* we must find two functions *u* and *v* that satisfy definition 5. Since I have proposed to identify *y* with *HIST*(*y*), the natural choice is $u(y) = HIST(y)$ and $v(y, t) = t$. It is then easy to verify that *u* and *v* satisfy definition 5.

THEOREM 12 *(any irreversible system is realized by a reversible system)*

For any irreversible system MDS, *there is a reversible system* R(MDS) *such that* R(MDS) *realizes* MDS *and* MDS(R(MDS)) *is isomorphic to MDS.*

PROOF. Let $MDS = \langle T^{+}, M, \{g^t\}\rangle$ be irreversible, and $R(MDS) = \langle T, E, \{h^{\lambda}\}\rangle$ be the reversible system defined above. For any $y \in M$, let $HIST(y) = \{\eta$: *for some* $s \in T$ *and* $x \in M$, $\eta = evol(s, x)$ *and* $\langle s, y\rangle \in evol(s, x)\}$. I show first that, if $y \neq z$, $HIST(y) \cap HIST(z) = \varnothing$. Suppose $y \neq z$, $evol(s, x) \in HIST(y)$, and $evol(s, x) \in HIST(z)$. Then, $\langle s, y\rangle \in evol(s, x)$ and $\langle s, z\rangle \in evol(s, x)$. By the definition of $evol(s, x)$, $y = z$, contrary to the hypothesis. Let us now define $u(y) = HIST(y)$ and $v(y, t) = t$. I now show that u and v satisfy definition 5. Conditions *(1)*, *(2a)*, and *(2b)* of definition 5 obviously hold. As for condition *(2c)*, suppose $evol(s, x) \in u(y) = HIST(y)$. Thus, $h^{v(y,t)}(evol(s, x)) = h^{t}(evol(s, x)) = evol(s + t, x) \in HIST(g^{t}(y)) = u(g^{t}(y))$. Concerning condition *(2d)*, suppose $evol(s, x) \in u(a)$, $evol(r, y) \in u(b)$, and $h^{\lambda}(evol(s, x)) = evol(r, y)$, where $\lambda \geq 0$. Hence, $evol(s + \lambda, x) = evol(r, y)$. Therefore, $evol(s + \lambda, x) \in u(b)$. By the definition of u, since $evol(s, x) \in u(a)$ and $evol(s + \lambda, x) \in u(b)$, $g^{\lambda}(a) = b$. Furthermore, by the definition of v, $v(a, \lambda) = \lambda$. Therefore, condition *(2d)* holds, and $R(MDS)$ thus realizes MDS. Finally, by theorem 11, $MDS(R(MDS))$ is isomorphic to MDS.

q.e.d.

I proved in section 6 that all universal computational systems are strongly irreversible. This result depends on the fact that I defined universal computational systems by means of the emulation relation. However, by using the realization relation, we can now obtain a more comprehensive concept of universality. A *universal system* is a mathematical dynamical system that realizes all computational systems. An immediate consequence of this definition, of the existence of universal computational systems, of theorem 12, and of corollary 10.1, is the existence of *reversible* universal systems. Let *UCS* be a universal computational system. Then *UCS* is irreversible.[28] Therefore, by theorem 12, *R*(*UCS*) realizes *UCS*. Also, *UCS* emulates all computational systems. Therefore, since the realization relation is transitive with respect to the emulation relation (corollary 10.1), *R*(*UCS*) realizes all computational systems. *R*(*UCS*) is thus a reversible universal system.

8 Appendix: Proofs of selected theorems

THEOREM 2
The relation of isomorphism is an equivalence relation on the set of all mathematical dynamical systems.

Proof. We must prove that the relation of isomorphism between mathematical dynamical systems is (1) reflexive, (2) symmetric, and (3) transitive.

Proof of (*1*). Let f be the identity function on the state space. MDS_1 is thus isomorphic to MDS_1, for f obviously satisfies definition 2.

Proof of (*2*). Suppose MDS_1 is isomorphic to MDS_2. Consider $f^{-1}: M_1 \to M_2$. Then, f^{-1} is a bijection and, for any $t \in T$ and $y \in M_1$, $g^t(f^{-1}(y)) = g^t(f^{-1}(f(x))) = g^t(x) = f^{-1}(f(g^t(x))) = f^{-1}(h^t(f(x))) = f^{-1}(h^t(y))$. Therefore, since $f^{-1}(h^t(y)) = g^t(f^{-1}(y))$, MDS_2 is isomorphic to MDS_1.

Proof of (*3*). Let $MDS_1 = \langle T, M_1, \{g_1^t\}\rangle$, $MDS_2 = \langle T, M_2, \{g_2^t\}\rangle$, $MDS_3 = \langle T, M_3, \{g_3^t\}\rangle$. Suppose MDS_1 is isomorphic to MDS_2 and MDS_2 is isomorphic to MDS_3. Let $f_1: M_2 \to M_1$ and $f_2: M_3 \to M_2$ satisfy definition 2. Consider $f_3 = f_2 \circ f_1$. Then, f_3 is a bijection from M_3 to M_1 and, for any $t \in T$ and $x \in M_3$, $g_1^t(f_3(x)) = g_1^t(f_1(f_2(x))) = f_1(g_2^t(f_2(x))) = f_1(f_2(g_3^t(x)) = f_3(g_3^t(x))$. Therefore, since $f_3(g_3^t(x)) = g_1^t(f_3(x))$, MDS_1 is isomorphic to MDS_3.

q.e.d.

Theorem 3

The emulation relation is a quasi-ordering on the set of all mathematical dynamical systems.

Proof. We must prove that the relation of emulation between mathematical dynamical systems is (1) reflexive, and (2) transitive.

Proof of (*1*). Let $u: M \to M$ be the identity function on M. Let $v: M \times T \to T$ be defined by $v(x, t) = t$. Obviously, u and v satisfy conditions (*2a*) and (*2b*) of definition 4. Condition (*2c*) is also satisfied, for $u(g^t(x)) = g^t(x) = g^{v(x,t)}(u(x))$. As for condition (*2d*), suppose $g^t(u(x)) = u(y)$. Thus, $g^t(x) = y$, and $v(x, t) = t$.

Proof of (*2*). Let $MDS_1 = \langle T_1, M_1, \{g_1^t\}\rangle$, $MDS_2 = \langle T_2, M_2, \{g_2^t\}\rangle$, $MDS_3 = \langle T_3, M_3, \{g_3^t\}\rangle$. Suppose MDS_1 mulates MDS_2 and MDS_2 emulates MDS_3. Let $u_1: M_2 \to M_1$, $u_2: M_3 \to M_2$, $v_1: M_2 \times T_2 \to T_1$, $v_2: M_3 \times T_3 \to T_2$ satisfy definition 4. Let $u_3 = u_2 \circ u_1$. Thus, u_3 is injective from M_3 to M_1. Therefore, condition (*2a*) of definition 4 is satisfied. Let $v_3: M_3 \times T_3 \to T_1$ be defined by $v_3(z, t) = v_1(u_2(z), v_2(z, t))$. Thus, v_3 satisfies condition (*2b*) of definition 4 because, first, $v_3(z, 0) = v_1(u_2(z), v_2(z, 0)) = v_1(u_2(z), 0) = 0$. Second, suppose $w < t$. By the definition of v_3, $v_3(z, w) = v_1(u_2(z), v_2(z, w))$ and $v_3(z, t) = v_1(u_2(z), v_2(z, t))$. Since $w < t$ and v_2 satisfies definition 4,

$v_2(z, w) < v_2(z, t)$. Thus, since v_1 satisfies definition 4, $v_1(u_2(z), v_2(z, w)) < v_1(u_2(z), v_2(z, t))$. Therefore, $v_3(z, w) < v_3(z, t)$. The functions u_3 and v_3 also satisfy condition (2*c*) of definition 4, because $u_3(g_3^t(z)) = u_1(u_2(g_3^t(z))) = u_1(g_2^{v_2(z,t)}(u_2(z))) = g_1^{v_1(u_2(z), v_2(z,t))}(u_1(u_2(z))) = g_1^{v_3(z,t)}(u_3(z))$. As for condition (2*d*), suppose $g_1^t(u_3(x)) = u_3(y)$. Thus, by the definition of u_3, $g_1^t(u_1(u_2(x))) = u_1(u_2(y))$. Hence, since u_1 and v_1 satisfy definition 4, there is w such that $g_2^w(u_2(x)) = u_2(y)$ and $t = v_1(u_2(x), w)$. Thus, since u_2 and v_2 satisfy definition 4, there is s such that $g_3^s(x) = y$ and $w = v_2(x, s)$. Therefore, there is s such that $g_3^s(x) = y$ and $t = v_1(u_2(x), v_2(x, s))$. Hence, by the definition of v_3, there is s such that $g_3^s(x) = y$ and $t = v_3(x, s)$.

q.e.d.

THEOREM 9

1. *If* MDS_2 *has periodic orbits and* MDS_1 *emulates* MDS_2, *then* MDS_1 *has periodic orbits;*
2. *if* MDS_2 *has aperiodic orbits,* MDS_1 *emulates* MDS_2, *and* MDS_1 *is a cascade, then* MDS_1 *has aperiodic orbits;*
3. *if* MDS_2 *has eventually periodic orbits and* MDS_1 *emulates* MDS_2, *then* MDS_1 *has eventually periodic orbits;*
4. *if* MDS_2 *has merging orbits and* MDS_1 *emulates* MDS_2, *then* MDS_1 *has merging orbits.*

PROOF OF (*1*). Suppose MDS_2 has periodic orbits and MDS_1 emulates MDS_2. Since MDS_2 has periodic orbits, there is x and $t > 0$ such that $g^t(x) = x$. Since MDS_1 emulates MDS_2, by conditions (2*c*) and (2*b*) of definition 4, $u(g^t(x)) = h^{v(x,t)}(u(x))$ and $v(x, t) > 0$. Hence, since $g^t(x) = x$, $u(x) = h^{v(x,t)}(u(x))$ and $v(x, t) > 0$. Therefore, MDS_1 has periodic orbits.

q.e.d.

PROOF OF (2). Suppose MDS_2 has aperiodic orbits, MDS_1 emulates MDS_2, and MDS_1 is a cascade. Suppose for *reductio* that MDS_1 does not have aperiodic orbits. Since MDS_2 has aperiodic orbits, there is x such that $orb(x)$ is aperiodic. Since MDS_1 does not have aperiodic orbits, $orb(u(x))$ is either periodic or eventually periodic. Therefore, there is $s \geq 0$, such that, for any $w \geq s$, $orb(h^w(u(x)))$ is periodic. Since MDS_1 is a cascade, there is a finite number of state transitions h^k such that $0 \leq k < s$. Let $orb^+(x) = \{y: g^t(x) = y$, for some $t \geq 0\}$. Since $orb(x)$ is aperiodic, for any t and r such that $t \neq r, g^t(x) \neq g^r(x)$. Therefore, $orb^+(x)$ has an infinite number of states. Furthermore, since MDS_1 emulates MDS_2, by condition (2*c*) of definition 4, for any t, $u(g^t(x)) = h^{v(x,t)}(u(x))$. Since u is injective, $orb^+(x)$ has an infinite number of states, and there is a finite number of state transitions h^k such that $0 \leq k < s$, it follows that there is t such that $u(g^t(x)) = h^{v(x,t)}(u(x))$, and $v(x, t) \geq s$. Therefore, $orb(u(g^t(x)))$ is periodic. Thus, there is $p > 0$ such that $h^p(u(g^t(x))) = u(g^t(x))$. Since MDS_1 emulates MDS_2, by condition (*2d*) of definition 4, there is q such that $g^q(g^t(x)) = g^t(x)$ and $v(g^t(x), q) = p$. By condition (*2b*) of definition 4, since $p > 0$, $q > 0$. Therefore, $orb(g^t(x))$ is periodic. But, since $orb(x)$ is aperiodic, $orb(g^t(x))$ is not periodic. We have thus reached a contradiction. Therefore, MDS_1 has aperiodic orbits.

q.e.d.

PROOF OF (*3*). Suppose MDS_2 has eventually periodic orbits and MDS_1 emulates MDS_2. Since MDS_2 has eventually periodic orbits, there are x, y, and t such that $orb(x)$ is not periodic, $g^t(x) = y$, and $orb(y)$ is periodic. Since MDS_1 emulates MDS_2, by condition (*2c*) of definition 4, $u(g^t(x)) = h^{v(x,t)}(u(x))$. Hence, since $g^t(x) = y$ and $orb(y)$ is periodic, $h^{v(x,t)}(u(x)) = u(y)$ and $orb(u(y))$ is periodic. Suppose for *reductio* that $orb(u(x))$ is periodic. Thus, there is $s > 0$ such that $h^s(u(x)) = u(x)$. Hence, since MDS_1 emulates MDS_2, by condition (*2d*) of definition 4, there is a time w such that $g^w(x) = x$ and $v(x, w) = s$. Since $v(x, w) = s$ and $s > 0$, by condition (*2b*) of definition 4, $w > 0$. Hence, $orb(x)$ is periodic. But $orb(x)$ is not periodic. Thus, $orb(u(x))$ is not periodic, $h^{v(x,t)}(u(x)) = u(y)$, and $orb(u(y))$ is periodic. Therefore, MDS_1 has eventually periodic orbits.

q.e.d.

PROOF OF (*4*). By theorem 8 and corollary 5.1.

q.e.d.

THEOREM 10

The realization relation is a quasi-ordering on the set of all mathematical dynamical systems.

PROOF. We must prove that the relation of realization between mathematical dynamical systems is (1) reflexive, and (2) transitive.

Proof of (*1*). For any state x of a mathematical dynamical system MDS, let $u(x) = \{x\}$. Note that, by identifying x with $\{x\}$, the realization relation reduces to the emulation relation. Therefore, by theorem 3, the realization relation is reflexive.

Proof of (2). Let $MDS_1 = \langle T_1, M_1, \{g_1^t\}\rangle$, $MDS_2 = \langle T_2, M_2, \{g_2^t\}\rangle$, $MDS_3 = \langle T_3, M_3, \{g_3^t\}\rangle$. Suppose MDS_1 realizes MDS_2 and MDS_2 realizes MDS_3. Let u_1: $M_2 \to D_1$ and v_1: $M_2 \times T_2 \to T_1$ satisfy definition 5. Let u_2: $M_3 \to D_2$ and v_2: $M_3 \times T_3 \to T_2$ satisfy definition 5. For any $z \in M_3$ and $t \in T_3$, let f: $M_3 \to M_2$ satisfy $f(z) \in u_2(z)$ and $f(g_3^t(z)) = g_2^{v_2(z,t)}(f(z))$. For any $z \in M_3$, let $u_3(z) = u_1(f(z))$. Let D be the image of u_3. By the definition of u_3, D is a set of mutually disjoint subsets of M_1, and u_3 is a bijection from M_3 to D. Condition (*2a*) of definition 5 is thus satisfied. Let v_3: $M_3 \times T_3 \to T_1$ be defined by $v_3(z, t) = v_1(f(z), v_2(z, t))$. Thus, v_3 satisfies condition (*2b*) of definition 5 because, first, $v_3(z, 0) = v_1(f(z), v_2(z, 0)) = v_1(f(z), 0) = 0$. Second, suppose $w < t$. By the definition of v_3, $v_3(z, w) = v_1(f(z), v_2(z, w))$ and $v_3(z, t) = v_1(f(z), v_2(z, t))$. Since $w < t$ and v_2 satisfies definition 5, $v_2(z, w) < v_2(z, t)$. Thus, since v_1 satisfies definition 5, $v_1(f(z), v_2(z, w)) < v_1(f(z), v_2(z, t))$. Therefore, $v_3(z, w) < v_3(z, t)$. The functions u_3 and v_3 also satisfy condition (*2c*) of definition 5. We must prove that, for any $\alpha \in u_3(z)$, $g_1^{v_3(z,t)}(\alpha) \in u_3(g_3^t(z))$. By the definition of v_3, $v_3(z, t) = v_1(f(z), v_2(z, t))$. By the definitions of u_3 and f, $u_3(g_3^t(z)) = u_1(f(g_3^t(z))) = u_1(g_2^{v_2(z,t)}(f(z)))$. By the definition of u_3, $u_3(z) = u_1(f(z))$. Since u_1 and v_1 satisfy condition (*2c*) of definition 5, for any $\alpha \in u_1(f(z))$, $g_1^{v_1(f(z),v_2(z,t))}(\alpha) \in u_I(g_2^{v_2(z,t)}(f(z)))$. Therefore, for any $\alpha \in u_3(z)$, $g_1^{v_3(z,t)}(\alpha) \in u_3(g_3^t(z))$. As for condition (*2d*), suppose $\alpha \in u_3(x)$, $\beta \in u_3(y)$, and $g_1^t(\alpha) = \beta$. Thus, by the definition of u_3, $\alpha \in u_1(f(x))$, $\beta \in u_1(f(y))$, and $g_1^t(\alpha) = \beta$. Hence, since u_1 and v_1 satisfy condition (*2d*) of definition 5, there is w such that $g_2^w(f(x)) = f(y)$ and $t = v_1(f(x), w)$. Thus, by the definition of f, and since u_2 and v_2 satisfy condition (*2d*) of definition 5, there is s such that $g_3^s(x) = y$ and $w = v_2(x, s)$. Therefore, there is s such that $g_3^s(x) = y$ and $t = v_1(f(x), v_2(x, s))$. Hence, by the definition of v_3, there is s such that $g_3^s(x) = y$ and $t = v_3(x, s)$.

q.e.d.

Notes

1. The proof of this first kind of theorem is frequently given as a part of the proof that a certain type of system can compute all (partial) recursive functions.

2. Several authors have studied computational devices whose basic operations are transformations of real numbers or, even more generally, transformations that define some abstract mathematical structure on some set (Blum et al. 1989; Friedman 1971; Shepherdson 1975, 1985, 1988). These devices may not be computational systems in the standard sense, for an operation on real numbers involves the manipulation of an infinite amount of information; therefore it may not in general be possible to effectively describe the basic

operations of these machines. Within standard computation theory it is possible to define computable functions on the real numbers, but the values of these functions can never be exactly computed. Rather, these values are calculable to any desired degree of accuracy (Turing 1965; Pour-El and Richards 1989). By contrast, the basic operations of the devices mentioned above are assumed to have infinite precision, in the sense that they yield the exact values of a real-valued function. Other devices that may not be standard computational systems are unrestricted cellular automata. These cellular automata either operate on arrays with an infinite number of cells in a nonblank state, or they do not satisfy the restriction that a neighborhood whose cells are all in the blank state never changes the state of its central cell.

3. Alvy Ray Smith defines the emulation relation between cellular automata and Turing machines (1971, def. 4). However, his definition only applies to cellular automata emulating Turing machines, not to the converse case.

4. The main difference is that cellular automata are able to emulate each step of a Turing machine in real time, while Turing machines take several steps to emulate one step of a cellular automaton. Furthermore, a Turing machine will, in general, emulate different steps of a cellular automaton in different times.

5. The operation of a standard digital computer is based on the storage and interaction of electrical currents. These electrical activities are continuous, and their behavior is described by differential equations. These equations thus specify a continuous dynamical model of a particular physical system (i.e., the digital computer at the level of its physical operation). On the other hand, the information-processing level of the digital computer is described by an appropriate computational system. This system is thus a computational dynamical model of a particular information-processing system (i.e., the digital computer at its information-processing level). Thus, the two different levels of the digital computer are described by two different types of mathematical dynamical systems: a continuous system describes the physical level, while a computational system describes the information-processing level. It is usually believed that, if we had a detailed description of these two dynamical models, we would find that, with appropriate identifications, the second is reducible to the first. In this sense, then, a computational system would be realized by a dynamical model of a physical system.

6. This does not contradict the result of section 6, that all universal computational systems are strongly irreversible. Universal systems can be defined in two ways, depending on whether they *emulate* or *realize* all computational systems. If we choose the first definition, all universal systems turn out to be strongly irreversible. The second definition, instead, allows for reversible universal systems.

7. A nonempty set X is a *commutative group* with respect to a binary operation $\otimes$: $X \times X \to X$ if and only if $\otimes$ is associative and commutative, and there is $e \in X$ such that, for any $x \in X$, there is $x^{-1} \in X$ such that $e \otimes x = x$

and $x \otimes x^{-1} = e$. The element e is called the *unity*, and x^{-1} is called the *inverse of x relative to* $\otimes$.

8. A nonempty set X is a *commutative monoid* with respect to a binary operation $\otimes$: $X \times X \rightarrow X$ if and only if $\otimes$ is associative and commutative, and there is $e \in X$ such that, for any $x \in X$, $e \otimes x = x$. The element e is called the *unity*.

9. This property expresses the fact that in *irreversible systems* (that is, systems where time is limited to the nonnegative portion of R, Q, or Z) there may be merging orbits, but no intersecting orbits.

10. Koçak (1986, p. 23). For a complete analysis of the dynamical behavior of the logistic function see Devaney (1989).

11. This definition of a Turing machine is apparently more restrictive than the usual one that allows *any* consistent set of quadruples, but in fact it is not. If a consistent set of quadruples does not contain a quadruple beginning with q_ia_j, we simply add the quadruple $q_ia_ja_jq_i$, and we adopt a slightly different convention to determine when a Turing machine stops. A Turing machine stops if and only if the position of the head, the internal state of the control unit, and all the symbols on the tape no longer change. This is equivalent to requiring that the Turing machine's state no longer change.

12. If G is a consistent set of mn quadruples, $g[G]$ is a function defined for all states of the Turing machine C. If G were allowed to be *any* consistent set of quadruples, $g[G]$ might be undefined for some state.

13. For example, an equivalent approach uses the concept of recursive function.

14. I take a Turing machine C to compute a function f: $X \rightarrow Y$ (where $X, Y \subseteq P(A)$) if and only if \$ and # are two symbols that do not belong to the alphabet A and, for any finite string $x \in X$, when C is started in internal state q_0, on the left marker \$ of a tape whose content is . . . *bb\$x#bb* . . . , C stops on the left marker \$ of a tape whose content is . . . *bb\$f(x)#bb*. . . .

I take the characteristic function of $M_1 \subseteq P(A)$ to be χ: $P(A) \rightarrow \{b, bb\}$, where b is the string that only contains one blank, bb is the string obtained by concatenating two blanks, and $\chi(x) = bb$ if $x \in M_1$, $\chi(x) = b$ if $x \notin M_1$.

15. If either condition is not satisfied, an infinite number of cells may need to be updated in one time step. No Turing machine could thus compute this step in a finite time. Cellular automata that do not satisfy one of these conditions may thus be more powerful than Turing machines, and they may not be computational systems in the sense of definition 3.

16. C is a $\langle n, m \rangle$ linear cellular automaton just in case each cell has n possible states and the updating of each cell depends on a neighborhood of radius m.

17. Also note that condition (*2d*) is in fact equivalent to: For any $t \in T_1^+$, if $h^t(u(x)) = u(y)$, there is a time $w \in T_2$ such that $v(x, w) = t$. I have chosen (*2d*) instead of this simpler formulation because (*2d*) makes the proofs of some theorems easier (i.e., theorems 3, 8, and 9).

18. One might also wonder what the relationship is between definition 4 and that of isomorphism (definition 2). First, note that the relation of isomorphism is a special case of emulation (if MDS_1 is isomorphic to MDS_2, choose $u = f$, and v to be the function that, for any x and t, satisfies $v(x, t) = t$). Second, in this special case, $u = f$ is injective and surjective (i.e., it is a bijection) and, for any $x \in M_2$, $v_x(t) = v(x, t) = t$ is injective and surjective too (recall that, by definition 2, $T_2 = T_1$). However, in the general case, surjectivity for either u or v_x is not ensured (condition (*2a*) of definition 4 only requires injectivity for u; similarly, condition (*2b*) entails that, for any x, v_x is injective, but not necessarily surjective). Third, condition (*2c*) is the obvious generalization of the second part of condition (*2*) of the definition of isomorphism.

As for condition (*2d*), one might wonder why it does not seem to correspond to any clause of definition 2. The reason is that, by taking $T_2 = T_1$ and $v_x(t) = v(x, t) = t$, v_x turns out to be surjective for any x, and thus condition (*2d*) is automatically satisfied. But, since the general case does not ensure the surjectivity of v_x, condition (*2d*) may not be automatically satisfied, and we thus need to explicitly require it.

These considerations make plausible that condition (*2d*) is in fact independent of the other conditions of definition 4. However, I have not been able to actually prove this point. To show the independence of (*2d*) we should exhibit two mathematical dynamical systems MDS_1 and MDS_2, and two functions u and v, which satisfy conditions (*1*), (*2a*), (*2b*), and (*2c*) but do not satisfy condition (*2d*). For this to be possible, however, the emulating system MDS_1 cannot be a cascade. This fact makes the search of a proof much harder.

19. This construction is simple and extremely natural, but it is not the most economical one. If C_1 has n symbols and m internal states, C_0 has $n + m$ cell states. It is possible to reduce this number to $max(n + 1, m + 1)$ (Smith 1971, th. 3).

20. This means that different copies of a may represent different symbols of the alphabet A. Therefore, a is not a variable.

21. Suppose $orb(x)$ is merging, and assume for *reductio* that $orb(x)$ is periodic. Since $orb(x)$ is merging, there is $y \neq x$ such that $orb(x) \cap orb(y) \neq \varnothing$, $orb(x) \not\subseteq orb(y)$, and orb(y) $orb(x)$. Thus, there is z such that $z \in orb(x)$ and $z \in orb(y)$. Since $orb(x)$ is periodic, and $z \in orb(x)$, $orb(z) = orb(x)$. Since $z \in orb(y)$, $orb(z) \subseteq orb(y)$. Thus, $orb(x) \subseteq orb(y)$. But $orb(x) \not\subseteq orb(y)$. Therefore, $orb(x)$ is not periodic.

22. Also note that the class of all logically reversible Turing machines is decidable. In fact, an arbitrary state transition of a Turing machine is injective if and only if the function determined by the quadruples of the Turing machine is injective, and we can decide this condition by inspecting the quadruples. If M is the state space of the Turing machine, each of its quadruples is an injective function from $X \subset M$ to M, and the domains of any two of its quadruples are disjoint. Therefore, the function determined by the quadruples is injective if and only if the images of any two quadruples do not overlap.

Furthermore, the following conditions hold: (1) two quadruples $q_j a_i a_m q_n$ and $q_s a_r a_k q_l$ have overlapping images if and only if $m = k$ and $n = l$; (2) two quadruples $q_j a_i L q_n$ and $q_s a_r L q_l$ ($q_j a_i R q_n$ and $q_s a_r R q_l$) have overlapping images if and only if $n = l$ and $i = r$; (3) two quadruples $q_j a_i L q_n$ and $q_s a_r a_k q_l$ ($q_j a_i R q_n$ and $q_s a_r a_k q_l$) have overlapping images if and only if $n = l$; (4) two quadruples $q_j a_i L q_n$ and $q_s a_r R q_l$ have overlapping images if and only if $n = l$. Obviously, these conditions allow us to decide whether there is a pair of quadruples with overlapping images. If no such pair exists, the Turing machine is logically reversible, and its halting problem is thus decidable. For example, a simple logically reversible Turing machine is specified by the quadruples $G = \{q_0 bRq_0, q_0 1 q_1, q_1 bb q_1, q_1 1 R q_2, q_2 b R q_2, q_2 1 R q_0\}$.

23. Let C be a Turing machine that computes the state transition h^1 of $MDS_1 = \langle T, M_1, \{h^t\}\rangle$. Thus, for any state $x \in M_1$, if C is started in internal state q_0, on the left marker $ of a tape whose content is . . . *bb$x#bb* . . . , C stops on the left marker $ of a tape whose content is . . . $bb\$h^t(x)\#bb$. . . . Since C stops on the left marker $, the set of quadruples of C must contain some quadruple of the form $q_i\$\$q_i$. If one of these quadruples is $q_0\$\$q_0$, let us replace it with the two quadruples $q_0\$\$q_{stop}$ and $q_{stop}\$\$q_{stop}$, where q_{stop} is not an internal state of C. We thus obtain a second machine C' which also computes h^1, but never stops at time 0 when started in state . . . $bbq_0\$x\#bb$. . . . Let us then replace each quadruple of C' of the form $q_i\$\$q_i$ with $q_i\$\$q_0$. We thus obtain a third machine C″ that emulates MDS_1. To verify this fact, let u and v be defined as follows: $u(x) =$ . . . $bbq_0\$x\#bb$ . . . ; $v(x, 0) = 0$, $v(x, 1) =$ the time at which the computation of C' that starts with . . . $bbq_0\$x\#bb$ . . . stops, and $v(x, t + 1) = v(x, t) + v(h^t(x), 1)$. It is then easy to verify that u and v satisfy definition 4.

24. We can obtain a proof of this fact by following the lines of one of the standard proofs of the existence of a universal Turing machine.

25. For example, the Turing machine specified by $\{q_0 0 1 q_1, q_0 1 1 q_0, q_1 0 1 q_1, q_1 1 1 q_1\}$ is strongly irreversible, for this Turing machine has merging orbits. To see this point, consider the orbits of the two states . . . $0q_0 0$ . . . and . . . $0q_1 0$. . . . These two orbits are merging, for they are not in the subset relation and their intersection is not empty.

26. All the orbits of the Turing machine specified by $\{q_0 0 0 q_0, q_0 1 1 q_0\}$ are periodic. All the orbits of the Turing machine specified by $\{q_0 0 R q_0, q_0 1 R q_0\}$ are aperiodic. The Turing machine specified by $\{q_0 0 1 q_1, q_0 1 1 q_0, q_1 0 0 q_1, q_1 1 1 q_1\}$ has eventually periodic orbits (for example, the orbit of state . . . $0q_0 0$ . . .). The Turing machine specified by $\{q_0 0 1 q_1, q_0 1 1 q_0, q_1 0 1 q_1, q_1 1 R q_1\}$ has merging orbits (for example, the orbits of states . . . $0q_0 0$ . . . and . . . $0q_1 0$ . . .).

27. The existence of this function is guaranteed by the fact that u_2 and v_2 satisfy condition (2*c*) of definition 5.

28. Recall that any universal computational system is strongly irreversible, and thus irreversible (see section 6).

TWO

Generalized Computational Systems

1 Introduction

The definition of a computational system that I proposed in chapter 1 (definition 3) employs the concept of Turing computability. In this chapter, however, I will show that this concept is not absolute, but instead depends on the relational structure of the support on which Turing machines operate. Ordinary Turing machines operate on a linear tape divided into a countably infinite number of adjacent squares. But one can also think of Turing machines that operate on different supports. For example, we can let a Turing machine work on an infinite checkerboard[1] or, more generally, on some n-dimensional infinite array. I call an arbitrary support on which a Turing machine can operate a *pattern field*. Depending on the pattern field F we choose, we in fact obtain different concepts of computability. At the end of this chapter (section 6), I will thus propose a new definition of a computational system (a computational system on pattern field F) that takes into account the relativity of the concept of Turing computability. If F is a doubly infinite tape, however, computational systems on F reduce to computational systems.

Turing (1965) presented his machines as an idealization of a human being that transforms symbols by means of a specified set of rules. Turing based his analysis on four hypotheses:

1. The capacity to recognize, transform, and memorize symbols and rules is finite. It thus follows that any transformation of a complex symbol must always be reduced to a series of simpler transformations. These operations on elementary symbols are of three types: recognizing a symbol, replacing a symbol, and shifting the attention to a symbol that is contiguous to the symbol which has been considered earlier.
2. The series of elementary operations that are in fact executed is determined by three factors: first, the subject's mental state at a given time; second, the symbol which the subject considers at that time; third, a rule chosen from a finite number of alternatives. Turing assumed that the number of possible mental states is finite,[2] and that the rules are of two different types: (1) If the mental state at a given time is q_i, and the symbol considered at that time is a_j, replace a_j by a_k, and change mental state from q_i to q_l; and (2) if the mental state at a given time is q_i, and the symbol considered at that time is a_j, shift the attention to a contiguous symbol (to the right, to the left, above, below, etc.) and change mental state from q_i to q_l.
3. The elementary symbols are written on a support with an infinite capacity. This support (for example a sheet of paper that can be extended in any direction as needed) is divided into cells, and each cell may contain, at most, one elementary symbol. The number of cells that actually contain symbols is finite.
4. All different types of support can always be replaced by a tape divided into an infinite number of cells, and this replacement does not limit the computational capacity.

If we think of a transformation of symbols that a human being can perform by applying a finite number of rules, the first three of Turing's hypotheses appear to be adequate idealizations. The adequacy of the fourth hypothesis, however, is not so immediately apparent. For, first, we can imagine having a support whose cells satisfy the following condition: Each cell is connected to a fixed number of other cells or, more precisely, for an arbitrary cell, there are exactly s ($s > 0$) different *types of path* that lead to other cells. Second, if each type of path can always be distinguished from the others, we could use this support to perform a transformation of symbols that satisfies Turing's first three hypotheses. The rules would be of the two forms: (1) If the mental state at a given time is q_i, and the symbol considered at that time is a_j, replace a_j with a_k and change mental state from q_i to q_l; and (2) if the mental state at a given time is q_i, and the symbol considered at that time is a_i, shift the attention to the symbol at the end of the path of type r ($0 \leq r < s$) and change mental state from q_i to q_l. But then, a natural question arises. If the relational structure of the support were sufficiently complex, could it happen that the symbolic transformations performed on it would not be reducible to those of a simpler structure? Or, more precisely, are we sure that a support with a very complex arrangement of connections between its cells can always be replaced by a tape divided into an infinite number of cells, and that this replacement does not limit the computational capacity?

The standard answer to this question is based on empirical considerations. We can in fact prove that many different types of support are equivalent. As mentioned, we can let a Turing machine operate on an infinite checkerboard or, more generally, on some n-dimensional infinite array, and we can show that a Turing machine of this type is not more powerful than an ordinary one. On the base of this evidence, one then concludes that the computational power of Turing machines cannot depend on the type of support on which they operate.

Nevertheless, this argument is not convincing. The relational structure of the supports for which we can prove the equivalence is in fact quite simple. But what happens if the cells are connected in arbitrarily complex ways? The next four sections of this chapter allow us to give a definite answer to this question. One of the surprising results is that some Turing machines that operate on supports with a sufficiently complex relational structure are capable of computing numeric functions that are not recursive.[3] Therefore, these machines are more powerful than ordinary Turing machines, and we must thus conclude that Turing's fourth hypothesis is false.

2 Turing machines on pattern field F

I have informally characterized a pattern field as an arbitrary support on which a Turing machine can operate. Therefore, a pattern field (see figure 2-1) consists of a countably infinite set U of *cells* that satisfy the following condition: Each cell is connected to a fixed number of other cells or, in other words, for an arbitrary cell, there are exactly $s (s > 0)$ different types of path that lead to other cells. Each type of path can thus be identified with a function f_r: $U \rightarrow U$ ($0 \leq r < s$). I call the set of functions $\{f_r\}$ the *relational structure* of the pattern field $F = \langle U, \{f_r\}\rangle$, and I formally define F in definition 1 below. Graphic representations of examples 1 through 3 are shown in figure 2-2.

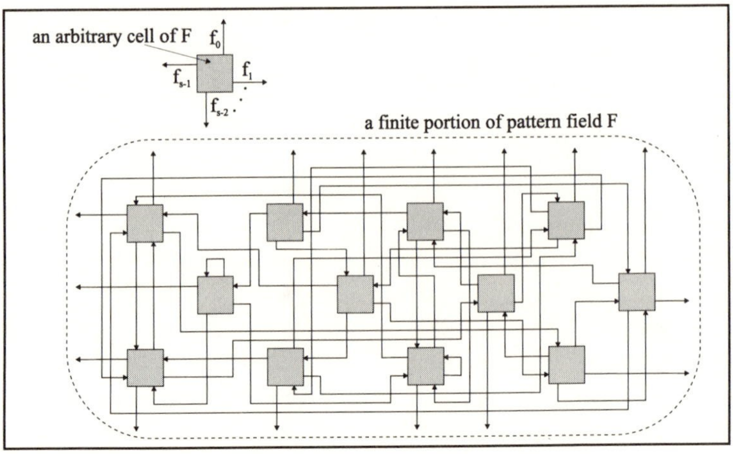

FIGURE 2-1 Pattern fields. Pattern field $F = \langle U, \{f_r\}\rangle$. U = set with a countably infinite number of elements (the cells of F). $\{f_r\}$ = set of s $(0 \leq r < s)$ functions from U to U (the relational structure of F).

DEFINITION 1 *(pattern fields)*

F = ⟨U, *{*f_r*}⟩ is a pattern field if and only if:*

1. U *is a set with a countably infinite number of elements. I call the elements of* U *the* cells *of the pattern field* F;

2. {f_r*} is a set of* s *(0 ≤* r *<* s*) functions from* U *to* U. *I call the functions {*f_r*} the* relational structure *of the pattern field* F.

EXAMPLE 1 (a tape infinite in one direction is a pattern field)

Let U = the set of all squares of a tape infinite in one direction (say to the right), and let $\{L, R\}$ satisfy these conditions: If x is not the leftmost square, $L(x)$ = the square to the left of square x; otherwise, $L(x) = x$; $R(x)$ = the square to the right of x. Then, by definition 1, $F_1 = \langle U, \{L, R\}\rangle$ is a pattern field.

EXAMPLE 2 (a tape infinite in two directions is a pattern field)

Let U = the set of all squares of a doubly infinite tape, and let $\{L, R\}$ satisfy these conditions: $L(x)$ = the square to the left of square x; $R(x)$ = the square to the right of x. Then, by definition 1, $F_2 = \langle U, \{L, R\}\rangle$ is a pattern field.

EXAMPLE 3 (an infinite checkerboard is a pattern field)

Let U = the set of all squares of an infinite checkerboard, and let $\{L, R, A, B\}$ satisfy these conditions: $L(x)$ = the square to the

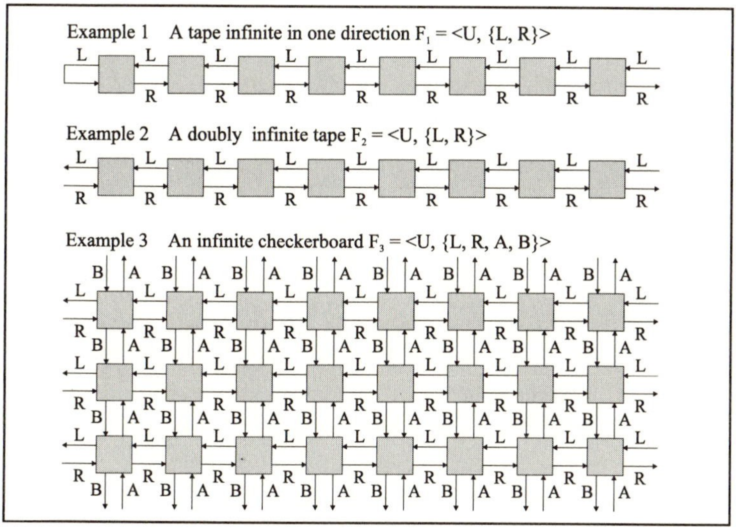

FIGURE 2-2 Three examples of pattern field.

left of square x; $R(x)$ = the square to the right of x; $A(x)$ = the square above x; $B(x)$ = the square below x. Then, by definition 1, $F_3 = \langle U, \{L, R, A, B\}\rangle$ is a pattern field.

Let $A = \{a_j\}$ be a finite alphabet with n $(0 \leq j < n)$ symbols. I call the first symbol a_0 of the alphabet the *blank*, and I often indicate a_0 by b. A *finite pattern* (or more simply a *pattern*) of a pattern field $F = \langle U, \{f_r\}\rangle$ relative to alphabet $A = \{a_j\}$ is a function from U to A that assigns nonblank symbols to a finite number of cells. Let us indicate the set of all finite patterns of F relative to alphabet A by $F(A)$.

I now define a *Turing machine C on pattern field F* as follows. Let $F = \langle U, \{f_r\}\rangle$ be a pattern field, and suppose a finite alphabet $A_C = \{a_j\}$ with n $(0 \leq j < n)$ symbols, and a set of internal states $Q_C = \{q_i\}$ with m $(0 \leq i < m)$ elements are given. An instruction is any quadruple of one of the two forms $q_i a_j a_k q_l$ or $q_i a_j f_r q_l$. A quadruple of the first form means: If the internal state is q_i and the symbol on the cell $x \in U$ where the machine is located is a_j, write symbol a_k on cell x and change internal state to q_l. A quadruple of the second form means: If the internal state is q_i and the symbol on the cell x where the machine is located is a_j, go to cell $f_r(x)$ and change internal state to q_l. Any Turing machine C on pattern field F is specified by a consistent set G_C of mn quadruples, where two different quadruples are consistent if and only if they do not begin with the same pair ⟨*internal state*, *symbol*⟩.

Intuitively, the *state* of a Turing machine C on pattern field F contains all the information sufficient (and necessary) for determining the future behavior of the machine (see figure 2-3). Therefore, the state is determined when a pattern $p \in F(A_C)$, a cell $x \in U$, and an internal state $q_i \in Q_C$ are fixed. It is, however, more convenient to identify the state with a special pattern. Suppose the state of a Turing machine C on F is determined by pattern p, cell x, and internal state q_i, and that the symbol on cell x is a_j. Consider now the pattern w such that, on cell x, w has the symbol q_ia_j, and w agrees with p on all other cells. Obviously, the state determined by p, x, and q_i can be identified with this pattern $w \in F(B_C)$, where B_C is the alphabet $A_C \cup \{q_ia_j\}$. The state of a Turing machine C on F is formally defined as follows.

Let $Q_C = \{q_i\}$ and $A_C = \{a_j\}$ be, respectively, the set of internal states and the alphabet of a Turing machine C on pattern field $F = \langle U, \{f_r\}\rangle$. Let m be the number of internal states that are members of Q_C, and let n be the number of symbols that are members of A_C. Let B_C be the set that contains all the symbols that are members of A_C and all the symbols q_ia_j such that $q_i \in Q_C$ and $a_j \in A_C$. Thus B_C has $n + mn$ members. I call this set the *extended alphabet of the Turing machine C*. Then, w is a *state of C* if and only if w is a function from U to B_C that assigns nonblank symbols to a finite number of cells, and there is exactly one cell $x \in U$ such that $w(x) = q_ia_j$, for some $q_i \in Q_C$ and

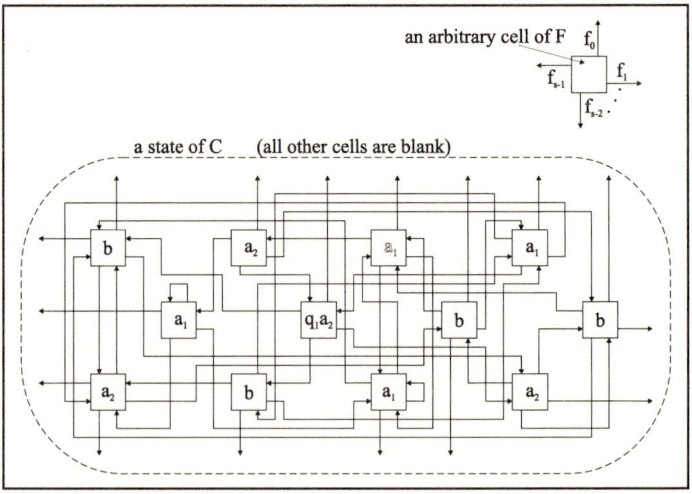

FIGURE 2-3 A state of a Turing machine C on pattern field F. Pattern field $F = \langle U, \{f_r\}\rangle$. C = Turing machine on F. $\{q_i\}$ = set of internal states of C. $\{a_j\}$ = alphabet of C. $a_0 = b$ = the blank.

$a_j \in A_C$. We thus see that the set of all states of Turing machine C is a proper subset M_C of the set $F(B_C)$ of all finite patterns of F relative to the extended alphabet B_C of the machine. If, at time t, the pattern is $p \in F(A_C)$, the Turing machine C is on cell x, and its internal state is q_i, then the state of C at t is the pattern $w \in F(B_C)$ such that $w(x) = q_ip(x)$ and, for any cell $y \neq x$, $w(y) = p(y)$.

If G_C is the set of quadruples that specifies a Turing machine C on F, G_C determines a function $g[G_C]$: $M_C \rightarrow M_C$, where $M_C \subset F(B_C)$ is the set of all states of C. We can thus identify C with the cascade[4] $\langle T, M_C, \{g^t\}\rangle$, where T is the set of the nonnegative integers Z^+, g^0 is the identity function on the state space M_C and, for any $t > 0$, the state transition g^t is obtained by iterating t times the function $g[G_C]$ (therefore, in particular, $g^1 = g[G_C]$). Once an initial state $w \in M_C$ is chosen, the Turing machine C performs a computation, and the *computation that starts with w stops* if and only if there is a time t such that $g^t(w) = g^1(g^t(w))$. Furthermore, I say that the *computation that starts with w stops at time t* if and only if $g^t(w) = g^1(g^t(w))$.

Let Z^{+n} $(1 \leq n)$ be the n-th Cartesian product of the nonnegative integers. By a *numeric function of n arguments* I mean any total or partial function from Z^{+n} to Z^+, and by a *numeric function* I mean any numeric function of one argument. Since we want to use Turing machines to compute numeric functions,[5] we first need to choose a format for their computation. A *format* Φ *for the computation of a numeric function f*: $Z^+ \rightarrow Z^+$ *on a pattern field* $F = \langle U, \{f_r\}\rangle$ consists of a convention that (1) specifies a finite alphabet A_Φ, and (2) for any Turing machine $C = \langle T, M_C, \{g^t\}\rangle$ on F with alphabet $A_C = A_\Phi$, specifies a function γ_C: $Z^+ \rightarrow M_C$ and a (partial) function δ_C: $M_C \rightarrow Z^+$. The function γ_C allows us to code an argument of the numeric function f we want to compute as an initial state of the machine C. The (partial) function δ_C, on the other hand, allows us to decode the value of the numeric function f from the state reached by the machine at the end of the computation.[6] Once we have chosen a format Φ, we can thus stipulate that *f is computable on F in format* Φ if and only if there is a Turing machine C on F with alphabet $A_C = A_\Phi$ such that, for any $n \in Z^+$, if $f(n)$ is defined, the computation that starts with $\gamma_C(n)$ stops and, if the final state of this computation is w, $\delta_C(w)$ is defined and $\delta_C(w) = f(n)$; if $f(n)$ is not defined, the computation that starts with $\gamma_C(n)$ does not stop.

For example, if the pattern field is $F_2 = \langle U, \{L, R\}\rangle$, that is, the doubly infinite tape of an ordinary Turing machine (see example 2), then a widely used format for the computation of a numeric function consists of the following convention (see Davis 1958):

1. The alphabet A_Φ only contains the two symbols b and 1.
2. Input number $n \in Z^+$ is represented by a tape with a block of $n + 1$ consecutive 1s, and which is otherwise blank; and the leftmost 1 is located on a fixed square x_0 of the tape.
3. Given a tape that represents input number n, an arbitrary Turing machine C on F_2 with alphabet $A_C = A_\Phi = \{b, 1\}$ starts its computation on square x_0, and in internal state q_0.
4. A state of the Turing machine C represents output number $m \in Z^+$ if and only if the tape that corresponds to this state has exactly m 1s on it.

It is thus clear that, for any Turing machine $C = \langle T, M_C, \{g^t\}\rangle$ on F_2 with alphabet $A_C = A_\Phi = \{b, 1\}$, this convention specifies two functions γ_C: $Z^+ \to M_C$ and δ_C: $M_C \to Z^+$. The coding function γ_C is specified by the conjunction of (2) and (3). More precisely, condition (2) specifies a function π_C: $Z^+ \to F_2(A_C)$, where $F_2(A_C)$ is the set of all finite patterns of F_2 relative to alphabet $A_C = A_\Phi = \{b, 1\}$. Condition (3), on the other hand, specifies a partial function σ_C: $F_2(A_C) \to M_C$. The coding function γ_C: $Z^+ \to M_C$ is thus the composition of π_C and σ_C. The decoding function δ_C is specified by condition (4). More precisely, δ_C: $M_C \to Z^+$ is the composition of two functions ϕ_C: $M_C \to F_2(A_C)$ and η_C: $F_2(A_C) \to Z^+$. The function ϕ_C assigns to any state $w \in M_C$ the finite pattern $p \in F_2(A_C)$ that corresponds to this state. The function η_C, on the other hand, assigns to pattern p the number of 1s of this pattern. I call this particular convention the *standard format* for the computation of a numeric function on a doubly infinite tape.

We should now note an important property of the standard format. Both the coding function γ_C and the decoding function δ_C specified by this format are *effective* in the following sense. Let e: $Z^+ \to U$ be the enumeration of the squares of the doubly infinite tape $F_2 = \langle U, \{L, R\}\rangle$ that assigns to number 0 the square x_0 specified by the standard format, to increasing even numbers the squares to its right, and to increasing odd numbers the squares to its left. I call this bijection e the *standard enumeration* of the tape. Then, both the coding function γ_C and the decoding function δ_C specified by the standard format are effective relative to the standard enumeration of the tape. To understand what this means, let us note first that, once the standard enumeration e is given, we can identify any state $w \in M_C \subset F_2(B_C)$ with a numeral $\mathbf{w}_e$ in base $2 + m2$, where m is the number of internal states of the Turing machine C whose alphabet is $A_C = A = \{b, 1\}$. The least significant digit of numeral $\mathbf{w}_e$ is the symbol member of the extended alphabet B_C that the state w assigns to square $e(0) = x_0$, its second digit is the symbol assigned to square $e(1)$, its third digit is the symbol assigned to square $e(2)$, etc. Its highest significant digit is thus the symbol assigned to square $e(u)$, where u is the smallest number such that for any $v > u$, the symbol assigned to square $e(v)$ is the blank. I indicate the number denoted by numeral $\boldsymbol{w_e}$ by w_e. Now, it is easy to verify (see examples 4 and 5) that the coding function γ_C: $Z^+ \to M_C$ and the decoding function δ_C: $M_C \to Z^+$ specified by the standard format respectively satisfy the following conditions: (1) there is a total recursive function γ_{Ce}: $Z^+ \to Z^+$ such that, for any $n \in Z^+$, if $\gamma_C(n) = w$, $\gamma_{Ce}(n) = w_e$; and (2) there is a total recursive function δ_{Ce}: $Z^+ \to Z^+$ such that, for any $w \in M_C$, if $\delta_C(w) = n$, $\delta_{Ce}(w_e) = n$. In this sense, then, both the coding function γ_C and the decoding function δ_C specified by the standard format are effective relative to the standard enumeration of the tape.

EXAMPLE 4 (the coding γ_C specified by the standard format for the computation of a numeric function on a doubly infinite tape is effective relative to the standard enumeration of the tape)

We have seen that the coding γ_C: $Z^+ \to M_C$ specified by the standard format is the composition of π_C: $Z^+ \to F_2(A_C)$ and σ_C: $F_2(A_C) \to M_C$, where $F_2(A_C)$ is the set of all finite patterns of a doubly infinite tape relative to alphabet $A_C = \{a_j\} = \{b, 1\}$, and M_C is the set of all states of Turing machine C. The function π_C assigns to number n the pattern p_n that has a block of $n + 1$ consecutive 1s, and is otherwise blank. The leftmost 1 is located on a fixed square x_0 of the tape. The partial function σ_C, on the other hand, assigns to pattern p_n the state w_n that, on square x_0, has the symbol $q_0 1$ and, on any other square $x \neq x_0$, has the symbol $p_n(x)$. Let e be the standard enumeration of the tape. Then, first, we can identify pattern p_n with a numeral $\boldsymbol{p_{ne}}$ in base 2. The number denoted by numeral $\boldsymbol{p_{ne}}$ is $p_{ne} = 1 \times 2^0 + 0 \times 2^1 + 1 \times 2^2 + 0 \times 2^3 + \ldots + 0 \times 2^{2n-1} + 1 \times 2^{2n}$. For any number n, let π_{Ce}: $Z^+ \to Z^+$ satisfy $\pi_{Ce}(n) = p_{ne}$. Therefore, by its definition, π_{Ce} is total recursive. Second, we can identify state w_n with a numeral $\boldsymbol{w_{ne}}$ in base $2 + m2$, where m is the number of internal states of Turing machine C. Let the extended alphabet $B_C = \{a_j\} \cup \{q_i a_j\}$ of Turing machine C be alphabetically ordered.[7] The number denoted by numeral $\boldsymbol{w_{ne}}$ is thus $w_{ne} = 3 \times (2 + m2)^0 + 0 \times (2 + m2)^1 + 1 \times (2 + m2)^2 + 0 \times (2 + m2)^3 + \ldots + 0 \times (2 + m2)^{2n-1} + 1 \times (2 + m2)^{2n}$. For any number k, let σ_{Ce}: $Z^+ \to Z^+$ satisfy this condition: If $k = p_{ne}$ for some n, $\sigma_{Ce}(k) = w_{ne}$; otherwise, $\sigma_{Ce}(k) = k$. Therefore, by its definition, σ_{Ce} is total recursive.[8] For any number n, let γ_{Ce}: $Z^+ \to Z^+$ satisfy $\gamma_{Ce}(n) = \sigma_{Ce}(\pi_{Ce}(n))$. Therefore, by its definition, γ_{Ce} is total recursive and, if $\gamma_C(n) = w_n$, $\gamma_{Ce}(n) = w_{ne}$. The coding γ_C is thus effective relative to the standard enumeration e.

EXAMPLE 5 (the decoding δ_C specified by the standard format for the computation of a numeric function on a doubly infinite tape is effective relative to the standard enumeration of the tape)

We have seen that the decoding δ_C: $M_C \rightarrow Z^+$ specified by the standard format is the composition of ϕ_C: $M_C \rightarrow F_2(A_C)$ and η_C: $F_2(A_C) \rightarrow Z^+$, where $F_2(A_C)$ is the set of all finite patterns of a doubly infinite tape relative to alphabet $A_C = \{a_j\} = \{b, 1\}$, and M_C is the set of all states of Turing machine C. The function ϕ_C assigns to state w the pattern p_w that corresponds to w. The function η_C, on the other hand, assigns to an arbitrary pattern p the number of 1s of this pattern. Let e be the standard enumeration of the tape. Then, first, we can identify state w with a numeral $\boldsymbol{w_e}$ in base $2 + m2$, where m is the number of internal states of Turing machine C. Let the extended alphabet $B_C = \{a_j\} \cup \{q_i a_j\}$ of Turing machine C be alphabetically ordered. The number denoted by numeral $\boldsymbol{w_e}$ is thus $w_e = c_0(2 + m2)^0 + c_1(2 + m2)^1 + \ldots + c_u(2 + m2)^u$, where exactly one coefficient c_v is equal to $2 + i2 + j$, for some i ($0 \leq i < m$) and j ($0 \leq j < 2$). Second, we can identify pattern p_w with a numeral $\boldsymbol{p_{we}}$ in base 2. The number denoted by numeral $\boldsymbol{p_{we}}$ is $p_{we} = d_0 2^0 + d_1 2^1 + \ldots + d_u 2^u$, where all the coefficients agree with the corresponding coefficients of w_e, except for the coefficient d_v which is equal to j. For any number n, let ϕ_{Ce}: $Z^+ \rightarrow Z^+$ satisfy this condition: If $n = w_e$ for some $w \in M_C$, $\phi_{Ce}(n) = p_{we}$; otherwise, $\phi_{Ce}(n) = n$. Therefore, by its definition, ϕ_{Ce} is total recursive.[9] For any number k, let η_{Ce}: $Z^+ \rightarrow Z^+$ satisfy $\eta_{Ce}(k)$ = the number of 1s in the binary expression of k. Therefore, by its definition, η_{Ce} is total recursive. For any number n, let δ_{Ce}: $Z^+ \rightarrow Z^+$ satisfy $\delta_{Ce}(n) = \eta_{Ce}(\phi_{Ce}(n))$. Therefore, by its definition, δ_{Ce} is total recursive and, if $\delta_C(w) = h$, $\delta_{Ce}(w_e) = h$. The decoding δ_C is thus effective relative to the standard enumeration e.

Before going on, let me also point out an important property of the standard enumeration of the tape. Suppose that, given an arbitrary pattern field $F = \langle U, \{f_r\}\rangle$, there is a cell $x_0 \in U$ and a Turing machine C on F with alphabet $A_C \supset \{b\}$ such that, when C is started on a completely blank pattern, cell x_0, and in internal state q_0, C performs a computation that satisfies these conditions: (1) for any cell member of U, C replaces the initial blank with a nonblank symbol; (2) the first replacement of a blank with a nonblank symbol occurs on cell x_0; and

(3) C never replaces a nonblank symbol with a blank. It is thus clear that, since these three conditions are satisfied, this computation of the Turing machine C allows us to *construct* an enumeration of all the cells of U. By conditions (1) and (3), for any cell member of U, C replaces the blank with a nonblank symbol exactly one time. Therefore, we can actually construct an enumeration of all the cells by counting the successive replacements of a blank with a nonblank symbol, and by then assigning to replacement number n ($n \leq 0$) the cell where this replacement occurs. Also note that this enumeration of the cells is in fact a bijection e: $Z^+ \to U$ and that, since (2) holds, $e(0) = x_0$. I call any bijection e: $Z^+ \to U$ that can be constructed in this way a *regular enumeration* of the pattern field $F = \langle U, \{f_r\}\rangle$. Let us now consider again the pattern field $F_2 = \langle U, \{L, R\}\rangle$, that is, the doubly infinite tape of an ordinary Turing machine. It is then easy to verify that the standard enumeration of the tape is regular (see example 6).

EXAMPLE 6 (the standard enumeration of the tape is regular)

Let $F_2 = \langle U, \{L, R\}\rangle$ be the doubly infinite tape of an ordinary Turing machine (see example 2). I first show that there is a square $x_0 \in U$ and a Turing machine C on F_2 with alphabet $A_C \supset \{b\}$ such that, when C is started on a *completely blank* tape, square x_0, and in internal state q_0, C performs a computation that satisfies these conditions: (1) for any square, C replaces the initial blank with a nonblank symbol; (2) the first replacement of a blank with a nonblank symbol occurs on square x_0, and (3) C never replaces a nonblank symbol with a blank. Let C be specified by $G_C = \{q_0b1q_1, q_11Lq_1, q_1b1q_0, q_01Rq_0\}$. When C is started on a blank tape, an arbitrary square x_0, and internal state q_0, C writes a 1 on square x_0 and changes internal state to q_1. It then goes to the square to the left of x_0, where it writes a second 1 and changes internal state to q_0. Next, it moves to the right skipping all the 1s and, as soon as it finds a blank, writes a 1. It then moves to the left skipping all the 1s, replaces the first blank with a 1, and repeats. Therefore, this computation of the Turing machine C satisfies the three conditions. By counting the successive replacements of a blank with a nonblank symbol, and by then assigning to replacement number n ($0 \leq n$) the cell where this replacement occurs, we can thus use this computation to construct an enumeration e of the squares. The enumeration e assigns to number 0 the square x_0, to increasing even numbers the squares to its right, and to increasing odd numbers the squares to its left. Let x_0 be the square specified by the standard format. The enumeration e is thus the standard enumeration of the tape. Therefore, the standard enumeration of the tape is regular.

We have thus seen two important properties of the standard format for the computation of a numeric function on a doubly infinite tape. First, both the coding function γ_C and the decoding function δ_C specified by this format are effective relative to the standard enumeration of the tape and, second, this enumeration is regular. I will now generalize these observations to obtain a concept of computability that can be applied to an arbitrary pattern field $F = \langle U, \{f_r\}\rangle$ and, if the pattern field F is a doubly infinite tape, is equivalent to the concept of computability on a doubly infinite tape in standard format.

If $C = \langle T, M_C, \{g^t\}\rangle$ is a Turing machine on $F = \langle U, \{f_r\}\rangle$, a *coding* is any function γ_C from Z^+ to M_C, and a *decoding* is any (partial) function δ_C from M_C to Z^+. Let e: $Z^+ \rightarrow U$ be a bijection. Once this enumeration e of the cells is given, we can identify any state $w \in M_C \subset F_2(B_C)$ with a numeral $\boldsymbol{w_e}$ in base $n + mn$, where m is the number of internal states of the Turing machine C whose alphabet A_C has n symbols. The least significant digit of numeral $\boldsymbol{w_e}$ is the symbol member of the extended alphabet B_C that the state w assigns to cell $e(0)$; its second digit is the symbol assigned to cell $e(1)$; its third digit is the symbol assigned to cell $e(2)$, etc. Its highest significant digit is thus the symbol assigned to cell $e(u)$, where u is the smallest number such that for any $v > u$, the symbol assigned to cell $e(v)$ is the blank. I indicate the number denoted by numeral $\boldsymbol{w_e}$ by w_e. Then, a coding γ_C: $Z^+ \rightarrow M_C$ is *effective relative to e* if and only if there is a total recursive function γ_{Ce}: $Z^+ \rightarrow Z^+$ such that, for any $n \in Z^+$, if $\gamma_C(n) = w$, $\gamma_{Ce}(n) = w_e$, and a decoding δ_C: $M_C \rightarrow Z^+$ is *effective relative to e* if and only if there is a total recursive function δ_{Ce}: $Z^+ \rightarrow Z^+$ such that, for any $w \in M_C$, if $\delta_C(w)$ is defined and $\delta_C(w) = n$, $\delta_{Ce}(w_e) = n$. If Φ is a format for the computation of a numeric function on F, Φ *is regular relative to e* if and only if e is a regular enumeration of F and, for any Turing machine $C = \langle T, M_C, \{g^t\}\rangle$ on F with alphabet $A_C = A_\Phi$, both the coding γ_C: $Z^+ \rightarrow M_C$ and the decoding δ_C: $M_C \rightarrow Z^+$ specified by format Φ are effective relative to e. Therefore, by this definition, and by examples 4, 5, and 6, the standard format is regular relative to the standard enumeration.

Let f: $Z^+ \rightarrow Z^+$ be a numeric function, $F = \langle U, \{f_r\}\rangle$ be a pattern field, and e: $Z^+ \rightarrow U$ be a bijection. I then say that *f is computable on F relative to e* if and only if there is a format Φ such that Φ is regular relative to e, and f is computable on F in format Φ. Furthermore, I say that *f is computable on F* if and only if, for some *e*, *f* is computable on *F* relative to *e*.

> EXAMPLE 7 (all the numeric functions computable on a doubly infinite tape in standard format are computable on a doubly infinite tape relative to the standard enumeration)
>
> By the definition of computability on *F* relative to *e*, since the standard format is regular relative to the standard enumeration, if a numeric function *f* is computable on a doubly infinite tape in standard format, then *f* is computable on a doubly infinite tape relative to the standard enumeration.

Let me finally anticipate that the concept of computability on pattern field *F* is a generalization of the concept of computability on a doubly infinite tape in standard format. In fact, we will see later that, if the pattern field *F* is a doubly infinite tape, the concept of computability on *F* is equivalent to the concept of computability on a doubly infinite tape in standard format (theorem 6).

3 Is the concept of computability on pattern field *F* reducible to the usual concept of Turing computability?

In the previous section, I defined a concept of computability that applies to an arbitrary pattern field $F = \langle U, \{f_r\}\rangle$, and I then anticipated that, if *F* is a doubly infinite tape, the concept of computability on *F* is equivalent to the concept of computability on a doubly infinite tape in standard format (see theorem 6). On the other hand, a numeric function *f* is computable on a doubly infinite tape in standard format if and only if *f* is recursive (Davis, 1958). Therefore, if *F* is a doubly infinite tape, the concept of computability on *F* is in fact equivalent to the usual concept of computability.

In this section, I will consider the following question: If a numeric function *f* is computable on an arbitrary pattern field *F*, is *f* computable on a doubly infinite tape? If we accept Turing's fourth hypothesis (see section 1 and figure 2-4) the answer to this question must be affirmative. For, according to this hypothesis, all different types of support can always be replaced by a tape divided into an infinite number of cells, and this replacement does not limit the computational capacity. However, before accepting this answer, we should take a closer look at those capabilities of a Turing machine that depend on the relational structure of the pattern field on which the machine

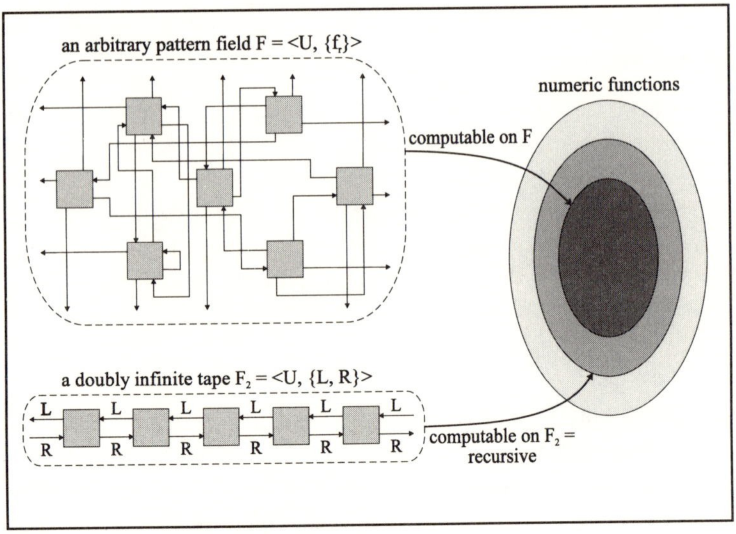

FIGURE 2-4 Turing's fourth hypothesis.

operates. A doubly infinite tape has a very simple relational structure. But what happens if the connections between the cells are more complicated? Could a more complex relational structure allow a Turing machine to compute nonrecursive functions?

The surprising answer to this question is "yes": There are Turing machines that can compute nonrecursive functions. More precisely, for any numeric function f that is not recursive, there is a pattern field $F = \langle U, \{f_r\}\rangle$ on which f turns out to be computable. This result crucially depends on the fact that some pattern fields have a relational structure essentially more complex than the structure of the tape of an ordinary Turing machine. This basic intuition can be expressed as follows: Given a doubly infinite tape, and an arbitrary regular enumeration of its squares, the functions *left* and *right* correspond to two numeric functions, and these two functions turn out to be recursive. However, if the pattern field $F = \langle U, \{f_r\}\rangle$ is more complicated, there may be a regular enumeration that allows us to represent some function f_r as a nonrecursive function. Now, if this is the case, this nonrecursive power contained in the pattern field may be used by a Turing machine that operates on it to compute nonrecursive functions. Therefore, it is false that all different types of support can always be replaced by a tape divided into an infinite number of cells, and that this replacement does not limit the computational capacity. We must thus reject Turing's fourth hypothesis. Before proving these claims, however, I need to precisely define the idea of a pattern field whose relational structure is recursive.

Let $F = \langle U, \{f_r\}\rangle$ be a pattern field, and let e: $Z^+ \to U$ be a bijection. To each function f_r: $U \to U$ $(0 \le r < s)$ thus corresponds a numeric function f_{re}: $Z^+ \to Z^+$ that, for any $n \in Z^+$, satisfies $f_{re}(n) = e^{-1}(f_r(e(n)))$. I then define: (1) *F is recursive relative to e* if and only if e is not a regular enumeration of F or, for any r, f_{re} is recursive; (2) *F is recursive* if and only if, for any e, F is recursive relative to e. By (1) we obtain: (3) F is not recursive relative to e if and only if e is a regular enumeration of F and, for some r, f_{re} is not recursive. By (2) and (3) we obtain: (4) F is not recursive if and only if, for some e, e is a regular enumeration of F and, for some r, f_{re} is not recursive.

Example 8 (a doubly infinite tape is recursive relative to the standard enumeration[10])

Let e be the standard enumeration of the tape. By example 6, the standard enumeration e is regular. Therefore, by the definition of recursive pattern field relative to e, a doubly infinite tape is recursive relative to the standard enumeration e if the numeric functions L_e and R_e that correspond to the functions *left* and *right* are recursive. Since e is the standard enumeration, the numeric functions L_e and R_e respectively satisfy these conditions: (1) If $n = 0$, $L_e(n) = 1$; if n is odd, $L_e(n) = n + 2$; if n is even, $L_e(n) = n - 2$; and (2) if $n = 0$ or n is even, $R_e(n) = n + 2$; if $n = 1$, $R_e(n) = 0$; if n is odd and $n \neq 1$, $R_e(n) = n - 2$. Both L_e and R_e are thus recursive. Therefore, a doubly infinite tape is recursive relative to the standard enumeration.

Example 9 (an example of a pattern field that is not recursive)

Let $F = \langle Z^+, \{s, f\}\rangle$, where Z^+ are the nonnegative integers, s is the successor function, and f: $Z^+ \to Z^+$ is an arbitrary total nonrecursive function. Let us consider the Turing machine C on F with alphabet $A_C \supset \{b\}$ whose set of quadruples is $G_C = \{q_0b1q_0, q_01sq_0\}$. When C is started on a completely blank pattern, cell 0, and in state q_0, C replaces all the initial blanks with a nonblank symbol, the first replacement of a blank with a nonblank symbol occurs on cell 0, and C never replaces a nonblank symbol with a blank. Therefore, by counting the successive replacements of a blank with a nonblank symbol, and by then assigning to replacement number n $(0 \le n)$ the cell where this replacement occurs, this computation of C allows us to construct an enumeration e of Z^+. The enumeration e is in fact the identity function on Z^+. The identity function on Z^+ is thus a regular enumeration of F. Furthermore, since e is the identity function on Z^+, the numeric function f_e that corresponds to f is f itself. Hence, since f is not recursive, f_e is not recursive. Therefore, by the definition of recursive pattern field, F is not recursive.

I will now prove that, for any numeric function f that is not recursive, there is a pattern field $F = \langle U, \{f_r\}\rangle$ on which f is computable. However, the relational structure of this pattern field turns out to be nonrecursive as well (theorem 1). The proof of this theorem is based on the following idea: We let the cells of the pattern field F be the integers themselves, so that we can take f (the numeric function we want to compute) to be one of the functions $\{f_r\}$. We then add two more functions, namely, the successor function s and the predecessor function v (where $v(0) = 0$). If f is *total*, this is sufficient for proving the theorem. In other words, an arbitrary total function f: $Z^+ \to Z^+$ that is not recursive is computable on the pattern field $F = \langle Z^+, \{s, v, f\}\rangle$. To prove the general case (f either total or partial), however, we need to slightly modify this idea. Instead of the pattern field $\langle Z^+, \{s, v, f\}\rangle$ we consider the pattern field $\langle Z^+, \{s, v, f'\}\rangle$ where f': $Z^+ \to Z^+$ is the total function that, for any $n \in Z^+$, satisfies these conditions: If $n = 0$, $f'(n) = 0$; if $n \neq 0$ and $f(n-1)$ is defined, $f'(n) = f(n-1) + 1$; if $n \neq 0$ and $f(n-1)$ is undefined, $f'(n) = 0$. (For example, suppose $f(0) = 3$, $f(1) =$ undefined, $f(2) = 123$, $f(3) = 0$, etc. Then, $f'(0) = 0$, $f'(1) = 4$, $f'(2) = 0$, $f'(3) = 124$, $f'(4) = 1$, etc.)

THEOREM 1

For any numeric function f, *if* f *is not recursive, there is a pattern field* F *such that* f *is computable on* F, *and* F *is not recursive.*

PROOF. Let $F = \langle Z^+, \{s, v, f'\}\rangle$, where Z^+ are the nonnegative integers, s is the successor function, v is the predecessor function (where $v(0) = 0$), and f' is the total function defined above. By the definition of f', and since f is not recursive, f' is total but not recursive.[11] Let e be the identity function on Z^+. By example 9, e is a regular enumeration of F. Since e is the identity function on Z^+, the numeric function f'_e that corresponds to f' is f' itself. Thus, since f' is not recursive, f'_e is not recursive. Therefore, F is not recursive.

I will now show that there is a format Φ such that Φ is regular relative to e, and f is computable on F in format Φ. Let Φ consist of the following convention: (1) the alphabet A_Φ only contains the two symbols b and 1; (2) a pattern $p \in F(A_\Phi)$ represents input (or output) number $n \in Z^+$ if and only if p has exactly $n + 1$ 1s, and the first 1 is on cell 0, the second 1 is on cell 1, the third 1 is on cell 2, etc.; (3) given a pattern that represents input number n, an arbitrary Turing machine on F with alphabet $A_C = A_\Phi = \{b, 1\}$ starts its computation on cell 0, and in internal state q_0; (4) a state of the Turing machine C represents output number $m \in Z^+$ if and only if the pattern that corresponds to this state represents output number m. It is thus clear that, for any Turing machine $C = \langle T, M_C, \{g^t\}\rangle$ on F with alphabet $A_C = A_\Phi = \{b, 1\}$, this convention specifies a coding γ_C: $Z^+ \to M_C$ and a decoding δ_C: $M_C \to Z^+$. The coding γ_C is specified by the conjunction of (*2*) and (*3*). More precisely, condition (*2*) specifies a function π_C: $Z^+ \to F(A_C)$, where $F(A_C)$ is the set of all finite patterns of F relative to alphabet $A_C = A_\Phi = \{b, 1\}$. Condition (*3*), on the other hand, specifies a partial function σ_C: $F_2(A_C) \to M_C$. The coding γ_C: $Z^+ \to M_C$ is thus the composition of π_C and σ_C. The decoding δ_C is specified by the conjunction of (*4*) and (*2*). More precisely, δ_C: $M_C \to Z^+$ is the composition of Φ_C: $M_C \to F_2(A_C)$ and η_C: $F_2(A_C) \to Z^+$. The function Φ_C assigns to any state $w \in M_C$ the finite pattern $p \in F_2(A_C)$ that corresponds to this state. On the other hand, η_C assigns to pattern p the output number represented by p. However, if p does not represent any output number, that is, if p does not satisfy condition (*2*), $\eta_C(p)$ is undefined. Therefore, η_C is partial and, since its domain is strictly included in the image of ϕ_C, δ_C is partial as well. It is now easy to verify that both the coding γ_C and the decoding δ_C are effective relative to e = the identity function on Z^+ (the proof is similar to examples 4 and 5). Therefore, since e is a regular enumeration of F, the format Φ is regular relative to e. Let us then consider the Turing machine C whose set of quadruples is $G_C = \{q_0 1 s q_1, q_1 1 b q_2, q_2 b s q_1, q_1 b f' q_3, q_3 1 1 q_4, q_4 1 1 q_3, q_3 b v q_5, q_5 b 1 q_6, q_6 1 v q_5, q_5 1 1 q_7\}$. If we start C in state q_0, on cell 0, and on a pattern that represents number n, C first moves to cell 1 (and thus leaves the marker 1 on cell 0), and then deletes all other 1s. As soon as C finds the first blank (on cell $n + 1$), it jumps according to f'. The pattern is now completely blank except for the marker 1 on cell 0, and the machine is on cell $f(n) + 1$, if $f(n)$ is defined; otherwise it is on cell 0 where it scans a 1. The machine now checks whether it is scanning a 1. If yes, it enters an infinite loop (it stays indefinitely on cell 0 scanning a 1, and switching the two internal states q_3 and q_4). If not, the machine first goes to cell $f(n)$, and it then writes a 1 on each blank cell, going back until it finds the 1 on cell 0. At this point, it stops in internal state q_7. Thus, if we start C in state q_0, on cell 0, and on a pattern that represents number n, then, if $f(n)$ is defined, this computation stops and the final pattern represents number $f(n)$; if $f(n)$ is not defined, this computation does not stop. Therefore, f is computable on F in format Φ. Since Φ is regular relative to e, f is thus computable on F relative to e. Therefore, by the definition of computability on F, f is computable on F.

q.e.d.

We have just seen (theorem 1) that nonrecursive pattern fields of a simple kind allow the computation of nonrecursive functions. This special result thus suggests a more general conjecture, namely, that being a nonrecursive pattern field might be a sufficient condition for computing nonrecursive functions. This conjecture turns out to be true (theorem 2). To prove this theorem, however, we need to consider first a different question. Let $F = \langle U, \{f_r\}\rangle$ be a pattern field, and e: $Z^+ \rightarrow U$ be a bijection. To each function f_r: $U \rightarrow U$ $(0 \leq r < s)$ thus corresponds a numeric function f_{re}: $Z^+ \rightarrow Z^+$ that, for any $n \in Z^+$, satisfies $f_{re}(n) = e^{-1}(f_r(e(n)))$. I call the set of numeric functions $\{f_{re}\}$ a *numeric representation* of the relational structure of F, and I say that $\{f_{re}\}$ is computable on F if and only if, for any r, f_{re} is computable on F. It is then interesting to ask under what conditions a numeric representation $\{f_{re}\}$ of the relational structure of F turns out to be computable on F itself. A sufficient condition is that e be a regular enumeration of F (lemma 2.1). The proof of this lemma is based on the following idea: Since e is a regular enumeration of F, there is a cell $x_0 \in U$ and a Turing machine C_e on F with alphabet $A_e \supset \{b\}$ such that, when C_e is started on a completely blank pattern, cell x_0, and in internal state q_0, C_e performs a computation that satisfies these conditions: (1) for any cell member of U, C_e replaces the initial blank with a nonblank symbol; (2) the first replacement of a blank with a nonblank symbol occurs on cell x_0; and (3) C_e never replaces a nonblank symbol with a blank. Furthermore, by counting the successive replacements of a blank with a nonblank symbol, and by then assigning to replacement number n $(0 \leq n)$ the cell where this replacement occurs, this computation of C_e allows us to construct the enumeration e. By slightly modifying the Turing machine C_e, and by choosing an appropriate format Φ, we can then show that, for any r, f_{re} is computable on F in format Φ. This is sufficient to prove the lemma, because the chosen format Φ turns out to be regular relative to e.

LEMMA 2.1

If e *is a regular enumeration of* $\mathrm{F} = \langle \mathrm{U}, \{\mathrm{f_r}\}\rangle$, *then* $\{\mathrm{f_{re}}\}$ *is computable on* F.

PROOF. Let e be a regular enumeration of pattern field $F = \langle U, \{f_r\}\rangle$. Therefore, there is a cell $x_0 \in U$ and a Turing machine C_e on F with alphabet $A_e \supset \{b\}$ such that, when C_e is started on a completely blank pattern, cell x_0, and in internal state q_0, C_e performs a computation that satisfies these conditions: (1) for any cell member of U, C_e replaces the initial blank with a nonblank symbol; (2) the first replacement of a blank with a nonblank symbol occurs on cell x_0; and (3) C_e never replaces a nonblank symbol with a blank. Furthermore, by counting the successive replacements of a blank with a nonblank symbol, and by then assigning to replacement number n $(0 \leq n)$ the cell where this replacement occurs, this computation of C_e allows us to construct the enumeration e. I will now show that there is a format Φ such that Φ is regular relative to e and, for any r, f_{re} is computable on F in format Φ.

Let the format Φ consist of the following convention: (1) the alphabet A_Φ is $A_e \cup \{\#\} = \{a_j\}$, where $\# \notin A_e$; (2) pattern $p \in F(A_\Phi)$ represents input number n if and only if p is completely blank, except for marker # on cell $e(n)$; (3) given a pattern that represents input number n, an arbitrary Turing machine C on F with alphabet $A_C = A_\Phi = A_e \cup \{\#\}$ starts its computation on cell $e(0)$, and in internal state q_0; (4) pattern $p \in F(A_\Phi)$ represents output number m if and only if p assigns marker # to exactly one cell, and this cell is $e(m)$; (5) a state of the Turing machine C represents output number m if and only if the pattern that corresponds to this state represents output number m. It is thus clear that, for any Turing machine $C = \langle T, M_C, \{g^t\}\rangle$ on F with alphabet $A_C = A_\Phi = A_e \cup \{\#\}$, this convention specifies a coding γ_C: $Z^+ \to M_C$ and a decoding δ_C: $M_C \to Z^+$. The coding γ_C is specified by the conjunction of (2) and (3). More precisely, condition (2) specifies a function π_C: $Z^+ \to F(A_C)$, where $F(A_C)$ is the set of all finite patterns of F relative to alphabet $A_C = A_\Phi = A_e \cup \{\#\}$. Condition (3), on the other hand, specifies a partial function σ_C: $F(A_C) \to M_C$. The coding γ_C: $Z^+ \to M_C$ is thus the composition of π_C and σ_C. The decoding δ_C is specified by the conjunction of (5) and (4). More precisely, δ_C: $M_C \to Z^+$ is the composition of ϕ_C: $M_C \to F(A_C)$ and η_C: $F(A_C) \to Z^+$. The function ϕ_C assigns to any state $w \in M_C$ the finite pattern $p \in F(A_C)$ that corresponds to this state. On the other hand, η_C assigns to pattern p the output number represented by p. However, if p does not represent any output number, that is, if p does not satisfy condition (4), $\eta_C(p)$ is undefined. Therefore, η_C is partial and, since its domain is strictly included in the image of ϕ_C, δ_C is partial as well. It is now easy to verify that both the coding γ_C and the decoding δ_C are effective relative to e.

Suppose that $A_C = A_\Phi = A_e \cup \{\#\} = \{a_j\}$ has z elements, that the blank $b = a_0$, and that the marker $\# = a_{z-1}$. The function π_C assigns to number n the pattern p_n which is completely blank, except for marker # on cell $e(n)$. The partial function σ_C, on the other hand, assigns to pattern p_n the state w_n that, on cell $e(0) = x_0$, has the symbol $q_0p_n(x_0)$ and, on any other cell $x \neq x_0$, has the symbol $p_n(x)$. Then, first, we can identify pattern p_n with a numeral $\boldsymbol{p_{ne}}$ in base z. The number denoted by numeral $\boldsymbol{p_{ne}}$ is $p_{ne} = c_0z^0 + c_1z^1 + \ldots + c_nz^n$, where coefficient c_n $(0 \leq n)$ is equal to $z - 1$ and any other coefficient (if any) is equal to 0. For any number n, let π_{Ce}: $Z^+ \rightarrow Z^+$ satisfy $\pi_{Ce}(n) = p_{ne}$. Therefore, by its definition, π_{Ce} is total recursive. Second, we can identify state w_n with a numeral $\boldsymbol{w_{ne}}$ in base $z + mz$, where m is the number of internal states of Turing machine C. Let the extended alphabet $B_C = \{a_j\} \cup \{q_ia_j\}$ of Turing machine C be alphabetically ordered.[12] The number denoted by numeral $\boldsymbol{w_{ne}}$ is thus $w_{ne} = d_0(z + mz)^0 + d_1(z + mz)^1 + \ldots + d_n(z + mz)^n$, where coefficient $d_0 = z + c_0$, and any other coefficient d_v (if any) is equal to the corresponding coefficient c_v of p_{ne}. For any number k, let σ_{Ce}: $Z^+ \rightarrow Z^+$ satisfy this condition: If $k = p_{ne}$ for some n, $\sigma_{Ce}(k) = w_{ne}$; otherwise, $\sigma_{Ce}(k) = k$. Therefore, by its definition, σ_{Ce} is total recursive.[13] For any number n, let γ_{Ce}: $Z^+ \rightarrow Z^+$ satisfy $\gamma_{Ce}(n) = \sigma_{Ce}(\pi_{Ce}(n))$. Therefore, by its definition, γ_{Ce} is total recursive and, if $\gamma_C(n) = w_n$, $\gamma_{Ce}(n) = w_{ne}$. The coding γ_C is thus effective relative to e.

We have seen above that the decoding δ_C: $M_C \rightarrow Z^+$ specified by format Φ is the composition of ϕ_C: $M_C \rightarrow F(A_C)$ and η_C: $F(A_C) \rightarrow Z^+$. The function ϕ_C assigns to state w the pattern p_w that corresponds to w. The function η_C, on the other hand, assigns to an arbitrary pattern p the output number represented by p. However, if p does not represent any output number, that is, if p does not satisfy condition (4), $\eta_C(p)$ is undefined. Then, first, we can identify state w with a numeral $\boldsymbol{w_e}$ in base $z + mz$, where m is the number of internal states of Turing machine C, and z is the number of symbols of alphabet $A_C = A_\Phi = A_e \cup \{\#\} = \{a_j\}$. Let the extended alphabet $B_C = \{a_j\} \cup \{q_ia_j\}$ of Turing machine C be alphabetically ordered. The number denoted by numeral $\boldsymbol{w_e}$ is thus $w_e = c_0(z + mz)^0 + c_1(z + mz)^1 + \ldots + c_u(z + mz)^u$, where exactly one coefficient c_v is equal to $z + iz + j$, for some i $(0 \leq i < m)$ and j $(0 \leq j < z)$. In the second place, we can identify pattern p_w with a numeral $\boldsymbol{p_{we}}$ in base z. The number denoted by numeral $\boldsymbol{p_{we}}$ is $p_{we} = d_0z^0 + d_1z^1 + \ldots + d_uz^u$, where all the coefficients agree with the corresponding coefficients of w_e, except for the coefficient d_v which is equal to j. For any number n, let ϕ_{Ce}: $Z^+ \rightarrow Z^+$ satisfy this condition: If $n = w_e$ for some $w \in M_C$, $\phi_{Ce}(n) = p_{we}$; otherwise, $\phi_{Ce}(n) = n$. Therefore, by its definition, ϕ_{Ce} is total recursive.[14] Let η_{Ce}: $Z^+ \rightarrow Z^+$ be defined as follows: Given an arbitrary number k, let $d_0z^0 + d_1z^1 + \ldots + d_uz^u$ be its decomposition in base z. Let us then check whether exactly one coefficient d_y is equal to $z - 1$ (recall that $z - 1$ is the number that corresponds to marker #). If yes, $\eta_{Ce}(k)$ = the index y of this coefficient. Otherwise, $\eta_{Ce}(k) = 0$. Therefore, by its definition, η_{Ce} is total recursive. For any number n, let δ_{Ce}: $Z^+ \rightarrow Z^+$ satisfy $\delta_{Ce}(n) = \eta_{Ce}(\phi_{Ce}(n))$. Therefore, by its definition, δ_{Ce} is total recursive and, if $\delta_C(w) = h$, $\delta_{Ce}(w_e) = h$. The decoding δ_C is thus effective relative to e.

We have thus verified that both the coding γ_C and the decoding δ_C are effective relative to e. Therefore, since e is a regular enumeration of F, the format Φ is regular relative to e. Let us now consider again the Turing machine C_e (see the first paragraph of this proof), and let us construct a second machine C_{re} that satisfies these two conditions: (1) the alphabet of C_{re} is $A_\Phi = A_e \cup \{\#\} = \{a_s\} \cup \{\#\}$, and (2) if G_e is the set of quadruples of C_e, the set of quadruples of C_{re} is $G_{re} = G_e \cup \{q_l\#bq_{jump}, q_{jump}bf_rq_{mark}, q_{mark}a_s\#q_{stop}\}$, where q_{jump}, q_{mark}, and q_{stop} are three internal states that are not members of the set of internal states $Q_e = \{q_l\}$ of C_e. If we start C_{re} in internal state q_0, on cell $e(0)$, and on a pattern that represents input number n, C_{re} works exactly as C_e does until it finds the marker # on cell $e(n)$. At this point, C_{re} deletes the marker, jumps to cell $f_r(e(n))$, writes the marker # on this cell, and stops in state q_{stop}. Thus, if we start C_{re} in internal state q_0, on cell $e(0)$, and on a pattern that represents number n, this computation stops and the final pattern represents number $f_{re}(n)$. Therefore, for any r, f_{re} is computable on F in format Φ. Hence, since Φ is regular relative to e, for any r, f_{re} is computable on F relative to e. Therefore, by the definition of computability on F, for any r, f_{re} is computable on F.

q.e.d.

An immediate consequence of lemma 2.1 is that being a nonrecursive pattern field is a sufficient condition for computing nonrecursive functions. Suppose $F = \langle U, \{f_r\}\rangle$ is not recursive. Then, for some e, e is a regular enumeration of F, and at least one of the numeric functions $\{f_{re}\}$ is not recursive. By lemma 2.1, however, all these functions are computable on F. Therefore, any nonrecursive pattern field allows us to compute some nonrecursive function.

THEOREM 2 *(being a nonrecursive pattern field is sufficient for computing nonrecursive functions)*

If a pattern field F *is not recursive, there is a numeric function* f *such that* f *is not recursive and* f *is computable on* F.

PROOF. By lemma 2.1, and by the definition of recursive pattern field.

q.e.d.

Before concluding this section, let me contrast the way a Turing machine can compute a nonrecursive function with the way an oracle machine can achieve the same result. Oracle machines are ordinary Turing machines equipped with a special device (*oracle*) that always gives the right answer to questions of the form: Is number n a member of set X? In the course of a computation an oracle machine can pause and ask its oracle whether the number of 1s on the tape at that moment is a member of X. The machine then resumes the computation by choosing between two alternatives according to the answer of the oracle. Let $\{f_u\}$ be a finite set of total numeric functions. Then, a numeric function f of n arguments is *recursive relative to* $\{f_u\}$ if and only if (1) $f \in \{f_u\}$, or (2) f is one of the basic recursive functions (successor, zero function, and identity functions[15]), or (3) f can be obtained from $\{f_u\}$ and the set of basic recursive functions by applying a finite number of times the operations of composition, primitive recursion, and minimization.[16] Let f_x be the characteristic function of a fixed subset X of the nonnegative integers. If an ordinary Turing machine is equipped with an oracle that correctly answers questions about the membership in set X, I call this machine an *oracle machine of type X*. Davis (1958) proved[17] that oracle machines of type X can compute all, and only, the recursive functions relative to $\{f_X\}$. In particular, the function f_X is thus computable by some oracle machine of type X. Therefore, if f_X is not recursive, oracle machines of type X can compute nonrecursive functions.

The main difference between oracle machines and Turing machines is thus in the source of their nonrecursive power. The nonrecursive power of an oracle machine depends on its oracle. By contrast, the nonrecursive power of a Turing machine depends on the relational structure of the pattern field on which it operates. Nevertheless, given an arbitrary type of oracle machines, we can find a corresponding class of Turing machines with the same computational power. Let Z^+ be the nonnegative integers, s the successor function, v the predecessor function (where $v(0) = 0$), and let us consider all the oracle machines of type X. Then, the Turing machines on pattern field $F = \langle Z^+, \{s, v, f_X\}\rangle$ correspond to this type of oracle machines in the following sense: As mentioned, the class of the numeric functions computable by oracle machines of type X is identical to the class of the recursive functions relative to $\{f_X\}$. On the other hand, it is possible to prove that these are exactly the numeric functions computable on $\langle Z^+, \{s, v, f_X\}\rangle$ relative to the identity function on Z^+ (corollary 3.1 below). This is a direct consequence of two more general results. The first one affirms that the class of the recursive functions relative to $\{f_u\}$ is included in the class of the numeric functions computable on $\langle Z^+, \{s, v\} \cup \{f_u\}\rangle$ relative to the identity function on Z^+ (theorem 3 below). The second one (lemma 4.1 in the next section) affirms that the class of the numeric functions computable on an arbitrary pattern field $F = \langle U, \{f_r\}\rangle$ relative to an arbitrary bijection $e: Z^+ \to U$ is included in the class of the recursive functions relative to $\{f_{re}\}$ (where, for any r, f_{re} is the numeric function that corresponds to the function f_r).

The proof of theorem 3 is based on the following idea: In the first place, note that each cell $x \in Z^+$ can be identified with a square of a tape infinite in one direction, and that s and v thus correspond, respectively, to the *right* and *left* functions of Turing machines that operate on this kind of tape. We can then prove theorem 3 by modifying Boolos and Jeffrey's proof that any recursive function is computable by a Turing machine that operates on a tape infinite in one direction (Boolos and Jeffrey 1980, chapters 6 and 7). The details are in the appendix.

THEOREM 3

If $f: Z^+ \to Z^+$ *is a recursive function relative to* $\{f_u\}$*, then* f *is computable on* $\langle Z^+, \{s, v\} \cup \{f_u\}\rangle$ *relative to the identity function on* Z^+.

PROOF. See the appendix.

COROLLARY 3.1

Let f_X *be the characteristic function of a subset* X *of the nonnegative integers. Then a numeric function* f *is recursive relative to* $\{f_X\}$ *if and only if* f *is computable on* $\langle Z^+, \{s, v, f_X\}\rangle$ *relative to the identity function on* Z^+.

PROOF. Suppose that f is recursive relative to $\{f_X\}$. Therefore, by theorem 3, f is computable on $\langle Z^+, \{s, v, f_X\}\rangle$ relative to the identity function on Z^+.

Conversely, suppose that f is computable on $\langle Z^+, \{s, v, f_X\}\rangle$ relative to the identity function on Z^+. Let $e: Z^+ \to Z^+$ be the identity function on Z^+. Hence, by lemma 4.1 (see the next section), f is recursive relative to $\{s_e, v_e, f_{Xe}\}$. Since e is the identity function on Z^+, f is thus recursive relative to $\{s, v, f_X\}$. Therefore, since s and v are both recursive, f is recursive relative to $\{f_X\}$.

q.e.d.

4 Is a nonrecursive pattern field necessary for computing nonrecursive functions?

I proved in the previous section that being a nonrecursive pattern field is a sufficient condition for computing nonrecursive functions (theorem 2). The goal of this section is to show that this condition is not only sufficient but also necessary (theorem 4). To prove this theorem, however, I am going to consider first a preliminary question. Let $F = \langle U, \{f_r\}\rangle$ be a pattern field, $e: Z^+ \to U$ be a bijection, and suppose that a numeric function f is computable on F relative to e. Let us then ask whether f is recursive relative to $\{f_{re}\}$. We will see shortly that the answer to this question is affirmative (lemma 4.1), and that theorem 4 easily follows from this lemma.

The proof of lemma 4.1 is similar to the usual proof that any numeric function computable on a doubly infinite tape in standard format is recursive. Let $C = \langle T, M_C, \{g^t\}\rangle$ be a Turing machine on pattern field $F = \langle U, \{f_r\}\rangle$. For any $w \in M_C$, the computation that starts with state w either stops or does not stop. Let us then consider the (partial) function $\rho_C: M_C \to M_C$ that, for any state w, satisfies this condition: If the computation that starts with w stops, $\rho_C(w)$ = the final state of this computation; otherwise, $\rho_C(w)$ is undefined. Let $e: Z^+ \to U$ be a bijection. Recall that, once this enumeration e of the cells is given, we can identify any state $w \in M_C$ with a numeral $\boldsymbol{w_e}$ in base $n + mn$, where m is the number of internal states of the Turing machine C whose alphabet A_C has n symbols (see section 2). I indicate the number denoted by numeral $\boldsymbol{w_e}$ by w_e. Let us now consider the numeric function $\rho_{Ce}: Z^+ \to Z^+$ that, for any $n \in Z^+$, satisfies these conditions: If, for some state $w, n = w_e$ and $\rho_C(w)$ is defined, $\rho_{Ce}(n) = \rho_C(w)_e$; if, for some state $w, n = w_e$ and $\rho_C(w)$ is undefined, $\rho_{Ce}(n)$ is undefined; otherwise, $\rho_{Ce}(n) = n$. It is then not difficult to prove that ρ_{Ce} is recursive relative to $\{f_{re}\}$ (lemma 4.1.1). Lemma 4.1 is in fact a direct consequence of this result.

As for the proof of lemma 4.1.1, let us consider the function $g[G_C]$: $M_C \rightarrow M_C$. Recall that this is the function determined by the set of quadruples G_C of the Turing machine $C = \langle T, M_C, \{g^t\}\rangle$. Let $g[G_C]_e$: $Z^+ \rightarrow Z^+$ be the numeric function that, for any $n \in Z^+$, satisfies this condition: If, for some state $w \in M_C$, $n = w_e$, $g[G_C]_e(n) = g[G_C](w)_e$; otherwise, $g[G_C]_e(n) = n$. Then, first, $g[G_C]_e$ is recursive relative to $\{f_{re}\}$ (lemma 4.1.1.1) and, second, if $g[G_C]_e$ is recursive relative to $\{f_{re}\}$, then ρ_{Ce} is recursive relative to $\{f_{re}\}$ (lemma 4.1.1.2). Lemma 4.1.1 is thus an immediate consequence of these two results.

LEMMA 4.1.1.1

$g[G_C]_e$ is recursive relative to $\{f_{re}\}$.

PROOF. Let $A_C = \{a_j\}$ $(0 \leq j < z)$ be the alphabet of Turing machine $C = \langle T, M_C, \{g^t\}\rangle$, and $Q_C = \{q_i\}$ $(0 \leq i < m)$ be the set of internal states of C. Let the elements of the extended alphabet $B_C = \{a_j\} \cup \{q_ia_j\}$ be alphabetically ordered.[18] The quadruples of C are of two types: $q_ia_ja_kq_l$ and $q_ia_jf_rq_l$. I first show that the partial numeric function that corresponds to each type of quadruple is partial recursive relative to $\{f_{re}\}$, and that its domain is a recursive subset of Z^+. Therefore, $g[G_C]_e$ can be defined by cases by means of these partial numeric functions, and it is thus recursive relative to $\{f_{re}\}$.

Since any state $w \in M_C$ can be identified with a numeral $\boldsymbol{w_e}$ in base $z + mz$, the number denoted by $\boldsymbol{w_e}$ is $w_e = c_0(z + mz)^0 + c_1(z + mz)^1 + \ldots + c_u(z + mz)^u$, where exactly one coefficient c_v is equal to $z + iz + j$, for some i $(0 \leq i < m)$ and j $(0 \leq j < z)$.

Let $[q_ia_ja_kq_l]_e$ be the partial numeric function that corresponds to a quadruple of the first type. For any number n, this function is defined as follows: If, for some $w \in M_C$, $n = w_e$, $[q_ia_ja_kq_l]_e(n)$ is equal to the number whose decomposition in base $z + mz$ is $d_0(z + mz)^0 + d_1(z + mz)^1 + \ldots + d_u(z + mz)^u$, where all the coefficients agree with the corresponding coefficients of w_e, except for $d_v = z + lz + k$; otherwise, $[q_ia_ja_kq_l]_e(n)$ is undefined. Therefore, $[q_ia_ja_kq_l]_e$ is partial recursive. Furthermore, its domain is a recursive subset of Z^+, for $[q_ia_ja_kq_l]_e(n)$ is defined if and only if the decomposition in base $z + mz$ of n has exactly one coefficient c_v equal to $z + jz + i$.

Let $\boldsymbol{f} = f_{re}$ be the numeric function that corresponds to the function f_r, and $[q_ia_jf_rq_l]_e$ be the partial numeric function that corresponds to a quadruple of the second type. For any number n, this function is defined as follows: If, for some $w \in M_C$, $n = w_e$, $[q_ia_jf_rq_l]_e(n)$ is equal to the number whose decomposition in base

$z+mz$ is $d_0(z+mz)^0 + d_1(z+mz)^1 + \ldots + d_y(z+mz)^y$ where, if $f(v) \neq v$, all the coefficients agree with the corresponding coefficients of w_e, except for $d_v = j$, and for $d_{f(v)} = z + lz + c_{f(v)}$. If $f(v) = v$, all the coefficients agree with the corresponding coefficients of w_e, except for $d_v = z + lz + j$. If, for any $w \in M_C$, $n \neq w_e$, $[q_i a_j f_r q_l]_e(n)$ is undefined. Therefore, $[q_i a_j f_r q_l]_e$ is partial recursive relative to $\{f_{re}\}$. Furthermore, its domain is a recursive subset of Z^+, for $[q_i a_j f_r q_l]_e(n)$ is defined if and only if the decomposition in base $z+mz$ of n has exactly one coefficient c_v equal to $z + jz + i$.

Finally, since the domains of the partial recursive functions relative to $\{f_{re}\}$ that correspond to each quadruple are recursive and mutually exclusive, $g[G_C]_e$ can be defined by cases by means of these partial functions. Therefore, $g[G_C]_e$ is recursive relative to $\{f_{re}\}$.

q.e.d.

LEMMA 4.1.1.2

If $g[G_C]_e$ *is recursive relative to* $\{f_{re}\}$, *then* ρ_{Ce} *is recursive relative to* $\{f_{re}\}$.

PROOF. Suppose that $g[G_C]_e$ is recursive relative to $\{f_{re}\}$. First, let us define the iteration of $g[G_C]_e$ up to time t $(0 \leq t)$ as follows: $\psi_e(n, 0) = n$, $\psi_e(n, t+1) = g[G_C]_e(\psi_e(n, t))$. Therefore, since $g[G_C]_e$ is recursive relative to $\{f_{re}\}$, ψ_e is recursive relative to $\{f_{re}\}$. Second, let us define a numeric function H_e that checks whether the computation that starts with state w stops at time t. This numeric function is 0 if the computation that starts with w stops at time t, otherwise it is 1. Recall that the computation that starts with w stops at time t if and only if the state at time t is identical to the state at time $t + 1$. H_e can thus be defined as follows: If $\psi_e(n, t) = \psi_e(n, t+1)$, $H_e(n, t) = 0$; otherwise, $H_e(n, t) = 1$. Therefore, since ψ_e is recursive relative to $\{f_{re}\}$, H_e is recursive relative to $\{f_{re}\}$. Third, let us now define a numeric function T_e that returns the least time at which the computation that starts with w stops. If this computation does not stop, T_e is undefined. Obviously, T_e can be obtained from H_e by applying the minimization operator, that is, $T_e(n)$ = the least t such that $H_e(n, t) = 0$. Therefore, since H_e is recursive relative to $\{f_{re}\}$, T_e is recursive relative to $\{f_{re}\}$. Finally, by the definitions of ρ_{Ce}, ψ_e, and T_e, $\rho_{Ce}(n) = \psi_e(n, T_e(n))$. Therefore, since ψ_e is recursive relative to $\{f_{re}\}$ and T_e is recursive relative to $\{f_{re}\}$, ρ_{Ce} is recursive relative to $\{f_{re}\}$.

q.e.d.

LEMMA 4.1.1

ρ_{Ce} is recursive relative to {f_{re}}.

PROOF. By lemmas 4.1.1.1 and 4.1.1.2.

q.e.d.

It is now easy to verify that lemma 4.1 is a direct consequence of lemma 4.1.1, of the definition of computability on F relative to e, and of the definitions of the (partial) function ρ_C and of the corresponding numeric function ρ_{Ce}.

LEMMA 4.1

If a numeric function f *is computable on pattern field* F = ⟨U, {f_r}⟩ *relative to* e, *then* f *is recursive relative to* {f_{re}}.

PROOF. Suppose that f is computable on F relative to e. Therefore, by the definition of computability on F relative to e, there is a format Φ such that Φ is regular relative to e, and f is computable on F in format Φ. Thus, by the definition of computability on F in format Φ, and by the definition of ρ_C, there is a Turing machine C on F with alphabet $A_C = A_\Phi$ such that, for any $n \in Z^+$, if $f(n)$ is defined, $\delta_C(\rho_C(\gamma_C(n)))$ is defined and $\delta_C(\rho_C(\gamma_C(n))) = f(n)$; if $f(n)$ is not defined, $\rho_C(\gamma_C(n))$ is not defined (where δ_C and γ_C are, respectively, the coding and the decoding specified by format Φ). Since Φ is regular relative to e, both the coding γ_C and the decoding δ_C are effective relative to e. Therefore, (1) there is a total recursive function γ_{Ce}: $Z^+ \to Z^+$ such that, for any $n \in Z^+$, if $\gamma_C(n) = w$, $\gamma_{Ce}(n) = w_e$; and (2) there is a total recursive function δ_{Ce}: $Z^+ \to Z^+$ such that, for any $w \in M_C$, if $\delta_C(w)$ is defined and $\delta_C(w) = n$, then $\delta_{Ce}(w_e) = n$. Hence, by (*1*), (*2*), and the definition of ρ_{Ce}, for any $n \in Z^+$, if $f(n)$ is defined, $\delta_{Ce}(\rho_{Ce}(\gamma_{Ce}(n)))$ is defined and $\delta_{Ce}(\rho_{Ce}(\gamma_{Ce}(n))) = f(n)$; if $f(n)$ is not defined, $\rho_{Ce}(\gamma_{Ce}(n))$ is not defined. Thus, the numeric function f is the composition of γ_{Ce}, ρ_{Ce}, and δ_{Ce}. By lemma 4.1.1, ρ_{Ce} is recursive relative to $\{f_{re}\}$. Therefore, since both γ_{Ce} and δ_{Ce} are recursive, f is recursive relative to $\{f_{re}\}$.

q.e.d.

Lemma 4.1, the definition of computability on F, and the definition of recursive pattern field allow us to prove theorem 4.

THEOREM 4 *(being a nonrecursive pattern field is a necessary condition for computing nonrecursive functions)*

If there is a numeric function f *such that* f *is not recursive and* f *is computable on pattern field* F, *then* F *is not recursive.*

PROOF. Assume that there is a numeric function f such that f is not recursive and f is computable on pattern field $F = \langle U, \{f_r\}\rangle$. Thus, by the definition of computability on F, for some e, f is computable on F relative to e. Therefore, by lemma 4.1, f is recursive relative to $\{f_{re}\}$. Assume for *reductio* that F is recursive. Thus, by the definition of recursive pattern field, e is not a regular enumeration of F or, for any r, f_{re} is recursive. By the definition of computability on F relative to e, and by the definition of regular format relative to e, if e is not a regular enumeration of F, no f is computable on F relative to e. But f is computable on F relative to e. Therefore, for any r, f_{re} is recursive. Since, for any r, f_{re} is recursive, the class of the recursive functions relative to $\{f_{re}\}$ is identical to the class of the recursive functions. Hence, since f is recursive relative to $\{f_{re}\}$, f is recursive. But f is not recursive. We have thus reached a contradiction. Therefore, F is not recursive.

q.e.d.

Theorem 4, together with theorem 2 of the previous section, implies that being a nonrecursive pattern field is a necessary and sufficient condition for computing nonrecursive functions.

COROLLARY 4.1 *(being a nonrecursive pattern field is a necessary and sufficient condition for computing nonrecursive functions)*

A pattern field F *is not recursive if and only if there is a numeric function* f *such that* f *is not recursive and* f *is computable on* F.

PROOF. By theorems 2 and 4.

q.e.d.

Finally, theorem 4 also implies that, for any recursive pattern field, the class of the numeric functions computable on it is included in the class of the recursive functions.

COROLLARY 4.2

If F *is a recursive pattern field, and a numeric function* f *is computable on* F, *then* f *is recursive.*

PROOF. Suppose that F is a recursive pattern field, and that f is computable on F. Suppose for *reductio* that f is not recursive. Hence, by theorem 4, F is not recursive. But F is recursive. Therefore, f is recursive.

q.e.d.

5 The concept of computability on pattern field F is a generalization of the usual concept of computability

At the end of the second section, I anticipated that, if a pattern field F is a doubly infinite tape, the concept of computability on F is equivalent to the concept of computability on a doubly infinite tape in standard format. This idea is stated in theorem 6. To prove theorem 6, however, we must first settle a preliminary question. Let F be a pattern field, and suppose that, for some regular enumeration e of F, F is recursive relative to e. Can we then conclude that the pattern field F is recursive? We will see below that the answer to this question is "yes" (theorem 5).

The proof of theorem 5 employs lemma 4.1 of the previous section and a new result (lemma 5.1) whose proof is similar to the one of lemma 2.1 of section 3. Let e^* and e be two arbitrary regular enumerations of pattern field $F = \langle U, \{f_r\}\rangle$, and let e^*/e be the composition of e^* and of the inverse e^{-1} of e. That is, for any number n, $e^*/e(n) = e^{-1}(e^*(n))$. The function e^*/e is thus a bijection from Z^+ to Z^+. Lemma 5.1 affirms that this numeric bijection is computable on F relative to e^*. The proof of this lemma is based on the following idea: Since e is a regular enumeration of F, there is a cell $x_0 \in U$ and a Turing machine C_e on F with alphabet $A_e \supset \{b\}$ such that, when C_e is started on a completely blank pattern, cell x_0, and in internal state q_0, C_e performs a computation that satisfies these conditions: (1) for any cell member of U, C_e replaces the initial blank with a nonblank symbol; (2) the first replacement of a blank with a nonblank symbol occurs on cell x_0; and (3) C_e never replaces a nonblank symbol with a blank. Furthermore, by counting the successive replacements of a blank with a nonblank symbol, and by then assigning to replacement number n $(0 \leq n)$ the cell where this replacement occurs, this computation of C_e allows us to construct the enumeration e. By slightly modifying the Turing machine C_e, and by choosing an appropriate format Φ, we can then show that e^*/e is computable on F in format Φ. This is sufficient to prove the lemma, because the chosen format Φ turns out to be regular relative to e^*.

Lemma 5.1

If e^* *and* e *are regular enumerations of a pattern field* F, *then the numeric bijection* e^*/e *is computable on* F *relative to* e^*.

Proof. Suppose that e^* and e are regular enumerations of a pattern field $F = \langle U, \{f_r\}\rangle$. Therefore, there is a cell x_0 and a Turing machine C_e on F with alphabet $A_e \supset \{b\}$ such that, when C_e is started on a completely blank pattern, cell x_0, and in internal state q_0, C_e performs a computation that satisfies these conditions: (1) for any cell member of U, C_e replaces the initial blank with a nonblank symbol; (2) the first replacement of a blank with a nonblank symbol occurs on cell x_0; and (3) C_e never replaces a nonblank symbol with a blank. Furthermore, by counting the successive replacements of a blank with a nonblank symbol, and by then assigning to replacement number n $(0 \leq n)$ the cell where this replacement occurs, this computation of C_e allows us to construct the enumeration e. I will now show that there is a format Φ such that Φ is regular relative to e^*, and e^*/e: $Z^+ \to Z^+$ is computable on F in format Φ.

Let the format Φ consist of the following convention: (1) the alphabet A_Φ is $A_e \cup \{\#\} = \{a_j\}$, where $\# \notin A_e$; (2) pattern $p \in F(A_\Phi)$ represents input number n if and only if p is completely blank, except for marker # on cell $e^*(n)$; (3) given a pattern that represents input number n, an arbitrary Turing machine C on F with alphabet $A_C = A_\Phi = A_e \cup \{\#\}$ starts its computation on cell $e(0) = x_0$, and in internal state q_0; (4) a state of the Turing machine C represents output number m if and only if the pattern $p \in F(A_\Phi)$ that corresponds to this state has exactly m nonblank symbols. It is thus clear that, for any Turing machine $C = \langle T, M_C, \{g^t\}\rangle$ on F with alphabet $A_C = A_\Phi = A_e \cup \{\#\}$, this convention specifies a coding γ_C: $Z^+ \to M_C$ and a decoding δ_C: $M_C \to Z^+$. The coding γ_C is specified by the conjunction of (2) and (3). More precisely, condition (2) specifies a function π_C: $Z^+ \to F(A_C)$, where $F(A_C)$ is the set of all finite patterns of F relative to alphabet $A_C = A_\Phi = A_e \cup \{\#\}$. Condition (3), on the other hand, specifies a partial function σ_C: $F(A_C) \to M_C$. The coding γ_C: $Z^+ \to M_C$ is thus the composition of π_C and σ_C. The decoding δ_C is specified by condition (4). More precisely, δ_C: $M_C \to Z^+$ is the composition of two functions ϕ_C: $M_C \to F(A_C)$ and η_C: $F(A_C) \to Z^+$. The function ϕ_C assigns to any state $w \in M_C$ the finite pattern $p \in F(A_C)$ that corresponds to this state. On the other hand, η_C assigns to pattern p the number of nonblank symbols of this pattern. It is now easy to verify that both the coding γ_C and the decoding δ_C are effective relative to e^*.

Suppose that $A_C = A_\Phi = A_e \cup \{\#\} = \{a_j\}$ has z elements, that the blank $b = a_0$, and that the marker $\# = a_{z-1}$. The function π_C assigns to number n the pattern p_n which is completely blank, except for marker # on cell $e^*(n)$. The partial function σ_C, on the other hand, assigns to pattern p_n the state w_n that, on cell $e(0) = x_0$, has the symbol $q_0 p_n(x_0)$ and, on any other cell $x \neq x_0$, has the symbol $p_n(x)$.

Then, first, we can identify pattern p_n with a numeral $\boldsymbol{p_{ne*}}$ in base z. The number denoted by numeral $\boldsymbol{p_{ne*}}$ is $p_{ne*} = c_0z^0 + c_1z^1 + \ldots + c_nz^n$, where coefficient c_n $(0 \leq n)$ is equal to $z - 1$ and any other coefficient (if any) is equal to *0*. For any number n, let π_{Ce*}: $Z^+ \rightarrow Z^+$ satisfy $\pi_{Ce*}(n) = p_{ne*}$. Therefore, by its definition, π_{Ce*} is total recursive. In the second place, we can identify state w_n with a numeral $\boldsymbol{w_{ne*}}$ in base $z + mz$, where m is the number of internal states of Turing machine C. Let the extended alphabet $B_C = \{a_j\} \cup \{q_ia_j\}$ of Turing machine C be alphabetically ordered,[19] and let $v = e^{*-1}(x_0)$. The number denoted by numeral $\boldsymbol{w_{ne*}}$ is thus $w_{ne*} = d_0(z + mz)^0 + d_1(z + mz)^1 + \ldots + d_u(z + mz)^u$, where all the coefficients agree with the corresponding coefficients of p_{ne*}, except for $d_v = z + c_v$. For any number k, let σ_{Ce*}: $Z^+ \rightarrow Z^+$ satisfy this condition: If $k = p_{ne*}$ for some n, $\sigma_{Ce*}(k) = w_{ne*}$; otherwise, $\sigma_{Ce*}(k) = k$. Therefore, by its definition, σ_{Ce*} is total recursive.[20] For any number n, let γ_{Ce*}: $Z^+ \rightarrow Z^+$ satisfy $\gamma_{Ce*}(n) = \sigma_{Ce*}(\pi_{Ce*}(n))$. Therefore, by its definition, γ_{Ce*} is total recursive and, if $\gamma_C(n) = w_n$, then $\gamma_{Ce*}(n) = w_{ne*}$. The coding γ_C is thus effective relative to $e*$.

We have seen above that the decoding δ_C: $M_C \rightarrow Z^+$ specified by format Φ is the composition of ϕ_C: $M_C \rightarrow F(A_C)$ and η_C: $F(A_C) \rightarrow Z^+$. The function ϕ_C assigns to state w the pattern p_w that corresponds to w. The function η_C, on the other hand, assigns to an arbitrary pattern p the number of nonblank symbols of this pattern. Then, first, we can identify state w with a numeral $\boldsymbol{w_{e*}}$ in base $z + mz$, where m is the number of internal states of Turing machine C, and z is the number of symbols of alphabet $A_C = A_\Phi = A_e \cup \{\#\} = \{a_j\}$. Let the extended alphabet $B_C = \{a_j\} \cup \{q_ia_j\}$ of Turing machine C be alphabetically ordered. The number denoted by numeral $\boldsymbol{w_{e*}}$ is thus $w_{e*} = c_0(z + mz)^0 + c_1(z + mz)^1 + \ldots + c_u(z + mz)^u$, where exactly one coefficient c_v is equal to $z + iz + j$, for some i $(0 \leq i < m)$ and j $(0 \leq j < z)$. Second, we can identify pattern p_w with a numeral $\boldsymbol{p_{we*}}$ in base z. The number denoted by numeral $\boldsymbol{p_{we*}}$ is $p_{we*} = d_0z^0 + d_1z^1 + \ldots + d_uz^u$, where all the coefficients agree with the corresponding coefficients of w_{e*}, except for the coefficient d_v which is equal to j. For any number n, let ϕ_{Ce*}: $Z^+ \rightarrow Z^+$ satisfy this condition: If $n = w_{e*}$ for some $w \in M_C$, then $\phi_{Ce*}(n) = p_{we*}$; otherwise, $\phi_{Ce*}(n) = n$. Therefore, by its definition, ϕ_{Ce*} is total recursive.[21] Let η_{Ce*}: $Z^+ \rightarrow Z^+$ be defined as follows. Given an arbitrary number k, let $d_0z^0 + d_1z^1 + \ldots + d_uz^u$ be its decomposition in base z. Then, $\eta_{Ce}(k)$ = the number of coefficients d_y $(0 \leq y \leq u)$ such that $d_y \neq 0$. Therefore, by its definition, η_{Ce*} is total recursive. For any number n, let δ_{Ce*}: $Z^+ \rightarrow Z^+$ satisfy $\delta_{Ce*}(n) = \eta_{Ce*}(\phi_{Ce*}(n))$. Therefore, by its definition, δ_{Ce^*} is total recursive and, if $\delta_C(w) = h$, then $\delta_{Ce^*}(w_{e^*}) = h$. The decoding δ_C is thus effective relative to e^*.

We have thus verified that both the coding γ_C and the decoding δ_C are effective relative to e^*. Therefore, since e^* is a regular enumeration of F, the format Φ is regular relative to e^*. Let us now consider again the Turing machine C_e (see the first paragraph of this proof), and let us construct a second machine $C_{e^*/e}$ as follows. First, the alphabet of $C_{e^*/e}$ is $A_\Phi = A_e \cup \{\#\}$. Second, let a_s and a_c be arbitrary nonblank symbols of alphabet A_e, and let q_l and q_a be arbitrary internal states of C_e. The quadruples of C_e are thus of the five types $q_l a_s f_r q_a$, $q_l a_s a_c q_a$, $q_l b f_r q_a$, $q_l b b q_a$, $q_l b a_c q_a$. Then, the quadruples of $C_{e^*/e}$ are all the quadruples of C_e and, in addition, the following quadruples: For each quadruple of type $q_l b f_r q_a$, we add $q_l \# f_r q_a$; for each quadruple of type $q_l b b q_a$, we add $q_l \#\# q_a$; and for each quadruple of type $q_l b a_c q_a$, we add $q_l \# b q_{stop}$, where q_{stop} is not an internal state of C_e. If we start $C_{e^*/e}$ in state q_0, on cell $e(0) = x_0$, and on a pattern that represents input number n, $C_{e^*/e}$ works exactly as C_e does until it executes a quadruple of type $q_l \# b q_{stop}$. Hence, since the marker # is on cell $e^*(n) = e(e^*/e(n))$, $C_{e^*/e}$ stops after exactly $e^*/e(n)$ replacements of a blank with a nonblank symbol. Thus, if we start $C_{e^*/e}$ in internal state q_0, on cell $e(0) = x_0$, and on a pattern that represents number n, this computation stops and the final pattern has exactly $e^*/e(n)$ nonblank symbols. Therefore, e^*/e is computable on F in format Φ. Since Φ is regular relative to e^*, e^*/e is thus computable on F relative to e^*.

q.e.d.

It is now easy to verify that theorem 5 is a direct consequence of lemma 5.1, of lemma 4.1, and of the definition of the numeric bijection e^*/e.

THEOREM 5

If there is e* *such that* e* *is a regular enumeration of* $F = \langle U, \{f_r\} \rangle$, *and* F *is recursive relative to* e*, *then* F *is recursive.*

PROOF. Suppose that, for some e^*, $F = \langle U, \{f_r\} \rangle$ is recursive relative to e^*, and e^* is a regular enumeration of F. By the definition of recursive pattern field, F is recursive if and only if for any regular enumeration e of F, and for any r, f_{re} is recursive. Let e be an arbitrary regular enumeration of F. Thus, by lemma 5.1, the numeric bijection e^*/e is computable on F relative to e^*. Therefore, by lemma 4.1, e^*/e is recursive relative to $\{f_{re^*}\}$. Since F is recursive relative to e^* and e^* is regular, for any r, f_{re^*} is recursive. Thus, the class of the recursive functions relative to $\{f_{re^*}\}$ is identical to the class of the recursive functions. Therefore, e^*/e is recursive and, since e^*/e is a bijection, also its inverse e/e^* is recursive.[22] Furthermore, by the definition of e^*/e, for any number n, $f_{re}(n) = e^*/e(f_{re^*}(e/e^*(n)))$. Hence, for any r, f_{re} is recursive. Therefore, F is a recursive pattern field.

q.e.d.

Recall that a doubly infinite tape is recursive relative to the standard enumeration (example 8). By theorem 5, we can now also conclude that a doubly infinite tape is a recursive pattern field.

COROLLARY 5.1
A doubly infinite tape is a recursive pattern field.

PROOF. Let $F_2 = \langle U, \{L, R\}\rangle$ be a doubly infinite tape (see example 2), and let e^* be the standard enumeration of the tape. By example 6, e^* is regular and, by example 8, F_2 is recursive relative to e^*. Therefore, by theorem 5, F_2 is a recursive pattern field.

q.e.d.

We are now in a position to prove theorem 6. This theorem is a straightforward consequence of corollary 5.1, corollary 4.2, example 7, and of the fact that any recursive function is computable on a doubly infinite tape in standard format.

THEOREM 6 *(the concept of computability on a doubly infinite tape is equivalent to the concept of computability on a doubly infinite tape in standard format)*
A numeric function f *is computable on a doubly infinite tape if and only if* f *is computable on a doubly infinite tape in standard format.*

PROOF. Let $F_2 = \langle U, \{L, R\}\rangle$ be a doubly infinite tape (see example 2). Suppose that f is computable on F_2. By corollary 5.1, F_2 is a recursive pattern field. Therefore, by corollary 4.2, f is recursive. But any recursive function is computable on a doubly infinite tape in standard format. Therefore, f is computable on a doubly infinite tape in standard format.

Conversely, suppose that f is computable on a doubly infinite tape in standard format. Hence, by example 7, f is computable on a doubly infinite tape relative to the standard enumeration.

Therefore, by the definition of computability on F, f is computable on a doubly infinite tape.

q.e.d.

Before concluding this section, let me draw a further consequence of theorem 5. Let $F = \langle U, \{f_r\}\rangle$ be a pattern field, and e: $Z^+ \rightarrow U$ be a bijection. I say that the numeric representation $\{f_{re}\}$ of the relational structure of F is *recursive* if and only if for any r, f_{re} is recursive. Therefore, by this definition, and by the definition of recursive pattern field, a pattern field $F = \langle U, \{f_r\}\rangle$ is recursive if and only if for any regular enumeration e of F, the numeric representation $\{f_{re}\}$ of the relational structure of F is recursive. Theorem 5 allows us to deduce the analogous necessary and sufficient condition for an arbitrary nonrecursive pattern field.

THEOREM 7

A pattern field $F = \langle U, \{f_r\}\rangle$ *is not recursive if and only if for any regular enumeration* e *of* F, *the numeric representation* $\{f_{re}\}$ *of the relational structure of* F *is not recursive.*

PROOF. Suppose that F is not recursive. Thus, by theorem 5, for any regular enumeration e of F, F is not recursive relative to e. Hence, by the definition of recursive pattern field relative to e, for any regular enumeration e of F, there is r such that f_{re} is not recursive. Therefore, for any regular enumeration e of F, $\{f_{re}\}$ is not recursive. Conversely, suppose that, for any regular enumeration e of F, $\{f_{re}\}$ is not recursive. Thus, for any regular enumeration e of F, there is r such that f_{re} is not recursive. Therefore, by the definition of recursive pattern field, F is not recursive.

q.e.d.

6 Computational systems on pattern field *F*

In chapter 1, I proposed an explication of the intuitive notion of a computational system (definition 3) that employs the concept of Turing computability. In particular, this formal concept allowed me to make precise the idea of an *effective cascade*. In this chapter, however, I have shown that the concept of Turing computability is not absolute, but instead depends on the relational structure of the pattern field F on which a Turing machine operates. For, if F is the doubly infinite tape of an ordinary Turing machine, then the concept of computability on F is equivalent to the usual concept of Turing computability (theorem 6); but, if F is a nonrecursive pattern field, then the concept of computability on F includes numeric functions that are not Turing computable in the usual sense (see theorem 2). The goal of this section is to propose a new definition of a computational system (a computational system on pattern field F) that takes into account the relativity of the concept of Turing computability. If F is a doubly infinite tape, however, computational systems on F reduce to computational systems.

Recall that in chapter 1 I proposed to identify a computational system with a cascade $MDS = \langle T, M, \{g^t\}\rangle$ which is isomorphic to some effective cascade $MDS_1 = \langle T, M_1, \{h^t\}\rangle$. I then used the concept of Turing computability to make precise the condition that the cascade $MDS_1 = \langle T, M_1, \{h^t\}\rangle$ is effective or, in other words, that its state space M_1 is a *decidable* set, and that each state transition function h^t is *effective* or computable. By using the concept of computability on F, we can now obtain a more general concept of computational system (see figure 2-5).

DEFINITION 2 *(computational systems on pattern field* F*)*

MDS *is a computational system on pattern field* F *if and only if* $\mathrm{MDS} = \langle \mathrm{T}, \mathrm{M}, \{\mathrm{g}^t\}\rangle$ *is a cascade, and there is a second cascade* $\mathrm{MDS}_1 = \langle \mathrm{T}, \mathrm{M}_1, \{\mathrm{h}^t\}\rangle$ *such that* MDS_1 *is isomorphic to* MDS *and*

1. $\mathrm{M}_1 \subseteq \mathrm{Z}^+$ *and the characteristic function of* M_1 *is computable on* F*;*
2. *the state transition* h^1 *is computable on* F.

As mentioned, if the pattern field F is a doubly infinite tape, then the concept of computational system on F is equivalent to the concept of computational system (theorem 8). This theorem is a straight-

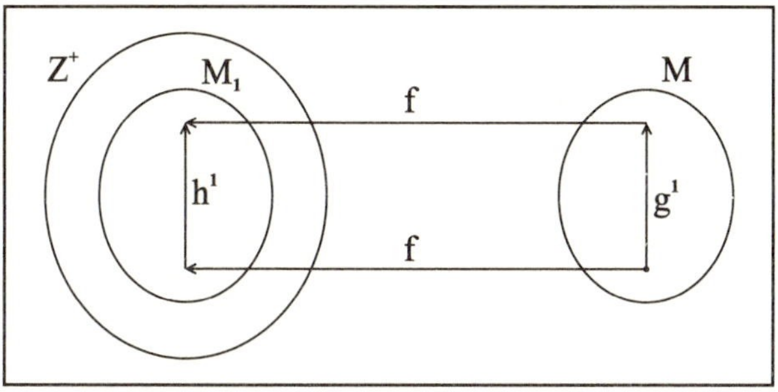

FIGURE 2-5 Computational systems on pattern field F. MDS = $\langle T, M, \{g^t\}\rangle$ and $\mathrm{MDS}_1 = \langle T, M_1, \{h^t\}\rangle$ are cascades. MDS_1 is isomorphic to MDS. f is a bijection from M to M_1. $F = \langle U, \{f_r\}\rangle$ is a pattern field. M_1 is a subset of the nonnegative integers Z^+. The characteristic function of M_1 is computable on F. The state transition h^1 is computable on F.

forward consequence of definition 2, of the definition of computational system, of corollaries 4.2 and 5.1, of theorem 6, and of the fact that any recursive function is computable on a doubly infinite tape in standard format. The detailed proof is in the appendix.

THEOREM 8 *(the concept of computational system on a doubly infinite tape is equivalent to the concept of computational system)*
MDS = ⟨T, M, $\{g^t\}$⟩ *is a computational system on a doubly infinite tape if and only if* MDS *is a computational system.*

PROOF. See the appendix.

Before concluding this chapter, let me make one further point. Recall that, in chapter 1, we verified that all ordinary Turing machines are computational systems (example 5). Therefore, by theorem 8, we can now affirm that all Turing machines on a *doubly infinite tape* are computational systems on a *doubly infinite tape*. It is then natural to ask to what *kind* of pattern field F we can generalize this result. On the one hand, it is obvious that the existence of a regular enumeration of F is a necessary condition. For, if there is no regular enumeration of F, the concept of computability on F is empty and thus, by definition 2, the concept of computational system on F is empty as well. On the other hand, the next theorem ensures that this condition is also sufficient. In other words, if there is a regular enumeration e of F, then any Turing machine on F is a computational system on F itself (theorem 9).

The proof of this theorem is based on the following idea: First, given an arbitrary Turing machine $C = \langle T, M_C, \{g^t\}\rangle$ on F, we can identify any state $w \in M_C$ with a numeral $\boldsymbol{w_e}$ in base $z + yz$, where y is the number of internal states of the Turing machine C and z is the number of symbols that are members of its alphabet. Second, we consider an isomorphic cascade $MDS_1 = \langle T, M_1, \{h^t\}\rangle$ whose state space M_1 is the set of all numbers m such that, for some $w \in M_C, m = w_e$, and we then show that both the characteristic function μ of M_1 and the state transition h^1 are computable on pattern field F. The proof that μ is computable on F is similar to the proofs of lemmas 2.1 and 5.1. Since e is a regular enumeration of F, there is a cell $x_0 \in U$ and a Turing machine C_e on F with alphabet $A_e \supset \{b\}$ such that, when C_e is started on a completely blank pattern, cell x_0, and in internal state q_0, C_e performs a computation that satisfies these conditions: (1) for any cell member of U, C_e replaces the initial blank with a nonblank symbol; (2) the first replacement of a blank with a nonblank symbol occurs on cell x_0; and (3) C_e never replaces a nonblank symbol with a blank. Furthermore, by counting the successive replacements of a blank with a nonblank symbol, and by then assigning to replacement number n $(0 \leq n)$ the cell where this replacement occurs, this computation of C_e allows us to construct the enumeration e. By appropriately modifying the Turing machine C_e, and by choosing a suitable format Φ, we can then show that μ is computable on F in format Φ. This implies that μ is computable on F, because the chosen format Φ turns out to be regular relative to e. We finally prove that the state transition h^1 is computable on F by modifying the Turing machine C, and by choosing a second format Θ. In this case also, the format Θ turns out to be regular relative to e, and h^1 to be computable on F in format Θ. The detailed proof of theorem 9 is in the appendix.

THEOREM 9

If C *is a Turing machine on pattern field* F, *then* C *is a computational system on* F *if and only if there is a regular enumeration* e *of* F.

PROOF. See the appendix.

By theorem 9, if a pattern field F has no regular enumeration, then no Turing machine C on F is a computational system on F itself. Nevertheless, C might be a computational system on some *other* pattern field. A direct consequence of theorem 9 (corollary 9.1) implies that this is true. Let $F = \langle U, \{f_r\}\rangle$ be a pattern field. I call a second pattern field $F^* = \langle U, \{f_u\}\rangle$ an *extension of F* if and only if there is a regular enumeration of F^*, and $\{f_r\} \subseteq \{f_u\}$. It is thus obvious that any pattern field F has some extension.[23] Let us now consider an arbitrary Turing machine C on F, and an arbitrary extension F^* of F. It is then easy to prove that C is a computational system on F^*.

COROLLARY 9.1

If C *is a Turing machine on* F, *and* F* *is an extension of* F, *then* C *is a computational system on* F*.

PROOF. Let $C = \langle T, M, \{g^t\}\rangle$ be a Turing machine on pattern field F, and F^* be an extension of F. Note first that, since C is a Turing machine on F, and F^* is an extension of F, C is a Turing machine on F^* as well. Second, since F^* is an extension of F, there is a regular enumeration e of F^*. Therefore, by theorem 9, C is a computational system on F^*.

q.e.d.

7 Appendix: Proofs of selected theorems

THEOREM 3

If f: $Z^+ \to Z^+$ *is a recursive function relative to* $\{f_u\}$, *then* f *is computable on* $\langle Z^+, \{s, v\} \cup \{f_u\}\rangle$ *relative to the identity function on* Z^+.

PROOF. First, note that each cell $x \in Z^+$ can be identified with a square of a tape infinite in one direction, and that s and v thus correspond, respectively, to the *right* and *left* functions of Turing machines that operate on this kind of tape. Let e be the identity function on Z^+. I will show that there is a format Φ such that Φ is regular relative to e and f is computable on $F = \langle Z^+, \{s, v\} \cup \{f_u\}\rangle$ in format Φ.

Let the format Φ consist of the following convention: (1) The alphabet A_Φ is $\{b, 1, b1, 11, \#_0, \#_1, \ldots, \#_{z-1}\} = \{\varsigma_\lambda\}$. A_Φ has thus z + 4 symbols (where $z > 0$); (2) input (or output) number n is represented by a block of $n + 1$ 1s, with the leftmost 1 on cell 2; (3) given a pattern that represents input number n, an arbitrary Turing machine C on F with alphabet $A_C = A_\Phi = \{\varsigma_\lambda\}$ starts its computation on cell 2, and in internal state q_0; (4) let ε be the number of internal states of the Turing machine C; a state w of C represents output number m if and only if for some r $(0 \le r < \varepsilon)$ and λ $(0 \le \lambda < z + 4)$, $w(2) = q_r\varsigma_\lambda$ and the pattern that corresponds to w represents output number m. It is thus clear that, for any Turing machine $C = \langle T, M_C, \{g^t\}\rangle$ on F with alphabet $A_C = A_\Phi = \{\varsigma_\lambda\}$, this convention specifies a coding γ_C: $Z^+ \to M_C$ and a decoding δ_C: $M_C \to Z^+$. The coding γ_C is specified by the conjunction of (2) and (3). More precisely, condition (2) specifies a function π_C: $Z^+ \to F(A_C)$, where $F(A_C)$ is the set of all finite patterns of F relative to alphabet $A_C = A_\Phi = \{\varsigma_\lambda\}$. Condition (3), on the other hand, specifies a partial function σ_C: $F(A_C) \to M_C$. The coding γ_C: $Z^+ \to M_C$ is thus the composition of π_C and σ_C. The decoding δ_C is specified by the conjunction of (4) and (2). More precisely, δ_C: $M_C \to Z^+$ is the composition of two partial functions ϕ_C: $M_C \to F(A_C)$ and η_C: $F(A_C) \to Z^+$. For any state $w \in M_C$ such that, for some r $(0 \le r < \varepsilon)$ and λ $(0 \le \lambda < z + 4)$, $w(2) = q_r\varsigma_\lambda$, ϕ_C assigns to w the finite pattern $p \in F(A_C)$ that corresponds to this state. If, for any r $(0 \le r < \varepsilon)$ and λ $(0 \le \lambda < z + 4)$, $w(2) \ne q_r\varsigma_\lambda$, then $\phi_C(w)$ is undefined. On the other hand, η_C assigns to pattern p the output number represented by p. However, if p does not represent any output number, that is, if p does not satisfy condition (2), $\eta_C(p)$ is undefined. Note that, since δ_C is the composition of two partial functions, δ_C is partial as well. It is now easy to verify that both the coding γ_Φ and the decoding δ_Φ are effective relative to e.

Recall that $A_C = A_\Phi = \{b, 1, b1, 11, \#_0, \#_1, \ldots, \#_{z-1}\} = \{\varsigma_\lambda\}$ has $z + 4$ elements. The function π_C assigns to number n the pattern p_n that has a block of $n + 1$ consecutive 1s, and is otherwise blank. The left-most 1 is on cell 2. The partial function σ_C, on the other hand, assigns to pattern p_n the state w_n that, on cell 2, has the symbol $q_0 1$ and, on any other cell $x \neq 2$, has the symbol $p_n(x)$. Then, first, we can identify pattern p_n with a numeral $\boldsymbol{p_{ne}}$ in base $z + 4$. The number denoted by numeral $\boldsymbol{p_{ne}}$ is $p_{ne} = 0(z + 4)^0 + 0(z + 4)^1 + 1(z + 4)^2 + 1(z + 4)^3 + \ldots + 1(z + 4)^{n+1} + 1(z + 4)^{n+2}$. For any number n, let π_{Ce}: $Z^+ \rightarrow Z^+$ satisfy $\pi_{Ce}(n) = p_{ne}$. Therefore, by its definition, π_{Ce} is total recursive. Second, we can identify state w_n with a numeral $\boldsymbol{w_{ne}}$ in base $(z + 4) + \varepsilon(z + 4)$, where ε is the number of internal states of Turing machine C. Let the extended alphabet $B_C = \{\varsigma_\lambda\} \cup \{q_r\varsigma_\lambda\}$ of Turing machine C be alphabetically ordered.[24] The number denoted by numeral $\boldsymbol{w_{ne}}$ is thus $w_{ne} = 0((z + 4) + \varepsilon(z + 4))^0 + 0((z + 4) + \varepsilon(z + 4))^1 + (z + 5)((z + 4) + \varepsilon(z + 4))^2 + 1((z + 4) + \varepsilon(z + 4))^3 + \ldots + 1((z + 4) + \varepsilon(z + 4))^{n+1} + 1((z + 4) + \varepsilon(z + 4))^{n+2}$. For any number k, let σ_{Ce}: $Z^+ \rightarrow Z^+$ satisfy this condition: If $k = p_{ne}$ for some n, $\sigma_{Ce}(k) = w_{ne}$; otherwise, $\sigma_{Ce}(k) = k$. Therefore, by its definition, σ_{Ce} is total recursive.[25] For any number n, let γ_{Ce}: $Z^+ \rightarrow Z^+$ satisfy $\gamma_{Ce}(n) = \sigma_{Ce}(\pi_{Ce}(n))$. Therefore, by its definition, γ_{Ce} is total recursive and, if $\gamma_C(n) = w_n$, then $\gamma_{Ce}(n) = w_{ne}$. The coding γ_C is thus effective relative to e.

We have seen above that the decoding δ_C: $M_C \rightarrow Z^+$ specified by format Φ is the composition of ϕ_C: $M_C \rightarrow F(A_C)$ and η_C: $F(A_C) \rightarrow Z^+$. For any state $w \in M_C$ such that, for some r $(0 \leq r < \varepsilon)$ and λ $(0 \leq \lambda < z + 4)$, $w(2) = q_r\varsigma_\lambda$, the partial function ϕ_C assigns to w the finite pattern $p \in F(A_C)$ that corresponds to this state. If, for any r $(0 \leq r < \varepsilon)$ and λ $(0 \leq \lambda < z + 4)$, $w(2) \neq q_r\varsigma_\lambda$, then $\phi_C(w)$ is undefined. The partial function η_C, on the other hand, assigns to an arbitrary pattern p the output number represented by p. However, if p does not represent any output number, that is, if p does not satisfy condition (2), $\eta_C(p)$ is undefined. Then, first, we can identify state w with a numeral $\boldsymbol{w_e}$ in base $(z + 4) + \varepsilon(z + 4)$, where ε is the number of internal states of Turing machine C, and $z + 4$ is the number of symbols of alphabet $A_C = A_\Phi = \{b, 1, b1, 11, \#_0, \#_1, \ldots, \#_{z-1}\} = \{\varsigma_\lambda\}$. Let the extended alphabet $B_C = \{\varsigma_\lambda\} \cup \{q_r\varsigma_\lambda\}$ of Turing machine C be alphabetically ordered. The number denoted by numeral $\boldsymbol{w_e}$ is thus $w_e = c_0((z + 4) + \varepsilon(z + 4))^0 + c_1((z + 4) + \varepsilon(z + 4))^1 + c_2((z + 4) + \varepsilon(z + 4))^2 + \ldots + c_\xi((z + 4) + \varepsilon(z + 4))^\xi$, where coefficient c_2 is equal to $(z + 4) + r(z + 4) + \lambda$, for some r $(0 \leq r < \varepsilon)$ and λ $(0 \leq \lambda < z + 4)$. Second, we can identify pattern p_w with a numeral $\boldsymbol{p_{we}}$ in base $z + 4$. The number denoted by numeral $\boldsymbol{p_{we}}$ is $p_{we} = d_0(z + 4)^0 + d_1(z + 4)^1 + d_2(z + 4)^2 + \ldots + d_\xi(z + 4)^\xi$, where all the coefficients agree with the corresponding coefficients of w_e, except for coefficient d_2 which is equal to λ. For any number n, let ϕ_{Ce}: $Z^+ \to Z^+$ satisfy this condition: If $n = w_e$ for some $w \in M_C$ such that, for some r $(0 \leq r < \varepsilon)$ and λ $(0 \leq \lambda < z + 4)$, $w(2) = q_r\varsigma_\lambda$, then $\phi_{Ce}(n) = p_{we}$; otherwise, $\phi_{Ce}(n) = n$. Therefore, by its definition, ϕ_{Ce} is total recursive.[26] Given an arbitrary number k, let $d_0(z + 4)^0 + d_1(z + 4)^1 + d_2(z + 4)^2 + \ldots + d_\xi(z + 4)^\xi$ be its decomposition in base $z + 4$. Let us then check whether coefficients d_0 and d_1 are equal to 0, and all other coefficients are equal to 1. If yes, $\eta_{Ce}(k) = \xi - 2$. Otherwise, $\eta_{Ce}(k) = k$. Therefore, by its definition, η_{Ce} is total recursive. For any number n, let δ_{Ce}: $Z^+ \to Z^+$ satisfy $\delta_{Ce}(n) = \eta_{Ce}(\phi_{Ce}(n))$. Therefore, by its definition, δ_{Ce} is total recursive and, if $\delta_C(w) = \tau$, then $\delta_{Ce}(w_e) = \tau$. The decoding δ_C is thus effective relative to e.

We have thus verified that both the coding γ_C and the decoding δ_C are effective relative to e. Therefore, since e is a regular enumeration of F, the format Φ is regular relative to e. I will now prove that any recursive function f: $Z^+ \to Z^+$ relative to $\{f_u\}$ is computable on $F = \langle Z^+, \{s, v\} \cup \{f_u\}\rangle$ in format Φ. This can be obtained by modifying Boolos and Jeffrey's proof that all recursive functions are Turing computable (1980, chapters 6 and 7). Boolos and Jeffrey first proved that all abacus computable functions are Turing computable (chapter 6), and then proved that all recursive functions are abacus computable (chapter 7).

An *abacus* is a machine with an infinite number of registers [1], [2], . . . , [k], ... Each register can hold an arbitrary nonnegative integer, and the machine performs just two types of operations on the registers: $\to$[k]— and $\to$[k]$—_1/—_2$. The first operation goes to register [k], adds 1 to the number in this register, and then exits along path —. The second operation goes to register [k] and checks whether the number n in this register is different from zero. If $n \neq 0$, it subtracts 1 from n, and then exits along path $—_1$. Otherwise, it simply exits along path $—_2$. Any abacus is specified by a *program*, that is, a flow graph that indicates the sequence in which these two types of operations are to be performed. A numeric function h with m $(1 \leq m)$ arguments is *abacus computable* if and only if there is an abacus such that, when it is started with the arguments $n_1, \ldots, n_m$ of the function in registers [1], . . . , [m], and with all other registers empty, it stops and the content of a specified register [k] is equal to $h(n_1, \ldots, n_m)$ if $h(n_1, \ldots, n_m)$ is defined. Otherwise, the abacus does not stop. It is then easy to prove that all recursive functions of m $(1 \leq m)$ arguments are abacus computable (see Boolos and Jeffrey 1980, chapter 7).

In fact, abacus machines can be modified so that they are able to compute all recursive functions relative to $\{f_u\}$. This can simply be obtained by adding the operation $\rightarrow f_u[k]$—, for any u. If the number in register $[k]$ is n, this operation goes to this register, changes n to $f_u(n)$, and then exits along path —. Let us call any abacus with these special operations an *$\{f_u\}$-abacus*. Then, it is obvious that all recursive functions relative to $\{f_u\}$ are $\{f_u\}$-abacus computable (the proof is analogous to the one for recursive functions).

According to Boolos and Jeffrey, a numeric function h with m $(1 \leq m)$ arguments is Turing computable if and only if there is a Turing machine with alphabet $\{b, 1\}$ that computes h according to the following conventions: (1) The tape is infinite in only one direction (say to the right), and input (output) number n is represented by a block of $n + 1$ 1s. The leftmost 1 is on the third square of the tape. If there is more than one input number, each of them is represented by the appropriate block of 1s, and two different blocks are separated by exactly one blank b; and (2) the Turing machine starts on the third square of the tape, in internal state q_0. Furthermore, it also stops on the same square. Boolos and Jeffrey proved that an arbitrary program of an abacus that computes a numeric function h with m $(1 \leq m)$ arguments can be transformed into the quadruples of a Turing machine that computes the same function according to conventions (*1*) and (*2*). Abacus programs are flow graphs with just two types of operations: $\rightarrow[k]$— and $\rightarrow[k]—_1/—_2$. Boolos and Jeffrey gave the quadruples of two Turing machines with alphabet $\{b, 1\}$ that correspond to these two types of operation. In broad outline, these machines work as follows: The number n in register $[k]$ is represented on the tape by a block of $n + 1$ 1s. This block is the kth block of 1s on the tape; two different blocks are separated by just one blank; and the leftmost 1 of the first block is on the third square of the tape. The machine that corresponds to the $\rightarrow[k]$— operation starts on the leftmost 1 (that is, on the third square) and then goes to the right until it finds the kth block. It then writes a 1 at the end of this block, shifts all the remaining blocks one square to the right, goes back to the third square, and stops. The machine that corresponds to the $\rightarrow[k]—_1/—_2$ operation starts on the leftmost 1 (on the third square) and then goes to the right until it finds the kth block. It then checks whether this block contains just one 1. If yes, it goes back to the third square and stops. Otherwise, it deletes the rightmost 1 of the kth block, shifts all the remaining blocks one square to the left, goes back to the third square, and stops. It is thus clear that, by appropriately combining these two types of machines, the program of an abacus that computes a numeric (partial) function h with m $(1 \leq m)$ arguments can be transformed into the quadruples of a Turing machine that computes the same function according to conventions (*1*) and (*2*).

I will now modify this proof in order to show that any program of a $\{f_u\}$-abacus that computes a numeric function h with m $(1 \leq m)$ arguments can be transformed into the quadruples of a Turing machine on $F = \langle Z^+, \{s, v\} \cup \{f_u\}\rangle$ that computes the same function according to conventions (*1*) and (*2*). The only difference between a $\{f_u\}$-abacus program and a normal abacus program is the presence of nodes of type $\rightarrow f_u[k]$—. Therefore, I must only describe a Turing machine C_u on F that corresponds to this type of node. Assume that the number n in register k is represented on the tape by the kth block of 1s, and that this block has $n + 1$ 1s. C_u has alphabet $\{b, 1, b1, 11, \#_0, \#_1, \ldots, \#_{z-1}\} = A_\Phi$, and it starts on the leftmost 1 (that is, on the third square = cell 2). It then goes to the right until it finds the kth block of 1s. Then, C_u makes a special copy of this block. Recall that the kth block has $n + 1$ 1s. C_u writes a copy of the kth block on the first $n + 1$ squares of the tape. This copy, however, is written without deleting the content of these squares. This is obtained by using the special symbols $b1$ and 11. That is, if square x $(0 \leq x < n + 1)$ contains symbol b, then C_u replaces b with $b1$; if square x contains symbol 1, then C_u replaces 1 with 11. To keep track of the progress of the copying process, C_u may use some of the markers $\#_0, \#_1, \ldots, \#_{z-1}$. All the markers, however, are deleted when the copying is complete and, at the end of this process, C_u is on the first square of the tape.

At this point, C_u starts a second routine that computes the function f_u. The quadruples of this routine are the following: $\{q_0(b1)sq_1$, $q_1(b1)bq_2$, $q_1(11)1q_2$, q_2bsq_1, q_21sq_1, q_1bvq_3, q_11vq_3, $q_3bf_uq_4$, $q_31f_uq_4$, $q_3(b1)f_uq_4$, $q_4b(b1)q_5$, $q_41(11)q_5$, $q_5(b1)vq_4$, $q_5(11)vq_4$, $q_4(b1)(b1)q_6\}$. At the end of this routine, C_u is on the first square, in state q_6, scanning $b1$. Each of the first $f_u(n) + 1$ squares contains the special symbol $b1$ or the special symbol 11. All other squares contain b or 1.

Finally, C_u must change the number of symbols in the kth block from $n + 1$ to $f_u(n) + 1$, and replace all the special symbols $b1$ and 11 with b and 1. This is accomplished by means of a third routine. This routine uses the special symbols on the first $f_u(n) + 1$ squares as a counter and, if necessary, keeps track of the progress of the computation by means of some of the markers $\#_0, \#_1, \ldots, \#_{z-1}$. When the kth block contains exactly $f_u(n) + 1$ symbols, all the markers and the special symbols $b1$ and 11 are replaced by either b or 1, and the machine finally goes back to the third square, where it stops.

I have thus described a Turing machine C_u on F that corresponds to the $\rightarrow f_u[k]$— operation of a $\{f_u\}$-abacus. Therefore, by appropriately combining this machine with the other two machines that correspond to the $\rightarrow[k]$— and $\rightarrow[k]—_1/—_2$ operations, the program of a $\{f_u\}$-abacus that computes a numeric function h with m $(1 \leq m)$ arguments can be transformed into the quadruples of a Turing machine C on $F = \langle Z^+, \{s, v\} \cup \{f_u\}\rangle$ that computes the same function according to conventions (*1*) and (*2*).

Let us now consider again the numeric function of one argument f. By the hypothesis of the theorem, f is recursive relative to $\{f_u\}$. Hence, since all recursive functions relative to $\{f_u\}$ are $\{f_u\}$-abacus computable, f is $\{f_u\}$-abacus computable. Furthermore, since f is $\{f_u\}$-abacus computable, there is a Turing machine C on $F = \langle Z^+, \{s, v\} \cup \{f_u\}\rangle$ that computes f according to conventions (*1*) and (*2*). Hence, f is computable on F in format Φ. Since Φ is regular relative to e, and e is the identity function on Z^+, f is thus computable on $\langle Z^+, \{s, v\} \cup \{f_u\}\rangle$ relative to the identity function on Z^+.

q.e.d.

THEOREM 8 *(the concept of computational system on a doubly infinite tape is equivalent to the concept of computational system)*

MDS = ⟨T, M, *{*g^t*}*⟩ *is a computational system on a doubly infinite tape if and only if* MDS *is a computational system.*

PROOF. Suppose that $MDS = \langle T, M, \{g^t\}\rangle$ is a computational system on a doubly infinite tape. Thus, by definition 2, MDS is a cascade, and there is a second cascade $MDS_1 = \langle T, M_1, \{h^t\}\rangle$ such that MDS_1 is isomorphic to MDS, $M_1 \subseteq Z^+$, the characteristic function of M_1 is computable on a doubly infinite tape, and the state transition h^1 is computable on a doubly infinite tape. By corollary 5.1, a doubly infinite tape is a recursive pattern field. Hence, by corollary 4.2, the characteristic function of M_1 is recursive, and the state transition h^1 is recursive as well. Let us now consider the cascade $MDS_{1*} = \langle T, M_{1*}, \{h^{t*}\}\rangle$ that satisfies the following conditions: (1) $x \in M_{1*}$ if and only if for some n $(0 \le n)$, x is a finite string that contains exactly $n + 1$ 1s and $n \in M_1$; and (2) let $f: M_1 \to M_{1*}$ satisfy this condition: For any $m \in M_1, f(m)$ = the finite string that contains exactly $m + 1$ 1s; then, for any $x \in M_{1*}$, let $h^{t*}(x) = f(h^t(f^{-1}(x)))$. Thus, by its definition, MDS_{1*} is isomorphic to MDS_1. Hence, since MDS_1 is isomorphic to MDS, MDS_{1*} is isomorphic to MDS. Also note that M_{1*} is a proper subset of the set $P(\{b, 1\})$ of all finite strings built out of the alphabet $\{b, 1\}$. I will now show that MDS_{1*} also satisfies conditions (1) and (2) of the definition of computational system (see definition 3 in chapter 1). Let $\mu: Z^+ \to \{0, 1\}$ be the characteristic function of M_1. Since μ is recursive, there is an ordinary Turing machine C_μ such that, when C_μ is started in internal state q_0, on the leftmost 1 of a block of $n + 1$ 1s on an otherwise blank tape, if $\mu(n) = 0$ (or $\mu(n) = 1$), C_μ stops on the leftmost 1 of a block of 1 (or 2) 1s on an otherwise blank tape.[27] Let z be an arbitrary string member of $P(\{b, 1\})$. Thus, by appropriately modifying C_μ, we can obtain a second machine[28] $C_{\mu*}$ such that, when $C_{\mu*}$ is started in internal state q_0, on the left marker $ of a tape whose content is . . . *bb$z#bb* . . . , if $z \notin M_{1*}$ (or $z \in M_{1*}$), $C_{\mu*}$ stops on the left marker $ of a tape whose content is . . . *bb$b#bb* . . . (or . . . *bb$bb#bb* . . .). Therefore, condition (1) of the definition of computational system is satisfied. As for condition (2), since h^1 is defined for any $m \in M_1$ and h^1 is recursive, for any $m \in M_1$, there is an ordinary Turing machine C such that, when C is started in internal state q_0, on the leftmost 1 of a block of $m + 1$ 1s on an otherwise blank tape, C stops on the leftmost 1 of a block of $h^1(m) + 1$ 1s on an otherwise blank tape. Thus, by appropriately modifying C, we can obtain a second machine C_* such that, for any $x \in M_{1*}$, when C_* is started in internal state q_0, on the left marker $ of a tape whose content is . . . *bb$x#bb* . . . , C_* stops on the left marker $ of a tape whose content is . . . *bb$h¹*(x)#bb*. . . . Finally, if $T = Z$, note first that h^{-1} is defined for any $m \in M_1$. Second, since the characteristic function μ of M_1 is recursive, and h^1 is recursive as well, then h^{-1} is also recursive.[29] Hence, the argument I have just given for h^{1*} also applies to h^{-1*}. Therefore, also condition (2) of the definition of computational system is satisfied, and MDS is thus a computational system.

Conversely, suppose that $MDS = \langle T, M, \{g^t\}\rangle$ is a computational system. Thus, by the definition of computational system, MDS is a cascade, and there is a second cascade $MDS_{1*} = \langle T, M_{1*}, \{h^{t^*}\}\rangle$ such that MDS_{1*} is isomorphic to MDS and (1) if $P(A)$ is the set of all finite strings built out of some finite alphabet A, then $M_{1*} \subseteq P(A)$, and there is an ordinary Turing machine $C_{\mu*}$ such that, for any finite string $z \in P(A)$, when $C_{\mu*}$ is started in internal state q_0, on the left marker $\$$ of a tape whose content is . . . $bb\$z\#bb$ . . . , if $z \notin M_{1*}$ (or $z \in M_{1*}$), $C_{\mu*}$ stops on the left marker $\$$ of a tape whose content is . . . $bb\$b\#bb$ . . . (or . . . $bb\$bb\#bb$ . . .); (2) there is also an ordinary Turing machine C_* such that, for any $x \in M_{1*}$, when C_* is started in internal state q_0, on the left marker $\$$ of a tape whose content is . . . $bb\$x\#bb$ . . . , C_* stops on the left marker $\$$ of a tape whose content is . . . $bb\$h^{1}*(x)\#bb$. . . . Let us now consider the cascade $MDS_1 = \langle T, M_1, \{h^t\}\rangle$ that satisfies the following conditions: (1) $m \in M_1$ if and only if for some finite string $z \in P(A)$, m is the number that corresponds to z in the alphabetical order of $P(A)$ and $z \in M_{1*}$; and (2) let f: $M_{1*} \rightarrow M_1$ satisfy this condition: For any $x \in M_{1*}$, $f(x)$ = the number that corresponds to string x in the alphabetical order of $P(A)$; then, for any $m \in M_1$, let $h^t(m) = f(h^{t^*}(f^{-1}(m)))$. Thus, by its definition, MDS_1 is isomorphic to MDS_{1*}. Hence, since MDS_{1*} is isomorphic to MDS, MDS_1 is isomorphic to MDS. Also note that M_1 is a subset of the nonnegative integers. I will now show that the characteristic function μ of M_1 and the state transition h^1 are both computable on a doubly infinite tape. Note first that, by appropriately modifying $C_{\mu*}$, we can obtain a second machine C_μ such that, when C_μ is started in internal state q_0, on the leftmost 1 of a string of $n + 1$ 1s on an otherwise blank tape, if the string z that corresponds to n in the alphabetical order of $P(A)$ is not member of M_{1*} (is member of M_{1*}), C_μ stops on the leftmost 1 of a block of 1 (or 2) 1s on an otherwise blank tape.[30] Therefore, the characteristic function μ of M_1 is recursive. Second, by appropriately modifying C_*, we can obtain a second machine C such that, for any $n \in Z^+$, when C is started in internal state q_0, on the leftmost 1 of a block of $n + 1$ 1s on an otherwise blank tape, if $n \in M_1$, C stops on the leftmost 1 of a block of $h^1(m) + 1$ 1s on an otherwise blank tape; if $n \notin M_1$, C does not stop.[31] Therefore, the state transition h^1 is recursive. Since any recursive function is computable on a doubly infinite tape in standard format, by theorem 6, both the characteristic function μ of M_1 and the state transition h^1 are thus computable on a doubly infinite tape. Therefore, MDS is a computational system on a doubly infinite tape.

q.e.d.

THEOREM 9

If C *is a Turing machine on pattern field* F, *then* C *is a computational system on* F *if and only if there is a regular enumeration* e *of* F.

PROOF. Suppose that C is a Turing machine on pattern field $F = \langle U, \{f_r\}\rangle$ and that, for any bijection e: $Z^+ \to U$, e is not a regular enumeration of F. Then, by the definition of computability on F, no numeric function is computable on F. Thus, neither conditions (1) nor (2) of definition 2 is satisfied. Therefore, C is not a computational system on F.

Conversely, suppose that $C = \langle T, M_C, \{g^t\}\rangle$ is a Turing machine on pattern field $F = \langle U, \{f_r\}\rangle$, and that there is a regular enumeration e of F. First, we can identify any state $w \in M_C$ with a numeral $\boldsymbol{w_e}$ in base $z + yz$, where y is the number of internal states that are members of $Q_C = \{q_i\}$ and z is the number of symbols that are members of $A_C = \{a_j\}$. I indicate the number denoted by numeral $\boldsymbol{w_e}$ by w_e. Let us then consider the cascade $MDS_1 = \langle T, M_1, \{h^t\}\rangle$ that satisfies the following conditions: (1) $M_1 \subseteq Z^+$, and $m \in M_1$ if and only if there is $w \in M_C$ such that $w_e = m$; (2) let f: $M_C \to M_1$ satisfy these conditions: For any $w \in M_C, f(w) = w_e$; then, for any $m \in M_1$, $h^t(m) = f(g^t(f^{-1}(m)))$. Thus, by its definition, the cascade MDS_1 is isomorphic to MDS, and $M_1 \subseteq Z^+$. I will now show that the characteristic function μ of M_1 and the state transition h^1 are both computable on pattern field F.

Since e is a regular enumeration of pattern field $F = \langle U, \{f_r\}\rangle$, there is a cell $x_0 \in U$ and a Turing machine C_e on F with alphabet $A_e = \{\alpha_u\} \supset \{b\}$ such that, when C_e is started on a completely blank pattern, cell x_0, and in internal state q_0, C_e performs a computation that satisfies these conditions: (1) for any cell member of U, C_e replaces the initial blank with a nonblank symbol; (2) the first replacement of a blank with a nonblank symbol occurs on cell x_0, and (3) C_e never replaces a nonblank symbol with a blank. Furthermore, by counting the successive replacements of a blank with a nonblank symbol, and by then assigning to replacement number n $(0 \leq n)$ the cell where this replacement occurs, this computation of C_e allows us to construct the enumeration e. I will now show that there is a format Φ such that Φ is regular relative to e and the characteristic function μ of M_1 is computable on F in format Φ.

Let the format Φ consist of the following convention:

a. The alphabet A_Φ is $\{a_j\alpha_u\} \cup \{q_i a_j \alpha_u\} \cup \{\#\} = \{\varsigma_\lambda\}$, where the marker # is neither a member of $A_C = \{a_j\}$, nor a member of $A_e = \{\alpha_u\}$. Let ξ be the number of symbols that are members of A_e. Thus, A_Φ has $z\xi + yz\xi + 1$ symbols.

b. For any number n, let $c_0(z + yz)^0 + c_1(z + yz)^1 + \ldots + c_v(z + yz)^v$ be the decomposition of n in base $z + yz$; then, pattern $p \in F(A_\Phi)$ represents input number n if and only if p assigns the marker # to cell $e(v + 1)$ and, for any ι $(v + 1 < \iota)$, p assigns $a_0\alpha_0$ to cell $e(\iota)$ and, for any ι $(0 \le \iota \le v)$, if $c_\iota = j$ $(0 \le j < z)$, then p assigns $a_j\alpha_0$ to cell $e(\iota)$; if $c_\iota = z + iz + j$ $(0 \le i < y)$, then p assigns $q_i a_j \alpha_0$ to cell $e(\iota)$.

c. Given a pattern that represents input number n, an arbitrary Turing machine C_Φ on F with alphabet $A_\Phi = \{\varsigma_\lambda\}$ starts its computation on cell $e(0)$, and in internal state q_0.

d. A state w of the Turing machine C_Φ represents output number 0 if and only if, for exactly one cell x, $w(x) = q_{no}\varsigma_\lambda$, for some λ $(0 \le \lambda < z\xi + yz\xi + 1)$; a state w of the Turing machine C_Φ represents output number 1 if and only if, for exactly one cell x, $w(x) = q_{yes}\varsigma_\lambda$, for some λ $(0 \le \lambda < z\xi + yz\xi + 1)$.

It is thus clear that, for any Turing machine $C_\Phi = \langle T, M_\Phi, \{g^t\}\rangle$ on F with alphabet $A_\Phi = \{\varsigma_\lambda\}$, this convention specifies a coding $\gamma_\Phi: Z^+ \to M_\Phi$ and a decoding $\delta_\Phi: M_\Phi \to Z^+$. The coding γ_Φ is specified by the conjunction of (b) and (c). More precisely, condition (b) specifies a function $\pi_\Phi: Z^+ \to F(A_\Phi)$, where $F(A_\Phi)$ is the set of all finite patterns of F relative to alphabet $A_\Phi = \{\varsigma_\lambda\}$. Condition ($c$), on the other hand, specifies a partial function $\sigma_\Phi: F(A_\Phi) \to M_\Phi$. The coding $\gamma_\Phi: Z^+ \to M_\Phi$ is thus the composition of π_Φ and σ_Φ. The decoding δ_Φ is specified by condition (d). Note that $\delta_\Phi: M_\Phi \to Z^+$ is a partial function. It is now easy to verify that both the coding γ_Φ and the decoding δ_Φ are effective relative to e.

Recall that $A_\Phi = \{a_j\alpha_u\} \cup \{q_i a_j \alpha_u\} \cup \{\#\} = \{\varsigma_\lambda\}$ has $z\xi + yz\xi + 1$ symbols. Let the blank $b = \varsigma_0 = a_0\alpha_0$, and the marker $\# = \varsigma_{z\xi + yz\xi}$. The function π_Φ assigns to $n \in Z^+$ the pattern $p_n \in F(A_\Phi)$ that represents input number n according to condition (b) above. The partial function σ_Φ, on the other hand, assigns to pattern p_n the state w_n that, on cell $e(0) = x_0$, has the symbol $q_0 p_n(x_0)$ and, on any other cell $x \neq x_0$, has the symbol $p_n(x)$. Then, first, we can identify pattern p_n with a numeral $\boldsymbol{p_{ne}}$ in base $z\xi + yz\xi + 1$. Let $c_0(z + yz)^0 + c_1(z + yz)^1 + \ldots + c_v(z + yz)^v$ be the decomposition of n in base $z + yz$. Then, the number denoted by numeral $\boldsymbol{p_{ne}}$ is $p_{ne} = d_0(z\xi + yz\xi + 1)^0$

$+ d_1(z\xi + yz\xi + 1)^1 + \ldots + d_v(z\xi + yz\xi + 1)^v + (z\xi + yz\xi)(z\xi + yz\xi + 1)^{v+1}$ where, for any ι $(0 \leq \iota \leq v)$, if $c_\iota = j$ $(0 \leq j < z)$, then $d_\iota = j\xi$, and if $c_\iota = z + iz + j$ $(0 \leq i < y)$, then $d_\iota = (z + iz + j)\xi$. For any number n, let $\pi_{\Phi e}$: $Z^+ \to Z^+$ satisfy $\pi_{\Phi e}(n) = p_{ne}$. Therefore, by its definition, $\pi_{\Phi e}$ is total recursive. Second, we can identify state w_n with a numeral $\boldsymbol{w_{ne}}$ in base $z\xi + yz\xi + 1 + \varepsilon(z\xi + yz\xi + 1)$, where ε is the number of internal states of Turing machine C_Φ. Let the extended alphabet $B_\Phi = \{\varsigma_\lambda\} \cup \{q_s\varsigma_\lambda\}$ of Turing machine C_Φ be alphabetically ordered.[32] The number denoted by numeral $\boldsymbol{w_{ne}}$ is thus $w_{ne} = (z\xi + yz\xi + 1 + d_0)(z\xi + yz\xi + 1 + \varepsilon(z\xi + yz\xi + 1))^0 + d_1(z\xi + yz\xi + 1 + \varepsilon(z\xi + yz\xi + 1))^1 + \ldots + d_v(z\xi + yz\xi + 1 + \varepsilon(z\xi + yz\xi + 1))^v + (z\xi + yz\xi)(z\xi + yz\xi + 1 + \varepsilon(z\xi + yz\xi + 1))^{v+1}$. For any number k, let $\sigma_{\Phi e}$: $Z^+ \to Z^+$ satisfy this condition: If $k = p_{ne}$ for some n, $\sigma_{\Phi e}(k) = w_{ne}$; otherwise, $\sigma_{\Phi e}(k) = k$. Therefore, by its definition, $\sigma_{\Phi e}$ is total recursive.[33] For any number n, let $\gamma_{\Phi e}$: $Z^+ \to Z^+$ satisfy $\gamma_{\Phi e}(n) = \sigma_{\Phi e}(\pi_{\Phi e}(n))$. Therefore, by its definition, $\gamma_{\Phi e}$ is total recursive and, if $\gamma_\Phi(n) = w_n$, $\gamma_{\Phi e}(n) = w_{ne}$. The coding γ_Φ is thus effective relative to e.

We have seen above that the decoding δ_Φ: $M_\Phi \to Z^+$ specified by format Φ is a partial function that, for any $w \in M_\Phi$, satisfies these conditions: (1) $\delta_\Phi(w)$ is defined if and only if, for exactly one cell x, $w(x) = q_{yes}\varsigma_\lambda$ or $w(x) = q_{no}\varsigma_\lambda$, for some λ $(0 \leq \lambda < z\xi + yz\xi + 1)$; (2) if $\delta_\Phi(w)$ is defined and, for some x and λ $(0 \leq \lambda < z\xi + yz\xi + 1)$, $w(x) = q_{yes}\varsigma_\lambda$, then $\delta_\Phi(w) = 1$; (3) if $\delta_\Phi(w)$ is defined and, for some x and λ $(0 \leq \lambda < z\xi + yz\xi + 1)$, $w(x) = q_{no}\varsigma_\lambda$, then $\delta_\Phi(w) = 0$. Then, first, we can identify state w with a numeral $\boldsymbol{w_e}$ in base $z\xi + yz\xi + 1 + \varepsilon(z\xi + yz\xi + 1)$, where ε is the number of internal states of Turing machine C_Φ, and $z\xi + yz\xi + 1$ is the number of symbols of alphabet $A_\Phi = \{\varsigma_\lambda\}$. Let the extended alphabet $B_\Phi = \{\varsigma_\lambda\} \cup \{q_s\varsigma_\lambda\}$ of Turing machine C_Φ be alphabetically ordered, $q_{no} = q_{\varepsilon-2}$, and $q_{yes} = q_{\varepsilon-1}$. Thus, $q_{no}\varsigma_\lambda$ corresponds to number $z\xi + yz\xi + 1 + (\varepsilon - 2)(z\xi + yz\xi + 1) + \lambda$, and $q_{yes}\varsigma_\lambda$ corresponds to number $(z\xi + yz\xi + 1) + (\varepsilon - 1)(z\xi + yz\xi + 1) + \lambda$. Second, for any number n, let $\delta_{\Phi e}$: $Z^+ \to Z^+$ satisfy these conditions: If, for some λ $(0 \leq \lambda < z\xi + yz\xi + 1)$ the decomposition in base $z\xi + yz\xi + 1 + \varepsilon(z\xi + yz\xi + 1)$ of n has exactly one coefficient equal to $(z\xi + yz\xi + 1) + (\varepsilon - 1)(z\xi + yz\xi + 1) + \lambda$, then $\delta_{\Phi e}(n) = 1$; if, for some λ $(0 \leq \lambda < z\xi + yz\xi + 1)$ the decomposition in base $z\xi + yz\xi + 1 + \varepsilon(z\xi + yz\xi + 1)$ of n has exactly one coefficient equal to $(z\xi + yz\xi + 1) + (\varepsilon - 2)(z\xi + yz\xi + 1) + \lambda$, then $\delta_{\Phi e}(n) = 0$; otherwise, $\delta_{\Phi e}(n) = n$. Therefore, by its definition, $\delta_{\Phi e}$ is total recursive and, if $\delta_{\Phi e}(w) = \tau \in \{0, 1\}$, $\delta_{\Phi e}(w_e) = \tau$. The decoding δ_C is thus effective relative to e^*.

We have thus verified that both the coding γ_Φ and the decoding δ_Φ are effective relative to e. Therefore, since e is a regular enumeration of F, the format Φ is regular relative to e. Let us now consider again the Turing machine C_e (see the third paragraph of this proof), and let us construct a second machine $C_{e\mu}$ as follows. First, the alphabet of $C_{e\mu}$ is $A_\Phi = \{a_j\alpha_u\} \cup \{q_ia_j\alpha_u\} \cup \{\#\} = \{\varsigma_\lambda\}$. Second, let α_u and α_c be arbitrary symbols of alphabet A_e, and let q_a and q_b be arbitrary internal states of C_e. The quadruples of C_e are thus of the two types $q_a\alpha_u\alpha_cq_b$ and $q_a\alpha_uf_rq_b$. Then, the quadruples of $C_{e\mu}$ are the following: For each quadruple of type $q_a\alpha_u\alpha_cq_b$, $C_{e\mu}$ has the quadruples $\{q_a(a_j\alpha_u)(a_j\alpha_c)q_b\} \cup \{q_a(q_ia_j\alpha_u)(a_j\alpha_c)q_{b\#}\} \cup \{q_{a\#}(a_j\alpha_u)(a_j\alpha_c)q_{b\#}\}$; for each quadruple of type $q_a\alpha_uf_rq_b$, $C_{e\mu}$ has the quadruples $\{q_a(a_j\alpha_u)f_rq_b\} \cup \{q_a(q_ia_j\alpha_u)(a_j\alpha_u)q_{br}\} \cup \{q_{br}(a_j\alpha_u)f_rq_{b\#}\} \cup \{q_{a\#}(a_j\alpha_u)f_rq_{b\#}\}$; in addition, $C_{e\mu}$ has the quadruples $\{q_a\#\#q_{no}, q_{a\#}\#\#q_{yes}\} \cup \{q_{a\#}(q_ia_j\alpha_u)(q_ia_j\alpha_u)q_{no}\}$. Let $p \in F(A_\Phi)$ be a pattern that represents input number n according to condition (b) above. There are three possible cases:

1. There is no cell x such that $p(x) = q_ia_j\alpha_0$, for some i $(0 \le i < y)$ and j $(0 \le j < z)$.
2. There is exactly one cell x such that $p(x) = q_ia_j\alpha_0$, for some i $(0 \le i < y)$ and j $(0 \le j < z)$.
3. There are at least two cells x and υ such that $p(x) = q_ia_j\alpha_0$ and $p(\upsilon) = q_la_k\alpha_0$, for some i $(0 \le i < y)$, j $(0 \le j < z)$, l $(0 \le l < y)$, and k $(0 \le k < z)$.

Note that $n \in M_1$ if and only if case 2 holds. If we start $C_{e\mu}$ in internal state q_0, on cell $e(0) = x_0$, and on a pattern $p \in F(A_\Phi)$ that represents input number n, then $C_{e\mu}$ moves from cell to cell looking for either the marker # or for a triple $q_ia_j\alpha_0$. If it finds the marker # first, it stops in internal state q_{no} (case 1). If it finds a triple $q_ia_j\alpha_0$ first, it memorizes this fact by going into internal state $q_{b\#}$, and then starts looking again for the marker or a second triple. If it finds the marker # first, it stops in internal state q_{yes} (case 2). Otherwise, it stops in state q_{no} (case 3). Thus, if we start $C_{e\mu}$ in state q_0, on cell $e(0) = x_0$, and on a pattern $p \in F(A_\Phi)$ that represents number n, this computation stops and, if $n \notin M_1$ (or $n \in M_1$), the final state represents number 0 (or 1). Hence, the characteristic function μ of M_1 is computable on F in format Φ. Since Φ is regular relative to e, μ is thus computable on F relative to e. Therefore, by the definition of computability on F, μ is computable on F.

I will now show that there is a format Θ such that Θ is regular relative to e and the transition function h^1 is computable on F in format Θ. Let the format Θ consist of the following convention:

1. The alphabet A_Θ is $\{a_j\} \cup \{q_ia_j\} = \{\varsigma_\lambda\}$ = the extended alphabet B_C of Turing machine C. Thus, A_Θ has $z + yz$ symbols.
2. Any pattern $p \in F(A_\Theta)$ can thus be identified with a numeral $\boldsymbol{p_e}$ in base $z + yz$. Then, for any n, pattern p represents input (or output) number n if and only if $p_e = n$.
3. Given a pattern $p \in F(A_\Theta)$ that represents input number n, if there is exactly one cell x such that $p(x) = q_ia_j$ for some i $(0 \le i < y)$ and j $(0 \le j < z)$, then an arbitrary Turing machine C_Θ on F with alphabet $A_\Theta = \{a_j\} \cup \{q_ia_j\}$ starts its computation on cell x and in internal state q_0; otherwise, C_Θ starts on cell $e(0) = x_0$ and in internal state $q_{\varepsilon-1}$, where ε is the number of internal states of Turing machine C_Θ.
4. A state of the Turing machine C_Θ represents output number m if and only if the pattern $p \in F(A_\Theta)$ that corresponds to this state represents output number m.

It is thus clear that, for any Turing machine $C_\Theta = \langle T, M_\Theta, \{g^t\}\rangle$ on F with alphabet $A_\Theta = \{a_j\} \cup \{q_ia_j\}$, this convention specifies a coding γ_Θ: $Z^+ \to M_\Theta$ and a decoding δ_Θ: $M_\Theta \to Z^+$. The coding γ_Θ is specified by the conjunction of (*2*) and (*3*). More precisely, condition (*2*) specifies a function π_Θ: $Z^+ \to F(A_\Theta)$, where $F(A_\Theta)$ is the set of all finite patterns of F relative to alphabet $A_\Theta = \{a_j\} \cup \{q_ia_j\}$. Condition (*3*), on the other hand, specifies a function σ_Θ: $F(A_\Theta) \to M_\Theta$. The coding γ_Θ: $Z^+ \to M_\Theta$ is thus the composition of π_Θ and σ_Θ. The decoding δ_Θ is specified by the conjunction of conditions (*4*) and (*2*). More precisely, δ_Θ: $M_\Theta \to Z^+$ is the composition of two functions Φ_Θ: $M_\Theta \to F(A_\Theta)$ and η_Θ: $F(A_\Theta) \to Z^+$. The function ϕ_Θ assigns to any state $w \in M_\Theta$ the finite pattern $p \in F(A_\Theta)$ that corresponds to this state. On the other hand, η_Θ assigns to pattern p the output number represented by this pattern. It is now easy to verify that both the coding γ_Θ and the decoding δ_Θ are effective relative to e.

Recall that $A_\Theta = \{a_j\} \cup \{q_ia_j\} = \{\varsigma_\lambda\}$ has $z + yz$ symbols. The function π_Θ assigns to $n \in Z^+$ the pattern $p_n \in F(A_\Theta)$ such that $p_{ne} = n$. On the other hand, if there is exactly one cell x such that $p_n(x) = q_ia_j$ for some i $(0 \le i < y)$ and j $(0 \le j < z)$, then the function σ_Θ assigns to pattern p_n the state w_n that, on cell x, has the symbol $q_0p_n(x)$ and, on any other cell $\zeta \ne x$, has the symbol $p_n(\zeta)$; otherwise σ_Θ assigns to pattern p_n the state w_n that, on cell $e(0) = x_0$, has the symbol $q_{\varepsilon-1}\,p_n(x_0)$ and, on any other cell $x \ne x_0$, has the symbol $p_n(x)$. First, for any number n, let $\pi_{\Theta e}$: $Z^+ \to Z^+$ satisfy $\pi_{\Theta e}(n) = p_{ne}$. Therefore, by its definition, $\pi_{\Theta e}$ is the identity function on Z^+, and it is thus total recursive. Second, we can identify state w_n with a numeral $\boldsymbol{w}_{ne}$ in base $z + yz + \varepsilon(z + yz)$, where ε is the number of internal states of Turing machine C_Θ. Let the extended alphabet $B_\Theta = \{\varsigma_\lambda\} \cup \{q_s\varsigma_\lambda\}$ of Turing machine C_Θ be alphabetically ordered,[34] and let $c_0(z + yz)^0 + c_1(z + yz)^1 + \ldots + c_v(z + yz)^v$ be the decomposition of n in base $z + yz$. If there is exactly one coefficient $c_\iota = z + iz + j$ for some i $(0 \le i < y)$ and j $(0 \le j < z)$, then the number denoted by numeral $\boldsymbol{w}_{ne}$ is $w_{ne} = d_0(z + yz + \varepsilon(z + yz))^0 + d_1(z + yz + \varepsilon(z + yz))^1 + \ldots + d_v(z + yz + \varepsilon(z + yz))^v$, where all the coefficients agree with the corresponding coefficients of the decomposition in base $z + yz$ of n, except for $d_\iota = (z + yz) + (z + iz + j)$; otherwise, the number denoted by numeral $\boldsymbol{w}_{ne}$ is $w_{ne} = d_0(z + yz + \varepsilon(z + yz))^0 + d_1(z + yz + \varepsilon(z + yz))^1 + \ldots + d_v(z + yz + \varepsilon(z + yz))^v$, where all the coefficients agree with the corresponding coefficients of the decomposition in base $z + yz$ of n, except for $d_0 = (z + yz) + (\varepsilon - 1)(z + yz) + c_0$. For any number n, let $\sigma_{\Theta e}$: $Z^+ \to Z^+$ satisfy $\sigma_{\Theta e}(n) = w_{ne}$. Therefore, by its definition, $\sigma_{\Theta e}$ is total recursive. For any number n, let $\gamma_{\Theta e}$: $Z^+ \to Z^+$ satisfy $\gamma_{\Theta e}(n) = \sigma_{\Theta e}(\pi_{\Theta e}(n))$. Therefore, by its definition, $\gamma_{\Theta e}$ is total recursive and, if $\gamma_\Theta(n) = w_n$, $\gamma_{\Theta e}(n) = w_{ne}$. The coding γ_Θ is thus effective relative to e.

We have seen that the decoding δ_Θ: $M_\Theta \to Z^+$ specified by format Θ is the composition of Φ_Θ: $M_\Theta \to F(A_\Theta)$ and η_Θ: $F(A_\Theta) \to Z^+$. The function Φ_Θ assigns to state w the pattern p_w that corresponds to w. The function η_Θ, on the other hand, assigns to an arbitrary pattern p the number p_e denoted by numeral $\boldsymbol{p}_e$. Then, first, we can identify state w with a numeral $\boldsymbol{w}_e$ in base $z + yz + \varepsilon(z + yz)$, where ε is the number of internal states of Turing machine C_Θ, and $z + yz$ is the number of symbols of alphabet $A_\Phi = \{a_j\} \cup \{q_ia_j\} = \{\varsigma_\lambda\}$. Let the extended alphabet $B_\Theta = \{\varsigma_\lambda\} \cup \{q_s\varsigma_\lambda\}$ of Turing machine C_Θ be alphabetically ordered. The number denoted by numeral $\boldsymbol{w}_e$ is thus $w_e = c_0(z + yz + \varepsilon(z + yz))^0 + c_1(z + yz + \varepsilon(z + yz))^1 + \ldots + c_v(z + yz + \varepsilon(z + yz))^v$, where exactly one coefficient c_ι is equal to $(z + yz) + s(z + yz) + \lambda$, for some s $(0 \le s < \varepsilon)$ and λ $(0 \le \lambda < z + yz)$. Second, we can identify pattern p_w with a numeral $\boldsymbol{p}_{we}$ in base $z + yz$. The number denoted by numeral $\boldsymbol{p}_{we}$ is $p_{we} = d_0(z + yz + \varepsilon(z + yz))^0 + d_1(z + yz + \varepsilon(z + yz))^1 + \ldots + d_v(z + yz + \varepsilon(z + yz))^v$, where all the coefficients agree with the corresponding coefficients of w_e, except for the coefficient d_ι which is equal to λ. For any number n, let $\phi_{\Theta e}$: $Z^+ \to Z^+$ satisfy this condition: If $n = w_e$ for some $w \in M_\Theta$, $\phi_{\Theta e}(n) = p_{we}$; otherwise, $\phi_{\Theta e}(n) = n$. Therefore, by its definition, $\phi_{\Theta e}$ is total recursive.[35] For any number k, let $\eta_{\Theta e}$: $Z^+ \to Z^+$ satisfy $\eta_{\Theta e}(k) = k$. Therefore, by its definition, $\eta_{\Theta e}$ is the identity function on Z^+, and it is thus total recursive. For any number n, let $\delta_{\Theta e}$: $Z^+ \to Z^+$ satisfy

$\delta_{\Theta e}(n) = \eta_{\Theta e}(\phi_{\Theta e}(n))$. Therefore, by its definition, $\delta_{\Theta e}$ is total recursive and, if $\delta_{\Theta}(w) = \tau$, $\delta_{\Theta e}(w_e) = \tau$. The decoding δ_{Θ} is thus effective relative to e.

We have thus verified that both the coding γ_{Θ} and the decoding δ_{Θ} are effective relative to e. Therefore, since e is a regular enumeration of F, the format Θ is regular relative to e. Let us now consider again the Turing machine C (see the second paragraph of this proof), and let us construct a second machine C_1 as follows: First, the alphabet of C_1 is $A_{\Theta} = \{a_j\} \cup \{q_i a_j\} = \{\varsigma_{\lambda}\}$. Second, the quadruples of C are of the two types $q_i a_j a_k q_l$ and $q_i a_j f_r q_l$. Then, the quadruples of C_1 are the following: for each quadruple of type $q_i a_j a_k q_l$, C_1 has the quadruple $q_0(q_i a_j)(q_l a_k)q_{stop}$; for each quadruple of type $q_i a_j f_r q_l$, C_1 has the quadruples $\{q_0(q_i a_j)a_j q_{move(l)}, q_{move(l)} a_j f_r q_{write(l)}, q_{write(l)} a_0 (q_l a_0) q_{stop}, \ldots, q_{write(l)} a_{z-1}(q_l a_{z-1}) q_{stop}\}$; in addition, C_1 has the quadruples $\{q_{loop} a_j a_j q_{loop*}, q_{loop*} a_j a_j q_{loop}\} \cup \{q_{loop}(q_i a_j)(q_i a_j) q_{loop*}, q_{loop*}(q_i a_j)(q_i a_j) q_{loop}\}$ where, if ε is the number of internal states of Turing machine C_1, $q_{loop} = q_{\varepsilon-1}$. On the one hand, if we start C_1 in internal state q_0, on a pattern $p \in F(A_{\Phi})$ that represents input number $m \in M_1$, and on the cell x such that $p(x) = q_i a_j$ for some i $(0 \le i < y)$ and j $(0 \le j < z)$, then C_1 operates as follows: If the pair $q_i a_j$ corresponds to a quadruple of type $q_i a_j a_k q_l$, then C_1 replaces $q_i a_j$ by $q_l a_k$ and then stops in internal state q_{stop}. Otherwise, C_1 first replaces $q_i a_j$ by a_j. It then moves to a new cell according to f_r, adds the symbol q_l to the symbol on this cell, and stops in internal state q_{stop}. On the other hand, if we start C_1 in internal state $q_{loop} = q_{\varepsilon-1}$, on a pattern $p \in F(A_{\Phi})$ that represents input number $m \notin M_1$, and on cell $e(0) = x_0$, then C_1 never stops. Thus, for any number n, if we start C_1 in state $\gamma_{\Theta}(n)$ and $h^1(n)$ is defined, this computation stops and, if the final state is w, then $\delta_{\Theta}(w) = h^1(n)$; if $h^1(n)$ is not defined, this computation does not stop. Hence, the transition function h^1 is computable on F in format Θ. Since Θ is regular relative to e, h^1 is thus computable on F relative to e. Therefore, by the definition of computability on F, h^1 is computable on F.

q.e.d.

Notes

1. Turing machines that operate on an infinite checkerboard have been discussed in Dewdney (1989). The only difference between these machines and ordinary ones is that they can also move upwards and downwards.

2. This follows from the hypothesis that the capacity of memorizing

symbols is finite. For, if the number of mental states were infinite, each of them might be used to memorize a different symbol.

3. By a *numeric function of n* ($1 \leq n$) *arguments* I mean any total or partial function from the n-th Cartesian product of the nonnegative integers to the nonnegative integers, and by a *numeric function* I mean any numeric function of one argument. Then, a numeric function f of n argument is *recursive* if and only it f is one of the basic recursive functions (successor, zero function, and identity functions), or if f can be obtained from the set of the basic recursive functions by applying a finite number of times the operations of composition, primitive recursion, and minimization.

For any nonnegative integer m, the successor function assigns $m + 1$ to m. The zero function is the constant function whose value is 0 for any nonnegative integer. For each positive integer n, there are n identity functions $id^n_1, \ldots,$ id^n_n of n arguments, whose values are the first, the second, . . . , the n-th of the arguments. In other words, for any i and n ($1 \leq i \leq n$), $id^n_i(m_1, \ldots, M_n) = m_i$.

If f is a numeric function of k ($1 \leq k$) arguments, and each of $f_1, \ldots, f_k$ is a numeric function of n ($1 \leq n$) arguments, then the numeric function of n arguments obtained from $f_1, \ldots, f_k$ and f by *composition* is h, where $h(m_1, \ldots, m_n) = f(f_1(m_1, \ldots, m_n), \ldots, f_k(m_1, \ldots, m_n))$.

If k is a nonnegative integer, g is a numeric function of two arguments, and s is the successor function, then the numeric function of one argument obtained from g by *primitive recursion* is h, where $h(0) = k$ and $h(s(m)) = g(m, h(m))$.

If f is a numeric function of n ($1 \leq n$) arguments, g is a numeric function of $n + 2$ arguments, and s is the successor function, then the numeric function of $n + 1$ arguments obtained from f and g by *primitive recursion* is h, where $h(m_1, \ldots, m_n, 0) = f(m_1, \ldots, m_n)$ and $h(m_1, \ldots, m_n, s(m)) = g(m_1, \ldots, m_n, m, h(m_1, \ldots, m_n, m))$.

If f is a numeric function of $n + 1$ ($1 \leq n$) arguments, then the numeric (partial) function of n arguments obtained from f by *minimization* is h, where $h(m_1, \ldots, m_n) =$ the smallest m such that $f(m_1, \ldots, m_n, m) = 0$ and $f(m_1, \ldots, m_n, k)$ is defined for all k less than m; $h(m_1, \ldots, m_n)$ is undefined if there is no such m.

4. Recall that a cascade is mathematical dynamical system with discrete time (see chapter 1, section 2).

5. I will only consider numeric functions of one argument, because any n-tuple of numbers can be recursively coded as one single number. More precisely, it can be proved that, for any n ($1 \leq n$), there is a recursive bijection ϕ: $Z^{+n} \rightarrow Z^+$. This bijection can thus be used to code any n-tuple $\langle m_1, \ldots, m_n \rangle$ as the number $\phi(m_1, \ldots, m_n)$ (Boolos and Jeffrey 1985, 161). For any numeric function f of n arguments, we can then consider the corresponding numeric function of one argument f_ϕ such that, if $f(m_1, \ldots, m_n)$ is defined, $f_\phi(\phi(m_1, \ldots, m_n)) = f_\phi(m_1, \ldots, m_n)$; otherwise, $f_\phi(\phi(m_1, \ldots, m_n))$ is unde-

fined. Therefore, any numeric function f of n arguments can always be identified with the corresponding numeric function f_ϕ of one argument.

6. I allow the decoding δ_C: $M_C \rightarrow Z^+$ to be partial because some widely used formats stipulate that only some states represent output numbers. For example, Boolos and Jeffrey (1980) adopt the following format for the computation of a numeric function on a doubly infinite tape $F_2 = \langle U, \{L, R\}\rangle$: (1) the alphabet A_Φ only contains the two symbols b and 1; (2) input (or output) number $n \in Z^+$ is represented by a tape with a block of $n + 1$ consecutive 1s, and which is otherwise blank. The leftmost 1 is located on a fixed square x_0 of the tape; (3) given a tape that represents input number n, an arbitrary Turing machine C on F_2 with alphabet $A_C = A_\Phi = \{b, 1\}$ starts its computation on square x_0, and in internal state q_0; (4) a state of the Turing machine C represents output number $m \in Z^+$ if and only if the tape that corresponds to this state represents output number m. If we adopt this format, the decoding δ_C is specified by the conjunction of (4) and (2). More precisely, δ_C: $M_C \rightarrow Z^+$ is the composition of ϕ_C: $M_C \rightarrow F_2(A_C)$ and η_C: $F_2(A_C) \rightarrow Z^+$, where $F_2(A_C)$ is the set of all finite patterns of a doubly infinite tape relative to alphabet $A_C = A_\Phi = \{b, 1\}$. The function ϕ_C assigns to any state $w \in M_C$ the finite pattern $p \in F_2(A_C)$ that corresponds to this state. On the other hand, η_C assigns to pattern p the output number represented by p. However, if p does not represent any output number, $\eta_C(p)$ is undefined. Therefore, η_C is partial, and its domain is strictly included in the image of ϕ_C. It thus follows that δ_C is partial as well.

7. Since $B_C = \{a_j\} \cup \{q_i a_j\}$ is alphabetically ordered, the symbol a_j ($0 \leq j < 2$) corresponds to number j, and the pair $q_i a_j$ ($0 \leq i < m$) corresponds to number $2 + i2 + j$.

8. For any number k, $k = p_{ne}$ for some n if and only if the decomposition in base 2 of k is of the form $1 \times 2^0 + 0 \times 2^1 + 1 \times 2^2 + 0 \times 2^3 + \ldots + 0 \times 2^{2n-1} + 1 \times 2^{2n}$. This condition is recursive. Therefore, σ_{Ce} is recursively defined by cases, and it is thus total recursive.

9. For any number n, $n = w_e$ for some $w \in M_C$ if and only if the decomposition in base $2 + m2$ of n has exactly one coefficient c_v which is equal to $2 + i2 + j$, for some i ($0 \leq i < m$) and j ($0 \leq j < 2$). This condition is recursive. Therefore, ϕ_{Ce} is recursively defined by cases, and it is thus total recursive.

10. We will see later that, besides being recursive relative to the standard enumeration, a doubly infinite tape is also an example of a recursive pattern field (corollary 5.1).

11. If f' were recursive, there would be an ordinary Turing machine $C_{f'}$ that computes f'. Therefore, we could construct a second ordinary Turing machine C_f that computes f. To obtain C_f, we add a routine that, when $C_{f'}$ stops, checks whether the output number is 0. If yes, C_f enters an infinite loop. If not, C_f stops. Since the ordinary Turing machine C_f computes f, f is recursive. By hypothesis, however, f is not recursive.

12. Since $B_C = \{a_j\} \cup \{q_i a_j\}$ is alphabetically ordered, the symbol a_j ($0 \leq j < z$) corresponds to number j, and the pair $q_i a_j$ ($0 \leq i < m$) corresponds to number $z + iz + j$.

13. For any number k, $k = p_{ne}$ for some n if and only if the decomposition in base z of k is of the form $c_0z^0 + c_1z^1 + \ldots + c_nz^n$, where coefficient c_n $(0 \leq n)$ is equal to $z - 1$ and all other coefficients (if any) are equal to 0. This condition is recursive. Therefore, σ_{Ce} is recursively defined by cases, and it is thus total recursive.

14. For any number n, $n = w_e$ for some $w \in M_C$ if and only if the decomposition in base $z + mz$ of n has exactly one coefficient c_v which is equal to $z + iz + j$, for some i $(0 \leq i < m)$ and j $(0 \leq j < z)$. This condition is recursive. Therefore, ϕ_{Ce} is recursively defined by cases, and it is thus total recursive.

15. See note 2.

16. See note 2.

17. See section 4 of chapter 1, chapter 2, section 1 of chapter 3, and section 2 of chapter 4 (in particular, corollary 2.3).

18. See note 12.

19. See note 12.

20. For any number k, $k = p_{ne*}$ for some n if and only if the decomposition in base z of k is of the form $c_0z^0 + c_1z^1 + \ldots + c_nz^n$, where coefficient c_n $(0 \leq n)$ is equal to $z - 1$ and all other coefficients (if any) is equal to 0. This condition is recursive. Therefore, σ_{Ce*} is recursively defined by cases, and it is thus total recursive.

21. For any number n, $n = w_{e*}$ for some $w \in M_C$ if and only if the decomposition in base $z + mz$ of n has exactly one coefficient c_v which is equal to $z + iz + j$, for some i $(0 \leq i < m)$ and j $(0 \leq j < z)$. This condition is recursive. Therefore, ϕ_{Ce*} is recursively defined by cases, and it is thus total recursive.

22. If an arbitrary bijection f: $Z^+ \rightarrow Z^+$ is recursive, then also its inverse f^{-1} is recursive. To verify this fact, let us define first a numeric function λ that, for any two numbers m and n, checks whether $f(n) = m$. This numeric function can thus be defined by cases: if $f(n) = m$, $\lambda(m, n) = 0$; otherwise, $\lambda(m, n) = 1$. Since f is recursive, λ is recursive. It is thus obvious that f^{-1} can be obtained from λ by applying the minimization operator, for $f^{-1}(m)$ = the least n such that $\lambda(m, n) = 0$. Therefore, since λ is recursive, f^{-1} is recursive.

23. Let $F = \langle U, \{f_r\}\rangle$ be a pattern field, and let $\langle U, \{\boldsymbol{L}, \boldsymbol{R}\}\rangle$ be isomorphic to a doubly infinite tape. Then, the pattern field $F^* = \langle U, \{f_r\} \cup \{\boldsymbol{L}, \boldsymbol{R}\}\rangle$ is an extension of $\boldsymbol{F}$.

24. Since $B_C = \{\varsigma_\lambda\} \cup \{q_r\varsigma_\lambda\}$ is alphabetically ordered, the symbol ς_λ $(0 \leq \lambda < z + 4)$ corresponds to number λ, and the pair $q_r\varsigma_\lambda$ $(0 \leq r < \varepsilon)$ corresponds to number $(z + 4) + r(z + 4) + \lambda$.

25. For any number k, $k = p_{ne}$ for some n if and only if the decomposition in base $z + 4$ of k is of the form $0(z + 4)^0 + 0(z + 4)^1 + 1(z + 4)^2 + 1(z + 4)^3 + \ldots + 1(z + 4)^{n+1} + 1(z + 4)^{n+2}$. This condition is recursive. Therefore, σ_{Ce} is recursively defined by cases, and it is thus total recursive.

26. For any number n, $n = w_e$ for some $w \in M_C$ such that, for some r $(0 \leq r < \varepsilon)$ and λ $(0 \leq \lambda < z + 4)$, $w(2) = q_r\varsigma_\lambda$ if and only if coefficient c_2 of the decomposition in base $(z + 4) + \varepsilon(z + 4)$ of n is equal to $(z + 4) + r(z + 4) +$

λ and all other coefficients are less than $z + 4$. This condition is recursive. Therefore, ϕ_{Ce} is recursively defined by cases, and it is thus total recursive.

27. This is an immediate consequence of the following result by Boolos and Jeffrey (1980, chapters 6 and 7): For any recursive function h with m $(1 \leq m)$ arguments there is a Turing machine with alphabet $\{b, 1\}$ that computes h according to the following conventions: (1) The tape is infinite in only one direction (say to the right), and input (output) number n is represented by a block of $n + 1$ 1s. The leftmost 1 is on the third square of the tape. If there is more than one input number, each of them is represented by the appropriate block of 1s, and two different blocks are separated by exactly one blank b. (2) The Turing machine starts on the third square of the tape, in internal state q_0. Furthermore, it also stops on the same square.

28. This second machine C_{μ^*} first checks whether the string z only contains 1s. If not, it replaces the string z with one blank b and stops. Otherwise, it deletes the markers \$ and #, positions itself on the leftmost 1 of the string z, and then starts a routine that works exactly as the machine C_μ. When this routine stops, it replaces the only 1 (or the block of two 1s) on the tape with $\$b\#$ (or $\$bb\#$), positions itself on the left marker \$, and stops.

29. Let X be a subset of Z^+. If the characteristic function μ_x of X is recursive, and an arbitrary bijection f: $X \to X$ is recursive, then also its inverse f^1: $X \to X$ is recursive. To verify this fact, let us define first a numeric function λ that, for any two numbers m and n, checks whether $f(n) = m$. This numeric function can thus be defined by cases: If $\mu_x(n) = 0$, then $\lambda(m, n) = 1$; if $\mu_x(n) = 1$ and $f(n) = m$, then $\lambda(m, n) = 0$; if $\mu_x(n) = 1$ and $f(n) \neq m$, then $\lambda(m, n) = 1$. Since both f and μ_x are recursive, λ is recursive. It is thus obvious that f^1 can be obtained from λ by applying the minimization operator, for $f^1(m)$ = the least n such that $\lambda(m, n) = 0$. Therefore, since λ is recursive, f^1 is recursive.

30. The machine C_μ first replaces the block of $n + 1$ 1s with the string $\$z\#$ (where $z \in P(A)$ corresponds to number n in the alphabetical order of $P(A)$), positions itself on the left marker \$, and then starts a routine that works exactly as the machine C_{μ^*}. When this routine stops, it replaces the string $\$b\#$ (or $\$bb\#$) with just one 1 (or with two 1s), positions itself on the leftmost 1, and stops.

31. First, the machine C starts a routine that works as the machine C_μ does, except that this routine does not delete the initial block of $n + 1$ 1s. At the end of this routine, if $n \notin M_1$ (or $n \notin M_1$) then C is on the leftmost 1 of a block of one (or two) 1s on a tape that also contains the initial block of $n + 1$ 1s. In the first case, C enters an infinite loop. In the second case, C deletes the block of two 1s, positions itself on the leftmost 1 of the block of $n + 1$ 1s, replaces the block of $n + 1$ 1s with the string $\$z\#$ (where $z \in P(A)$ corresponds to number n in the alphabetical order of $P(A)$), positions itself on the left marker \$, and then starts a routine that works exactly as the machine C_* does. When this routine stops, C replaces the string $\$h^{1*}(z)\#$ with a block of m + 1 1s (where m is the number that corresponds to string $h^{1*}(z)$ in the alphabetical order of $P(A)$), positions itself on the leftmost 1, and stops.

32. Since $B_\Phi = \{\varsigma_\lambda\} \cup \{q_r\varsigma_\lambda\}$ is alphabetically ordered, the symbol ς_λ $(0 \leq \lambda < z\xi + yz\xi + 1)$ corresponds to number λ, and the pair $q_s\varsigma_\lambda$ $(0 \leq s < \varepsilon)$ corresponds to number $(z\xi + yz\xi + 1) + s(z\xi + yz\xi + 1) + \lambda$.

33. For any number k, $k = p_{ne}$ for some n if and only if the decomposition of k in base $z\xi + yz\xi + 1$ is of the form $d_0(z\xi + yz\xi + 1)^0 + d_1(z\xi + yz\xi + 1)^1 + \ldots + d_v(z\xi + yz\xi + 1)^v + (z\xi + yz\xi)(z\xi + yz\xi + 1)^{v+1}$ where, for any ι $(0 \leq \iota \leq v)$, $d_i = j\xi$ or $d_\iota = (z + iz + j)\xi$, for some i $(0 < i < y)$ and j $(0 \leq j < z)$. This condition is recursive. Therefore, $\sigma_{\Phi e}$ is recursively defined by cases, and it is thus total recursive.

34. Since $B_\Phi = \{\varsigma_\lambda\} \cup \{q_s\varsigma_\lambda\}$ is alphabetically ordered, the symbol ς_λ $(0 \leq \lambda < z + yz)$ corresponds to number λ, and the pair $q_r\varsigma_\lambda$ $(0 \leq s < \varepsilon)$ corresponds to number $(z + yz) + s(z + yz) + \lambda$.

35. For any number n, $n = w_e$ for some $w \in M_\Theta$ if and only if the decomposition in base $z + yz + \varepsilon(z + yz)$ of n has exactly one coefficient c_t which is equal to $(z + yz) + s(z + yz) + \lambda$, for some s $(0 \leq s < \varepsilon)$ and λ $(0 \leq \lambda < z + yz)$. This condition is recursive. Therefore, $\phi_{\phi e}$ is recursively defined by cases, and it is thus total recursive.

THREE

Galilean Models and Explanations

1 Introduction

Given a natural kind K (for example, mechanical, chemical, biological, cognitive, etc.), I say that a real system is a K-system if and only if it has some K-property. The main goal of this chapter is to analyze a particular type of scientific explanation, which I call a Galilean explanation. This analysis is based on a more general view of scientific explanation, according to which scientific explanations are solutions of problems of a special type. This type of problem essentially consists of two parts: first, considering a certain K-system and, second, setting the goal of scientifically explaining some K-property of this system. A *scientific explanation* of a K-property of a K-system is an explanation obtained by studying a model of the K-system, and the type of scientific explanation we construct in general depends on the type of model that we are going to study. Galilean explanations are a particular type of scientific explanations, for they are based on the study of models of a special type. I call a model of this special type a *Galilean model* of a K-system. The next four sections of this chapter explain, exactly, what I mean by a Galilean model of a K-system.

A *Galilean explanation* of a K-property of a K-system is an explanation obtained by studying a Galilean model of the K-system. But if we need to study a Galilean model of the *K*-system, we must first specify or describe the model in such a way that we are able to use the model for constructing the explanation we seek. Therefore, the problem of constructing a Galilean explanation of a *K*-property of a *K*-system presupposes the problem of specifying a Galilean model of the *K*-system. We will see in section 6 that this second problem is equivalent to that of producing a *correct Galilean framework* of the *K*-system.

Thus, if our main goal is to produce a Galilean explanation of a particular *K*-property *P* of a fixed *K*-system *KRS*, we must first construct a correct Galilean framework of *KRS*. Furthermore, this correct framework must also be *P-explanatory*, in the sense that it must specify a Galilean model of *KRS* whose study will then allow us to produce an explanation of the particular *K*-property *P* we want to explain. Therefore, to achieve our main goal, we must first set the subgoal of constructing a correct Galilean framework of *KRS* which is *P*-explanatory. The last three sections of this chapter outline two standard methods for implementing this subgoal. Following a traditional terminology, I call the first procedure the inductive method, and the second one the deductive method.

2 Real dynamical systems versus mathematical dynamical systems

A *real dynamical system* is any real system that changes over time. Therefore, since any real system can be thought to change in time (in some respect), any real system is a real dynamical system. A *mathematical dynamical system*, on the other hand, is an abstract mathematical structure that can be used to *describe* the change of a real system as an evolution through a series of *states*. If the evolution of the real system is *deterministic*, that is, if the state at any future time is determined by the state at the present time, then the abstract mathematical structure consists of three elements, as discussed in chapter 1. The first element is a set *T* that represents time. *T* may be either the reals, the rationals, the integers, or the nonnegative portions of these structures. Depending on the choice of *T*, then, time is represented as continuous, dense, or discrete. In this chapter, however, I will only consider mathematical dynamical systems with continuous or discrete time. The second element is a nonempty set *M* that represents all possible states through which the system can evolve; *M* is called the *state space* (or sometimes the *phase space*) of the system. The third element is a set of functions $\{g^t\}$ that describes the state of the system at any instant t provided that the initial state is known; each function in $\{g^t\}$ is called a *state transition* (or a *t-advance*) of the system. For example, if the initial state is $x \in M$, the state at time t is given by $g^t(x)$, the state at time $u > t$ is given by $g^u(x)$, etc. The functions in the set $\{g^t\}$ must only satisfy two conditions. First, the function g^0 must be reflexive. For, if the initial state is x, the state $g^0(x)$ at time 0 obviously is x itself. Second, the composition of any two functions g^t and g^w must be equal to the function g^{t+w}. For, given an arbitrary initial state x, the state $g^{t+w}(x)$ reached at time $t + w$ can always be considered as the result of two successive state transitions, the first from state x to state $g^t(x)$, and the second from state $g^t(x)$ to state $g^w(g^t(x))$.

The distinction between real and mathematical dynamical systems is crucial to understanding how an abstract, timeless structure can be used to represent the change of a real system. Before going on, then, let me further illustrate this distinction by means of a classic example. Consider first those concrete objects (falling bodies, spheres on inclined planes, projectiles, etc.) which Galileo studied in the course of his investigations in the field of mechanics. These objects are examples of real dynamical systems of a special natural kind, namely, *mechanical systems*. Consider then Galileo's laws for the vertical position and velocity of a falling body: $S(t) = s + vt + (1/2)\boldsymbol{c}t^2$ and $V(t) = v + \boldsymbol{c}t$, where s and v are, respectively, the vertical position and velocity of the falling body at time 0, and $\boldsymbol{c}$ is a constant (the acceleration of a freely falling body under the influence of gravity). If we identify the state of a falling body with the values of its vertical position and velocity, it is easy to verify that these two laws specify a mathematical dynamical system $MDS_1 = \langle T, S \times V, \{g^t\}\rangle$, where each state transition g^t is defined by $g^t(s, v) = \langle s + vt + (1/2)\boldsymbol{c}t^2, v + \boldsymbol{c}t\rangle$ (see chapter 1, example 1).

3 Models of *K*-systems

What is the relation between the mathematical dynamical system MDS_1 specified by Galileo's laws and a real falling body? We all know that, within certain limits of precision, these two laws accurately describe how the vertical position and velocity of a real falling body change in time. Also, note that vertical position and velocity are *mechanical* properties of the falling body. Therefore, we may take the mathematical dynamical system MDS_1 to correctly describe one mechanical aspect of a particular mechanical system, that is, the change of vertical position and velocity of a falling body. However, it is important to note that, if we decided to focus on a different mechanical aspect of the falling body, a different mathematical dynamical system would in general be appropriate. For example, suppose we are interested in how the mass of the body changes over time. Then, since we may take the mass to be a constant $\boldsymbol{m}$, we obtain a different mathematical dynamical system $MDS_2 = \langle T, \{\boldsymbol{m}\}, \{h^t\}\rangle$, where each state transition h^t is the identity function on the state space $\{\boldsymbol{m}\}$, that is, for any $t \in T$, and any $m \in \{\boldsymbol{m}\}$, $h^t(m) = m$. We may thus claim that the mathematical dynamical system MDS_2 correctly describes a different mechanical aspect of the particular mechanical system we have considered, that is, the change of mass of a real falling body.

This example thus shows that different mathematical dynamical systems may correctly describe different mechanical aspects of the same mechanical system. Let me now generalize these observations by introducing terminology which will be useful later. Given a *natural kind K* (for example, mechanical, chemical, biological, cognitive, etc.), I say that a real system is a *K-system* if and only if it has some *K*-property. Then, a *K*-system *KRS instantiates* an abstract mathematical structure *MS* if and only if *MS* correctly describes some *K*-aspect of *KRS*. According to this definition, then, we may take a falling body to instantiate both mathematical dynamical systems MDS_1 and MDS_2 specified above. In general, a given *K*-system will instantiate many abstract mathematical structures, and each of these structures correctly describes a different *K*-aspect of the *K*-system. If a *K*-system *KRS* instantiates a mathematical structure *MS*, I call *MS* a *model of KRS* (see figure 3-1).

4 Galilean explanations and the traditional practice of dynamical modeling

Given a *K*-system, one of the most typical scientific tasks is trying to understand or explain those of its *K*-properties which seem most interesting, puzzling, or surprising. A *scientific explanation* of a *K*-property of a *K*-system is an explanation obtained by studying a model of the *K*-system (see figure 3-2). Galilean explanations are a particular type of scientific explanations, based on the study of models of a special type. The type of model on which Galilean explanations are based is perhaps the most widespread in science. I have in mind here a traditional way of using mathematical dynamical systems to describe the change of real systems. Simple examples of this type of

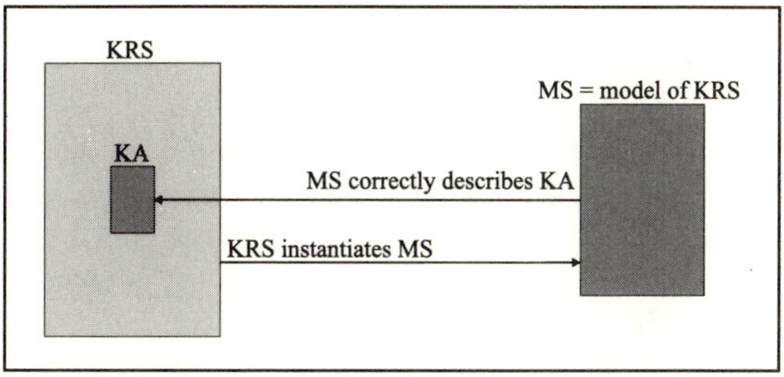

FIGURE 3-1 Model of a K-system. MS = mathematical structure. KRS = K-system. KA = K-aspect of KRS.

model can be found in many elementary books on differential or difference equations, and they cover such different fields as mechanics, electrodynamics, chemistry, population dynamics, engineering, etc.

For the moment, I wish to focus on just one basic aspect of traditional dynamical modeling, namely, the use of magnitudes in order to describe the change of a real system. A *magnitude of a real system* is a property that belongs to this system (or, if the system has more than one part, to one of its parts) and that, at different times, may assume different values. For example, consider the particular mechanical system that consists of the moon and the earth. Then, the position of the earth S_e and the gravitational force exerted on the moon by the earth $G_{m,e}$ are two different mechanical magnitudes of this particular mechanical system. These two magnitudes, however, are mechanical

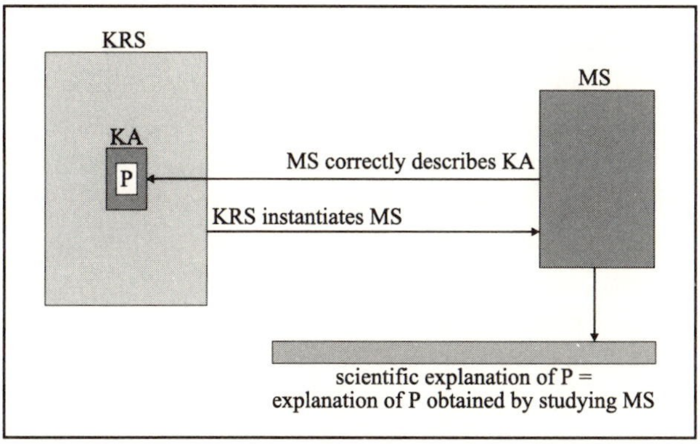

FIGURE 3-2 Scientific explanation of a K-property P of KRS. MS = model of KRS. KRS = K-system. KA = K-aspect of KRS. P = K-property of KRS.

properties that belong to different parts of the system. The first is a property of the earth, while the second is a relational property of the moon.

Each magnitude is always associated with two mathematical objects. First, the set of values that the magnitude can take at different times and, second, the set of its time evolution functions. Time is a special magnitude, for it is associated with a set of values, but not with a set of time evolution functions.

The *set of values* of a magnitude usually is the set of the real numbers; however, one may also think of magnitudes whose set of values is the domain of some other mathematical structure (for example, some magnitudes can only take discrete values, that is, their set of values is a subset of the integers).

A *time evolution function of a magnitude* M_i is any function $M_i(t)$ or $M_i[x_1, \ldots, x_n](t)$ $(1 \leq n)$ such that (1) the values of this function belong to the set of values of M_i; (2) the domain of the variable t is the set of values of the magnitude time; and (3) the domains of the variables $x_1, \ldots, x_n$ are, respectively, the sets of values of n magnitudes $M_1, \ldots, M_n$. I call the variables $x_1, \ldots, x_n$ the *parameters* of the function $M_i[x_1, \ldots, x_n](t)$, and any such function a *parametric function of time*. On the other hand, I call any function $M_i(t)$ with no parameter a *function of time*. Note that an arbitrary time evolution function $M_i[x_1, \ldots, x_n](t)$ with n $(1 \leq n)$ parameters determines a set of time evolution functions with no parameter, namely, all the functions of time $M_i(t)$ such that, for some $x_1, \ldots, x_n$, $M_i(t) = M_i[x_1, \ldots, x_n](t)$.

For example, let us consider again Galileo's law for the vertical position of a falling body: $S(t) = s + vt + (1/2)\boldsymbol{c}t^2$. In this equation, the variable t stands for an arbitrary instant, $\boldsymbol{c}$ is a constant (the acceleration due to gravity), while s and v are two parameters (the arbitrary initial values of the vertical position and velocity of the falling body). This equation is thus satisfied by a set of functions of time, namely, all the functions $S(t)$ such that, for some s and v, $S(t) = s + vt + (1/2)\boldsymbol{c}t^2$. Each of these functions of time is a time evolution function of the vertical position of a falling body. Note, however, that this set of time evolution functions is the set of functions of time determined by the parametric function $S[s, v](t)$ such that $S[s, v](t) = s + vt + (1/2)\boldsymbol{c}t^2$. According to the definition I have just given, this parametric function is also a time evolution function of the vertical position of a falling body.

Since certain magnitudes may be functions of other magnitudes, a time evolution function of a magnitude can often be expressed by using different parameters. Thus, since the vertical velocity of a falling body is the ratio of its vertical momentum and of its mass, that is $v = p/\mathbf{m} = V(p)$, the time evolution function of the vertical position that we have just considered can also be expressed by using the parameters s and p, that is, $S[s, v](t) = S[s, V(p)](t) = s + (p/\mathbf{m})t + (1/2)\mathbf{c}t^2 = S[s, p](t)$.

Given an arbitrary time evolution function of magnitude M_i with n $(0 \leq n)$ parameters, we can always introduce or eliminate *dummy parameters*, that is, any parameter on which the time evolution function of M_i does not depend. For example, a time evolution function of the vertical velocity of a falling body is the parametric function $V[v](t)$ such that $V[v](t) = v + \mathbf{c}t$. This function has only one parameter, namely, v. Thus, it does not depend on any other parameter. Sometimes, however, it may be useful to introduce the dummy parameter s, by setting, $V[s, v](t) = V[v](t)$. The two parametric functions, $V[s, v](t)$ and $V[v](t)$, are thus two equivalent ways of expressing the same time evolution function of the vertical velocity of a falling body.

When I want to make explicit the n $(1 \leq n)$ parameters I use to express a time evolution function of magnitude M_i, I indicate this function with the term $M_i[x_1, \ldots, x_n](t)$. If a time evolution function of M_i does not depend on any parameter, and I want to make explicit this fact, I use the term $M_i(t)$. For a matter of convenience, however, I sometimes indicate a time evolution function of magnitude M_i with the term in bold $\boldsymbol{M_i(t)}$. The context then makes clear which parameters (if any) I use to express this function.

5 Galilean explanations are based on Galilean models of *K*-systems

Let me now introduce a basic result that links the theory of magnitudes to dynamical systems theory, and is in fact one of the foundations of the traditional practice of dynamical modeling. Let us consider n $(n \geq 1)$ magnitudes $M_1, \ldots, M_n$ and, for each of these magnitudes, let us choose one of its time evolution functions. Let us also assume that the chosen functions can all be expressed by using the parameters $x_1, \ldots, x_n$, whose respective domains are the sets of values of the magnitudes $M_1, \ldots, M_n$. That is, the time evolution function $\boldsymbol{M_i(t)}$ that we choose for magnitude M_i $(1 \leq i \leq n)$ can be expressed as the parametric function $M_i[x_1, \ldots, x_n](t)$. Let us then consider the structure $G = \langle T, M_1 \times \ldots \times M_n, \{g^t\}\rangle$, where T is the set of values of the magnitude time, each component of the Cartesian product $M_1 \times \ldots \times M_n$ is the set of values of magnitude M_i, and, for any

$t \in T$, $g^t(x_1, \ldots, x_n) = \langle M_1[x_1, \ldots, x_n](t), \ldots, M_n[x_1, \ldots, x_n](t)\rangle$. I call G the structure *generated* by a choice of time evolution functions of the magnitudes $M_1, \ldots, M_n$. Then, the structure G is a mathematical dynamical system if and only if the choice of time evolution functions $\langle M_i[x_1, \ldots, x_n](t)\rangle$ of the magnitudes $M_1, \ldots, M_n$ satisfies these conditions: (1) $M_i[x_1, \ldots, x_n](0) = x_i$, and (2) $M_i[x_1, \ldots, x_n](t + w) = M_i[M_1[x_1, \ldots, x_n](t), \ldots, M_n[x_1, \ldots, x_n](t)](w)$ (for a proof, see theorem 1 in the appendix of this chapter).

Given a natural kind K and a K-system KRS, a *K-magnitude of KRS* is a K-property that belongs to KRS (or, if KRS has more than one part, to one of its parts) and that, at different times, may assume different values. By this definition, and by the definitions of K-system (see section 3) and of magnitude of a real system (see section 4), a K-magnitude of KRS is thus a *special type of magnitude* of the real system KRS.

Let us now consider n $(1 \leq n)$ K-magnitudes of an arbitrary K-system. Among all the choices of time evolution functions of these n K-magnitudes, there will be some that satisfy conditions (1) and (2) above. Each of these choices will thus generate a mathematical dynamical system MDS. I call any mathematical dynamical system MDS generated by a choice of time evolution functions of a finite number of K-magnitudes of a K-system a possible Galilean model of the K-system. Furthermore, I say that a possible Galilean model of a K-system is a Galilean model of the K-system if and only if the K-system instantiates the possible model. In other words, a *Galilean model of a K-system* is a possible Galilean model of the K-system which is instantiated by it (see figure 3-3). Therefore, by this definition, and by the definition of model (see section 3), any Galilean model of a K-system is a special type of model of the K-system.

I said earlier that Galilean explanations are a special type of scientific explanations, for they are based on the study of models of a special type. I can now add that these special models are the Galilean models of K-systems, and that a *Galilean explanation of a K-property of a K-system* is an explanation obtained by studying a Galilean model of the K-system (see figure 3-4).

6 Galilean frameworks of K-systems

We have just seen that, to obtain a Galilean explanation of a K-property of a K-system, we must study a Galilean model of the K-system. Obviously, if we need to study a Galilean model of the K-system, we need first to specify or describe the model, in such a way

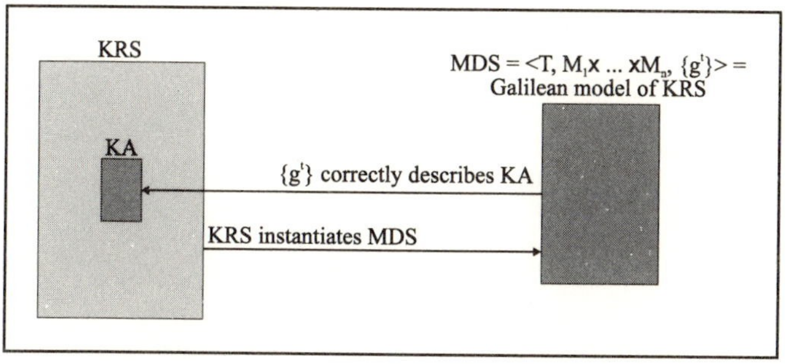

FIGURE 3-3 Galilean model of a K-system. KRS is a K-system. MDS = $\langle T, M_1 \times \ldots \times M_n, \{g^t\}\rangle$ is a mathematical dynamical system. $M_1, \ldots, M_n$ are n different K-magnitudes of KRS. $M_1[x_1, \ldots, x_n](t), \ldots, M_n[x_1, \ldots, x_n](t)$ is a choice of time evolution functions of $M_1, \ldots, M_n$. $g^t(x_1, \ldots, x_n) = \langle M_1[x_1, \ldots, x_n](t), \ldots, M_n[x_1, \ldots, x_n](t)\rangle$. KA = simultanueous variation in time of $M_1, \ldots, M_n$.

that we are then able to use the model for constructing the explanation we seek. Therefore, before constructing a Galilean explanation of a *K*-property of a *K*-system, we face the problem of specifying a Galilean model of the *K*-system.

Since a Galilean model of a *K*-system is a possible Galilean model of the *K*-system which is instantiated by it, the problem of specifying a Galilean model of a *K*-system can naturally be divided into two parts: We give a specification first of a possible Galilean model of the

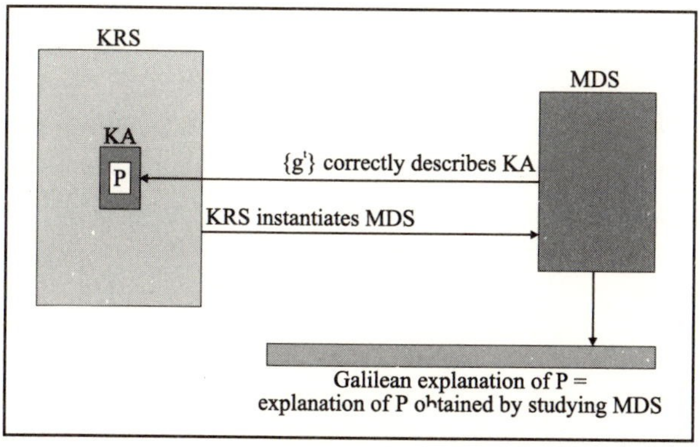

FIGURE 3-4 Galilean explanation of a K-property P of KRS. KRS = K-system. MDS = $\langle T, M_1 \times \ldots \times M_n, \{g^t\}\rangle$ = Galilean model of KRS. $M_1, \ldots, M_n$ = n different K-magnitudes of KRS. KA = simultaneous variation in time of $M_1, \ldots, M_n$. P = K-property of KRS.

K-system, and second of an empirical interpretation of the possible model which, together, allow us to decide whether the *K*-system instantiates the model. I call the result of these two steps a *Galilean framework of the K-system.*

Since a possible Galilean model of a *K*-system is a mathematical dynamical system $MDS = \langle T, M, \{g^t\}\rangle$ generated by a choice of time evolution functions of n $(1 \leq n)$ *K*-magnitudes $M_1, \ldots, M_n$ of the *K*-system, a specification of a possible Galilean model of a *K*-system consists of three parts: (1) a specification of the set of values T of the magnitude time; (2) a specification of the *K*-magnitudes $M_1, \ldots, M_n$ whose sets of values are the components of the state space $M = M_1 \times \ldots \times M_n$; and (3) a specification of the set of state transitions $\{g^t\}$.

A specification of an empirical interpretation of a possible Galilean model of a *K*-system, on the other hand, also consists of three parts:

1. A specification of experimental or observational techniques (preparation methods) which, given some initial state $\langle x_1, \ldots, x_n\rangle$ of the possible Galilean model, allow us to make the *K*-magnitudes $M_1, \ldots, M_n$ assume the values $x_1, \ldots, x_n$ at time 0.
2. A division of the *K*-magnitudes $M_1, \ldots, M_n$ into two groups: those *K*-magnitudes which we intend to measure (observable) and those which we do not plan to measure (nonobservable or theoretical). This division of the *K*-magnitudes,[1] however, must satisfy two conditions. First, there must be at least one observable *K*-magnitude and, second, if there are theoretical *K*-magnitudes, they must be *empirically relevant.* More precisely, for any theoretical *K*-magnitude, there must be some observable *K*-magnitude whose parametric time evolution function (as determined by the specified mathematical dynamical system *MDS*) depends on it.[2] In fact if this condition is violated, we can always obtain an empirically equivalent system by simply eliminating all those theoretical components which do not make any difference to the possible evolutions of any observable.
3. A specification of experimental or observational techniques (measurement methods) that allow us to simultaneously measure or detect the values of all the *K*-magnitudes that we classified observable.

Let us now see in what sense the conjunction of a specification of a possible Galilean model of a *K*-system, and a specification of an empirical interpretation of the possible model allows us to decide whether the *K*-system instantiates the model. By the definition of instantiation (see section 3), a *K*-system *KRS* instantiates a possible Galilean model of *KRS* if and only if the model correctly describes some *K*-aspect of *KRS*. First, note that the *K*-aspect of *KRS* that a possible Galilean model of *KRS* describes is the simultaneous variation in time of the *n* *K*-magnitudes of *KRS* whose sets of values are the components of the state space $M = M_1 \times \ldots \times M_n$ of the possible model. Second, the description of this variation is given by the set of state-transitions $\{g^t\}$ of the possible model. Third, this description is correct if and only if the possible model turns out to be an *empirically adequate model of KRS*, that is, if all the measurements of the observable *K*-magnitudes turn out to be consistent with the values we obtain from the specification of the set of state transitions $\{g^t\}$ (in conjunction with a specification of some initial state of the possible model). Therefore, given an arbitrary Galilean framework of a *K*-system *KRS*, *KRS* instantiates the possible Galilean model of *KRS* specified by the framework if and only if the possible model is an empirically adequate model of *KRS*. Thus, if a Galilean framework of *KRS* specifies a possible model that turns out to be an empirically adequate model of *KRS*, then *KRS* instantiates the possible model and, consequently, the possible model is a Galilean model of *KRS*. I call any such framework a *correct Galilean framework of KRS* (see figure 3-5).

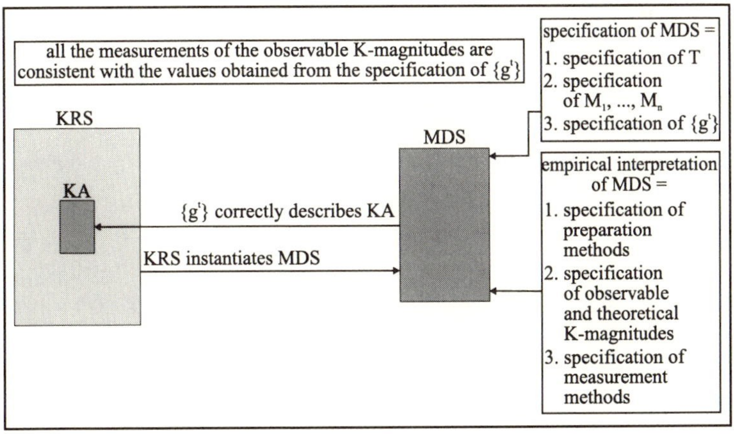

FIGURE 3-5 Correct Galilean framework of a K-system. KRS = K-system. MDS = $\langle T, M_1 \times \ldots \times M_n, \{g^t\}\rangle$ = Galilean model of KRS. $M_1, \ldots, M_n = n$ different K-magnitudes of KRS. KA = simultaneous variation in time of $M_1, \ldots, M_n$.

7 Explicit versus implicit specification of the set of state transitions of a possible Galilean model of a *K*-system

Thus far we have seen that the problem of constructing a Galilean explanation of a *K*-property of a *K*-system presupposes the problem of specifying a Galilean model of the *K*-system, and that this problem in fact reduces to that of producing a correct Galilean framework of the *K*-system. We must now consider whether there are standard methods or procedures for dealing with this problem. In fact, if we look at the traditional practice of dynamical modeling, we realize that there are at least two general methods that allow us to actually construct Galilean frameworks of *K*-systems. Furthermore, the frameworks produced by means of either method typically turn out to be correct. Following a traditional terminology, I call the first procedure the *inductive method*, and the second one the *deductive method*.

Usually, these two methods lead to the construction of two different types of Galilean frameworks. These two types of frameworks differ only with respect to the way of specifying the set of state transitions $\{g^t\}$ of a possible Galilean model of a *K*-system. Therefore, before we can analyze either method, we must first consider these two different ways of specifying the set of state transitions $\{g^t\}$.

Let us thus suppose that we want to specify the set of state transitions $\{g^t\}$ of a possible Galilean model of a *K*-system. Let us further assume that we have already specified the set of values T of the magnitude time, and also the *K*-magnitudes $M_1, \ldots, M_n$ $(1 \leq n)$ whose sets of values are the components of the state space $M = M_1 \times \ldots \times M_n$. Then, in order to specify $\{g^t\}$, we may in general follow two different paths.

First, we may state a system of n laws $\langle M_i(t) = \lambda_i \rangle$ $(1 \leq i \leq n)$. In general, a law $M_i(t) = \lambda_i$ determines the mathematical form of a set of time evolution functions of the magnitude M_i, where each of these functions is just a function of time. For example, let us consider again Galileo's law for the vertical velocity of a falling body: $V(t) = v + ct$. Since v is a parameter (the arbitrary initial value of the vertical velocity of the falling body), this law determines the mathematical form of all the functions of time $V(t)$ such that, for some v, $V(t) = v + ct$.

Second, we may instead state a system of n differential or difference equations $\langle D_t(M_i(t)) = \alpha_i \rangle$ (depending on whether we take time to be continuous or discrete). Unlike a law, which determines the mathematical form of a set of time evolution functions of a magnitude, a differential or difference equation expresses a mathematical relation between time evolution functions of several magnitudes, where each of these functions is just a function of time. For example, consider the particular mechanical system that consists of a body attached to a spring, where the only forces acting on the body are its weight and the restoring force of the spring. Since the restoring force of the spring is proportional to its extension (or compression), the differential equation $D_t(V(t)) = -(\boldsymbol{k}/\boldsymbol{m})\ S(t)$ expresses a mathematical relation between a time evolution function $V(t)$ of the vertical velocity of the body and a time evolution function $S(t)$ of its vertical position (measured from the equilibrium point). The two constants $\boldsymbol{k}$ and $\boldsymbol{m}$ are, respectively, the force constant of the spring, and the mass of the body.

The concepts of a law and that of a differential or difference equation are thus crucial to describe the two different ways of specifying the set of state transitions $\{g^t\}$ of a possible Galilean model of a *K*-system. However, to precisely understand what I mean when I talk of laws and differential or difference equations, we need to look first at the special type of mathematical language to which these two types of equations belong. I call this special type of language a *Galilean language of a K-system.*

The *alphabet* of a Galilean language of a *K*-system consists of six types of symbols. First, the *identity predicate* =. Second, a list of *mathematical operators* $O_1, \ldots, O_m, \ldots$. Third, the *constants* $c_1, \ldots, c_k, \ldots$ whose respective values belong to the domains $D_1, \ldots, D_k, \ldots$ of mathematical structures. Fourth, the *variable* t whose domain is the set of values of the magnitude time. Fifth, a finite number r $(1 \leq r)$ of variables (which I call *parameters*) $x_1, \ldots, x_r$ whose respective domains are the sets of values of r *K*-magnitudes $M_1, \ldots, M_r$ of a fixed *K*-system *KRS*. Sixth, the *r function constants* $M_1(\ ), \ldots, M_r(\ )$.

The *terms* of a Galilean language of a *K*-system are of three types. First, the *individual terms*, that is, the constants, the variable t, and the parameters. Second, all the *function terms* which are obtained from an arbitrary function constant $M_j(\ )$ $(1 \leq j \leq r)$ by inserting the variable t between the parentheses. Third, all the *complex terms* which are obtained by applying a mathematical operator to individual terms, function terms, or complex terms.[3] A *law term* is a term of a Galilean *K*-language of a *K*-system where no function term occurs.

A *formula* of a Galilean language of a *K*-system is an equation where terms occur on both sides. A *law* of a Galilean language of a *K*-system is a formula whose left-hand side is a function term and whose right-hand side is a law term (or *vice versa*). A *system of n laws* of a Galilean language of a K-system consists of n laws of this language $\langle M_i(t) = \lambda_i \rangle$ such that the n left-hand sides of these laws are n different function terms of the language. A *solution of a system of n laws* of a Galilean language of a K-system consists of n functions of time $\langle M_i(t) \rangle$ that, for some value of the parameters $x_1, \ldots, x_r$ of the language, satisfy the system. It is thus clear that a system of n laws of a Galilean language of a K-system always has at least one solution. However, since the law terms $\langle \lambda_i \rangle$ may contain parameters, this solution may not be unique.

If one of the mathematical operators of a Galilean language of a K-system is the derivative or the difference operator[4] $D_t(\ )$ (depending on whether we consider time to be continuous or discrete), a *differential or difference equation* of this language is a formula whose left-hand side (right-hand side) is a term of the form $D_t(M_j(t))$ (where $M_j(t)$ is an arbitrary function term of the language). A *system of n differential or difference equations* of a Galilean language of a K-system consists of n differential or difference equations of this language $\langle D_t(M_i(t)) = \alpha_i \rangle$ such that the n left-hand sides of these equations contain n different function terms of the language. A *solution of a system of n differential or difference equations* of a Galilean language of a K-system consists of n functions of time $\langle M_i(t) \rangle$ that, for some value of the parameters $x_1, \ldots, x_r$ of the language, satisfy the system. In general, if a system of n differential or difference equations of a Galilean language of a K-system has a solution, this solution is not unique.

Before going on, let me illustrate these abstract definitions by considering a simple example of a Galilean language of a K-system, and also some examples of systems of laws and differential equations that belong to this language. Let me assume that the K-system we consider is a falling body. I am now going to describe a very simple Galilean language of this particular mechanical system. I call this simple language GL_0.

The alphabet of GL_0 consists of: (1) the identity predicate =; (2) all the mathematical operators of elementary algebra and calculus, such as, for example, the four arithmetical operation signs +, −, ×, /, and the derivative operator $D_t(\ )$; (3) the usual mathematical constants, such as the real constant π, the numerals *1, 2, 3,* . . . etc.; let us also include one more constant **c**, whose value is a negative real number (the acceleration of a falling body under the influence of gravity); (4) the variable t whose domain is the set of the real numbers; (5) the two parameters s and v whose respective domains are the sets of values of the two mechanical magnitudes S = the vertical position of a falling body, and V = its vertical velocity; and (6) the two function constants $S(\ )$ and $V(\ )$.

Therefore, GL_0 has a denumerable number of individual terms (all the constants, the variable t, and the two parameters s and v), but it has only two function terms, that is, $S(t)$ and $V(t)$. The number of complex terms of GL_0, however, is denumerable, for a complex term can be obtained by applying a mathematical operator to individual terms, function terms, or complex terms. For example, $\mathbf{c} + \mathbf{c}$, $(\mathbf{c} + \mathbf{c}) + \mathbf{c}$, $((\mathbf{c} + \mathbf{c}) + \mathbf{c}) + \mathbf{c}, \ldots$ is a denumerable sequence of complex terms. Four more complex terms are $s + vt + (1/2)\mathbf{c}t^2$, $v + \mathbf{c}t$, $D_t(S(t))$, and $D_t(V(t))$. Of these four, the first two are law terms, for they do not contain function terms.

An example of a system of two laws of GL_0 is $\langle S(t) = s + vt + (1/2)\mathbf{c}t^2, V(t) = v + \mathbf{c}t\rangle$. A solution of this system consists of two functions of time $\langle S(t), V(t)\rangle$ such that, for some s and v, they satisfy $\langle S(t) = s + vt + (1/2)\mathbf{c}t^2, V(t) = v + \mathbf{c}t\rangle$.

Finally, an example of a system of two differential equations of GL_0 is $\langle D_t(S(t)) = V(t), D_t(V(t)) = \mathbf{c}\rangle$. A solution of this system consists of two functions of time $\langle S(t), V(t)\rangle$ that satisfy $\langle D_t(S(t)) = V(t), D_t(V(t)) = \mathbf{c}\rangle$. We know from calculus that this system has solutions, and that every solution has the form $\langle \kappa_2 + \kappa_1 t + (1/2)\mathbf{c}t^2, \kappa_1 + \mathbf{c}t\rangle$, where κ_1 and κ_2 are two arbitrary real numbers.

We have now the appropriate conceptual tools to look more closely at the two different ways of specifying the set of state transitions $\{g^t\}$ of a possible Galilean model. Let us thus suppose that we want to specify the set of state transitions $\{g^t\}$ of a possible Galilean model of a K-system KRS. Let us further assume that we have already specified the set of values T of the magnitude time, and also the n $(1 \leq n)$ K-magnitudes $M_1, \ldots, M_n$ whose sets of values are the components of the state space $M = M_1 \times \ldots \times M_n$ of the possible model. As mentioned earlier, in order to specify $\{g^t\}$, we may in general follow two different paths.

First, we may state a system of n laws $\langle M_i(t) = \lambda_i\rangle$ of a Galilean language of KRS. This system of n laws is an *explicit specification of* $\{g^t\}$ if and only if there is a choice of time evolution functions $\langle M_i[x_1, \ldots, x_n](t)\rangle$ of the K-magnitudes $M_1, \ldots, M_n$ such that

1. $\langle M_i(t)\rangle$ is a solution of $\langle M_i(t) = \lambda_i\rangle$ if and only if, for some $x_1, \ldots, x_n$, $M_i(t) = M_i[x_1, \ldots, x_n](t)$.
2. $M_i[x_1, \ldots, x_n](0) = x_i$.
3. $M_i[x_1, \ldots, x_n](t + w) = M_i[M_1[x_1, \ldots, x_n](t), \ldots, M_n[x_1, \ldots, x_n](t)](w)$.

Note that this definition is justified because, by theorem 1 (found in the appendix to this chapter), if (*1*), (*2*), and (*3*) are satisfied, we may explicitly define an arbitrary state transition g^t by means of the equation $g^t(x_1, \ldots, x_n) = \langle \lambda_1, \ldots, \lambda_n \rangle$.

Second, depending on whether we take time to be continuous or discrete, we may instead state a system of *n* differential or difference equations $\langle D_t(M_i(t)) = \alpha_i \rangle$ of a Galilean language of *KRS*. This system of *n* differential or difference equations is an *implicit specification of* $\{g^t\}$ if and only if there is a choice of time evolution functions $\langle M_i[x_1, \ldots, x_n](t) \rangle$ of the *K*-magnitudes $M_1, \ldots, M_n$ such that

1. $\langle M_i(t) \rangle$ is a solution of $\langle D_t(M_i(t)) = \alpha_i \rangle$ if and only if, for some $x_1, \ldots, x_n$, $M_i(t) = M_i[x_1, \ldots, x_n](t)$.
2. $M_i[x_1, \ldots, x_n](0) = x_i$.
3. $M_i[x_1, \ldots, x_n](t + w) = M_i[M_1[x_1, \ldots, x_n](t), \ldots, M_n[x_1, \ldots, x_n](t)](w)$.

This definition is justified because, by theorem 1 (see appendix), if (*2*) and (*3*) are satisfied, we know that the choice of time evolution functions $\langle M_i[x_1, \ldots, x_n](t) \rangle$ generates a mathematical dynamical system $\langle T, M_1 \times \ldots \times M_n, \{g^t\} \rangle$ such that each state transition g^t satisfies $g^t(x_1, \ldots, x_n) = \langle M_1[x_1, \ldots, x_n](t), \ldots, M_n[x_1, \ldots, x_n](t) \rangle$. Furthermore, in many cases, we may be able to prove that all three conditions hold *without actually solving* the system of *n* differential or difference equations $\langle D_t(M_i(t)) = \alpha_i \rangle$ (see theorems 2 and 3 in the appendix).

Finally, let us consider a concrete case that illustrates the two different ways of specifying the set of state transitions of a possible Galilean model of a *K*-system. Assume that we want to specify the set of state transitions $\{g^t\}$ of a possible Galilean model of a falling body, that the set of values *T* of the magnitude time is the set of the real numbers *R*, and the state space *M* of this possible model has the two components *S* = the set of values of the vertical position of a falling body = *R*, and *V* = the set of values of its vertical velocity = *R*. Then, (a) the system of two laws of GL_0 $\langle S(t) = s + vt + (1/2)\boldsymbol{c}t^2, V(t) = v + \boldsymbol{c}t \rangle$ is an explicit specification of $\{g^t\}$, and (b) the system of two differential equations of GL_0 $\langle D_t(S(t)) = V(t), D_t(V(t)) = \boldsymbol{c} \rangle$ is an implicit specification of $\{g^t\}$.

To see that (*a*) holds, consider the choice of time evolution functions $\langle S[s, v](t), V[s, v](t) \rangle$ such that $S[s, v](t) = s + vt + (1/2)\boldsymbol{c}t^2$, and $V[s, v](t) = v + \boldsymbol{c}t$. Then, first, $\langle S(t), V(t) \rangle$ is a solution of the system of two laws of GL_0 $\langle S(t) = s + vt + (1/2)\boldsymbol{c}t^2, V(t) = v + \boldsymbol{c}t \rangle$ if and only if, for some *s* and *v*, $S(t) = S[s, v](t)$, and $V(t) = V[s, v](t)$. Second,

$S[s, v](0) = s$, and $V[s, v](0) = v$. Third, $S[s, v](t + w) = s + v(t + w) + (1/2)\mathbf{c}(t + w)^2 = s + vt + (1/2)\mathbf{c}t^2 + vw + \mathbf{c}tw + (1/2)\mathbf{c}w^2 = S[s + vt + (1/2)\mathbf{c}t^2, v + \mathbf{c}t](w) = S[S[s, v](t), V[s, v](t)](w)$, and $V[s, v](t + w) = v + \mathbf{c}(t + w) = v + \mathbf{c}t + \mathbf{c}w = V[s + vt + (1/2)\mathbf{c}t^2, v + \mathbf{c}t](w) = V[S[s, v](t), V[s, v](t)](w)$. Therefore, the system of two laws of GL_0 $\langle S(t) = s + vt + (1/2)\mathbf{c}t^2, V(t) = v + \mathbf{c}t\rangle$ is an explicit specification of $\{g^t\}$.

To see that (*b*) holds, recall first that the system $\langle D_t(S(t)) = V(t), D_t(V(t)) = \mathbf{c}\rangle$ has solutions, and that every solution has the form $\langle \kappa_2 + \kappa_1 t + (1/2)\mathbf{c}t^2, \kappa_1 + \mathbf{c}t\rangle$, where κ_1 and κ_2 are two arbitrary real numbers. Let $\kappa_1 = v$, $\kappa_2 = s$, and consider the choice of time evolution functions $\langle S[s, v](t), V[s, v](t)\rangle$ such that $S[s, v](t) = s + vt + (1/2)\mathbf{c}t^2$, and $V[s, v](t) = v + \mathbf{c}t$. Then, first, $\langle S(t), V(t)\rangle$ is a solution of the system of two differential equations of GL_0 $\langle D_t(S(t)) = V(t), D_t(V(t)) = \mathbf{c}\rangle$ if and only if, for some s and v, $S(t) = S[s, v](t)$, and $V(t) = V[s, v](t)$. Second, we have already verified that the last two conditions of the definition of an implicit specification hold. Therefore, the system of two differential equations of GL_0 $\langle D_t(S(t)) = V(t), D_t(V(t)) = \mathbf{c}\rangle$ is an implicit specification of $\{g^t\}$.

8 The inductive method for constructing Galilean frameworks of *K*-systems

I said earlier (see section 7) that, if we look at the traditional practice of dynamical modeling, we realize that there are at least two general methods that allow us to actually construct Galilean frameworks of *K*-systems. These two procedures (the inductive and deductive methods) lead to the construction of two different types of Galilean frameworks, which differ only with respect to the way of specifying the set of state transitions $\{g^t\}$ of a possible Galilean model of a *K*-system. I can now add that the frameworks produced by means of the inductive method give an *explicit specification* of the set of state transitions $\{g^t\}$, while those which result from the deductive method give an *implicit specification* of $\{g^t\}$. In this section, I will focus on the *inductive method*. The *deductive* method will be the subject of section 9.

Suppose that our main goal is to produce a Galilean explanation of a particular *K*-property *P* of a fixed *K*-system *KRS*. We already know that, to achieve this goal, we must first construct a correct Galilean framework of *KRS* (see section 6). Furthermore, this correct framework must also be *P-explanatory*, in the sense that it must specify a Galilean model of *KRS* whose study will then allow us to produce an explanation of the particular *K*-property *P* (see figure 3-6). Therefore, to achieve our main goal, we must first set the subgoal of constructing a correct Galilean framework of *KRS* which is *P*-explanatory. Actually, the inductive method sketched below allows us to construct a correct Galilean framework of *KRS* that has a good chance of being *P*-explanatory.

Let us thus assume that we set the subgoal of constructing a correct Galilean framework of *KRS* which is *P*-explanatory. Then, to achieve this subgoal, we perform the following steps:

1. We specify the set of values T of the magnitude time.
2. We specify n $(1 \leq n)$ K-magnitudes $M_1, \ldots, M_n$ of *KRS* which are likely to be relevant to an explanation of the *K*-property *P*, and whose sets of values are the components of the state space $M = M_1 \times \ldots \times M_n$ of a possible Galilean model of *KRS*, $GI = \langle T, M, \{g^t\}\rangle$, whose set of state transitions $\{g^t\}$ we will specify later.
3. We specify experimental or observational techniques (preparation methods) which, given some state $\langle x_1, \ldots, x_n\rangle$ of GI, allow us to make the K-magnitudes $M_1, \ldots, M_n$ assume values $x_1, \ldots, x_n$ at time 0.
4. We divide the K-magnitudes $M_1, \ldots, M_n$ into two groups: those K-magnitudes which we intend to measure (observable) and

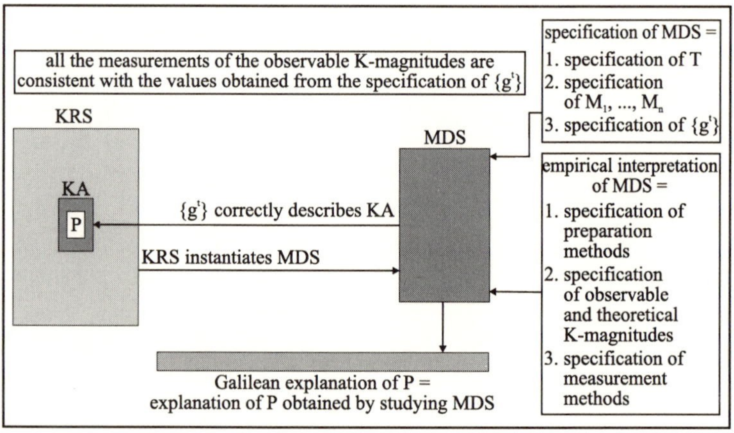

FIGURE 3-6 P-explanatory and correct Galilean framework of a K-system. KRS = K-system. MDS = $\langle T, M_1 \times \ldots \times M_n, \{g^t\}\rangle$ = Galilean model of KRS. $M_1, \ldots, M_n$ = n different K-magnitudes of KRS. KA = simultaneous variation in time of $M_1, \ldots, M_n$. P = K-property of KRS.

those which we do not plan to measure (nonobservable, or theoretical), keeping in mind that we must plan to measure at least one *K*-magnitude.

5. We specify experimental or observational techniques (measurement methods) that allow us to simultaneously measure or detect the values of all the *K*-magnitudes which we classified observable.
6. Given several measurements of the observable *K*-magnitudes, we *induce* on the base of these *available data* a system of *n* laws $\langle M_i(t) = \lambda_i \rangle$ of a Galilean language of *KRS*. This system of *n* laws must be an explicit specification of the set of state transitions $\{g^t\}$ of the possible Galilean model of *KRS* $GI = \langle T, M, \{g^t\} \rangle$.
7. We check that all the theoretical *K*-magnitudes are empirically relevant (see note 2).
8. We check that the possible model *GI* we specified is an empirically adequate model of *KRS*.

It is thus clear that, because of its design, the inductive method I have just sketched allows us to construct a Galilean framework of *KRS*. For, if we successfully complete the first seven steps, we actually produce a specification of a possible Galilean model of *KRS* (i.e., a specification of *GI*) and a specification of an empirical interpretation of *GI*. Then, if step (*8*) is also successful, *GI* is an empirically adequate model of *KRS*. Therefore, the Galilean framework we construct turns out to be correct. And, finally, since the *K*-magnitudes $M_1, \ldots, M_n$ are likely to be relevant to an explanation of the *K*-property *P*, this correct Galilean framework also has a good chance of being *P*-explanatory.

9 The deductive method for constructing Galilean frameworks of *K*-systems

Let us now suppose again that our main goal is to produce a Galilean explanation of a particular *K*-property *P* of a fixed *K*-system *KRS*, and that we set the subgoal of constructing a correct Galilean framework of *KRS* which is *P*-explanatory. Then, to achieve this subgoal, we perform the following steps:

1. We specify the set of values *T* of the magnitude time.
2. We specify *n* ($1 \leq n$) *K*-magnitudes $M_1, \ldots, M_n$ of *KRS* which are likely to be relevant to an explanation of the *K*-property

P, and whose sets of values are the components of the state space $M = M_1 \times \ldots \times M_n$ of a possible Galilean model of *KRS*, $GD = \langle T, M, \{g^t\}\rangle$, whose set of state transitions $\{g^t\}$ we will specify next.

3. Given a finite number of formulas of a Galilean language of *KRS*, we *deduce* from these *available hypotheses* a system of *n* differential or difference equations $\langle D_t(M_i(t)) = \alpha_i \rangle$ of this language. This system of *n* differential or difference equations must be an implicit specification of the set of state transitions $\{g^t\}$ of the possible Galilean model of *KRS* $GD = \langle T, M, \{g^t\}\rangle$.
4. We specify experimental or observational techniques (preparation methods) which, given some state $\langle x_1, \ldots, x_n \rangle$ of *GD*, allow us to make the *K*-magnitudes $M_1, \ldots, M_n$ assume values $x_1, \ldots, x_n$ at time 0.
5. We divide the *K*-magnitudes $M_1, \ldots, M_n$ into two groups: those *K*-magnitudes which we intend to measure (observable) and those which we do not plan to measure (nonobservable, or theoretical), keeping in mind that we must plan to measure at least one *K*-magnitude.
6. We check that all the theoretical *K*-magnitudes are empirically relevant (see note 2).
7. We specify experimental or observational techniques (measurement methods) which allow us to simultaneously measure or detect the values of all the *K*-magnitudes that we classified observable.
8. We check that the possible model *GD* we specified is an empirically adequate model of *KRS*.

It is thus clear that, because of its design, the deductive method I have just sketched allows us to construct a Galilean framework of *KRS*. For, if we successfully complete the first seven steps, we actually produce a specification of a possible Galilean model of *KRS* (i.e., a specification of *GD*) and a specification of an empirical interpretation of *GD*. Then, if step (*8*) is also successful, *GD* is an empirically adequate model of *KRS*. Therefore, the Galilean *K*-framework we construct turns out to be correct. And, finally, since the *K*-magnitudes $M_1, \ldots, M_n$ are likely to be relevant to an explanation of the *K*-property *P*, this correct Galilean framework also has a good chance of being *P*-explanatory.

If we now compare the deductive and the inductive methods (see figure 3-7), we see that step (*3*) of the deductive method is analogous to step (*6*) of the inductive method, while all other steps are identi-

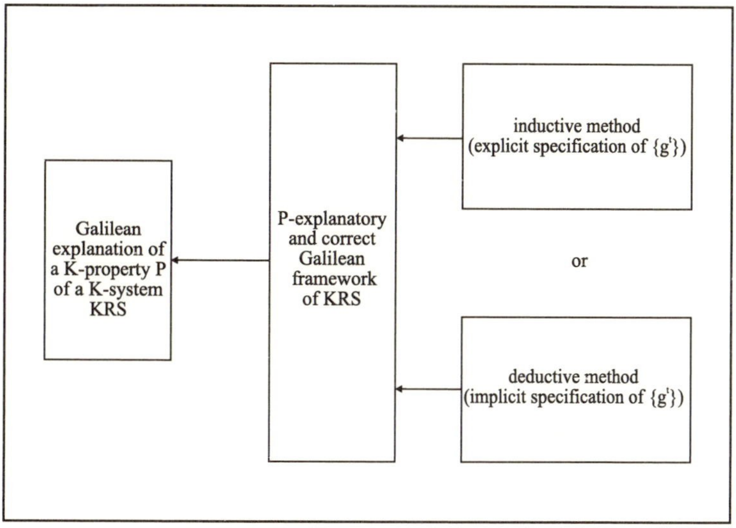

FIGURE 3-7 Two methods to obtain Galilean explanations.

cal, even though they are in a different order. Let me finally remark that I have only given the skeleton, or the basic structure, of the two methods. Therefore, in each concrete application, we should consider each step as a special problem, whose specific methods of solution will in general depend on the particular case.

10 Appendix: Proofs of selected theorems

THEOREM 1 *(necessary and sufficient conditions for the structure generated by a choice of time evolution functions of* n *magnitudes to be a mathematical dynamical system)*

Let $\langle M_i[x_1, \ldots, x_n](t)\rangle$ *be a choice of time evolution functions of the* n *magnitudes* $M_1, \ldots, M_n$. *Let us then consider the structure* $G = \langle T, M_1 \times \ldots \times M_n, \{g^t\}\rangle$, *where* T *is the set of values of the magnitude time, each component of the Cartesian product* $M_1 \times \ldots \times M_n$ *is the set of values of magnitude* M_i, *and, for any* $t \in T$, $g^t(x_1, \ldots, x_n) = \langle M_1[x_1, \ldots, x_n](t), \ldots, M_n[x_1, \ldots, x_n](t)\rangle$.

Then, the structure G *is a mathematical dynamical system if and only if the choice of time evolution functions* $\langle M_i[x_1, \ldots, x_n](t)\rangle$ *satisfies these conditions: (1)* $M_i[x_1, \ldots, x_n](0) = x_i$, *and (2)* $M_i[x_1, \ldots, x_n](t + w) = M_i[M_1[x_1, \ldots, x_n](t), \ldots, M_n[x_1, \ldots, x_n](t)](w)$.

PROOF. Suppose the choice of time evolution functions $\langle M_i[x_1, \ldots, x_n](t)\rangle$ satisfies (*1*) and (*2*). Then, $g^0(x_1, \ldots, x_n) = \langle M_1[x_1, \ldots, x_n](0), \ldots, M_n[x_1, \ldots, x_n](0)\rangle = \langle x_1, \ldots, x_n\rangle$, and $g^{t+w}(x_1, \ldots, x_n) = \langle M_1[x_1, \ldots, x_n](t+w), \ldots, M_n[x_1, \ldots, x_n](t+w)\rangle = \langle M_1[M_1[x_1, \ldots, x_n](t), \ldots, M_n[x_1, \ldots, x_n](t)](w), \ldots, M_n[M_1[x_1, \ldots, x_n](t), \ldots, M_n[x_1, \ldots, x_n](t)](w) = g^w(M_1[x_1, \ldots, x_n](t), \ldots, M_n[x_1, \ldots, x_n](t)) = g^w(g^t(x_1, \ldots, x_n))$. Therefore, G is a mathematical dynamical system.

Conversely, suppose G is a mathematical dynamical system. Then, $\langle M_1[x_1, \ldots, x_n](0), \ldots, M_n[x_1, \ldots, x_n](0)\rangle = g^0(x_1, \ldots, x_n) = \langle x_1, \ldots, x_n\rangle$, and $\langle M_1[x_1, \ldots, x_n](t+w), \ldots, M_n[x_1, \ldots, x_n](t+w)\rangle = g^{t+w}(x_1, \ldots, x_n) = g^w(g^t(x_1, \ldots, x_n)) = g^w(M_1[x_1, \ldots, x_n](t), \ldots, M_n[x_1, \ldots, x_n](t)) = \langle M_1[M_1[x_1, \ldots, x_n](t), \ldots, M_n[x_1, \ldots, x_n](t)](w), \ldots, M_n[M_1[x_1, \ldots, x_n](t), \ldots, M_n[x_1, \ldots, x_n](t)](w)\rangle$. Therefore, the choice of time evolution functions $\langle M_i[x_1, \ldots, x_n](t)\rangle$ satisfies (*1*) and (*2*).

q.e.d.

THEOREM 2 *(ordinary implicit specification of the set of state transitions{*g^t*} of a possible Galilean model of a* K*-system with discrete and nonnegative time)*

Assume that we want to specify the set of state transitions {g^t*} of a possible Galilean model of a* K*-system* KRS*, and that the set of values* T *of the magnitude time is the set of the nonnegative integers* Z^+*, and the sets of values of* n *(*$1 \le n$*)* K*-magnitudes* $M_1, \ldots, M_n$ *of* KRS *are the* n *components of the state space* $M = M_1 \times \ldots \times M_n$ *of this possible model.*

Let GL_1 *be a Galilean language of* KRS *such that (1) the domain of the variable* t *is* Z^+*; (2) the difference operator* $D_t(\ )$ *is one of the mathematical operators of* GL_1*; for any* i *(*$1 \le i \le n$*), (3)* $M_i(t)$ *is one of the function terms of* GL_1*, and (4) the parameter* x_i*, whose domain is the set of values of* K*-magnitude* M_i *of* KRS*, is one of the parameters of* GL_1*.*

Let $\alpha_i(x_1, \ldots, x_n)$ *be a law term of* GL_1 *such that (a) no parameter of* GL_1 *different from* $x_1, \ldots, x_n$ *occurs in it; (b) the variable* t *does not occur in it; and (c) the equation* $g_i(x_1, \ldots, x_n) = \alpha_i(x_1, \ldots, x_n)$ *is satisfied by exactly one function* $g_i(x_1, \ldots, x_n)$ *whose values belong to the set of values of* K*-magnitude* M_i*.*

Let $\alpha_i(M_1(t), \ldots, M_n(t))$ *be the term of* GL_1 *obtained from the law term* $\alpha_i(x_1, \ldots, x_n)$ *by replacing each occurrence of the parameters* $x_1, \ldots, x_n$ *(if any) with the function terms* $M_1(t), \ldots, M_n(t)$*.*

Then, the system of n *difference equations* $\langle D_t(M_i(t)) = \alpha_i(M_1(t), \ldots, M_n(t))\rangle$ *of* GL_1 *is an implicit specification of* $\{g^t\}$. *I will show below that the three conditions of the definition of an implicit specification hold without solving this system of* n *difference equations.*

PROOF. Consider the choice of time evolution functions $\langle M_i[x_1, \ldots, x_n](t)\rangle$ such that $M_i[x_1, \ldots, x_n](0) = x_i$, and $M_i[x_1, \ldots, x_n](t+1) = g_i(M_1[x_1, \ldots x_n](t), \ldots, M_n[x_1, \ldots x_n](t))$. Suppose that, for some $x_1, \ldots, x_n$, $M_i(t) = M_i[x_1, \ldots, x_n](t)$. Then, I must prove that $\langle M_i(t)\rangle$ is a solution of the system of n difference equations $\langle D_t(M_i(t)) = \alpha_i(M_1(t), \ldots, M_n(t))\rangle$. Let $\boldsymbol{x}_1, \ldots, \boldsymbol{x}_n$ be n values of $x_1, \ldots, x_n$ such that $M_i(t) = M_i[\boldsymbol{x}_1, \ldots, \boldsymbol{x}_n](t)$. Then, $D_t(M_i(t)) = M_i(t + 1) = M_i[\boldsymbol{x}_1, \ldots, \boldsymbol{x}_n](t+1) = g_i(M_1[\boldsymbol{x}_1, \ldots, \boldsymbol{x}_n](t), \ldots, M_n[\boldsymbol{x}_1, \ldots, \boldsymbol{x}_n](t)) = g_i(M_1(t), \ldots, M_n(t)) = \alpha_i(M_1(t), \ldots, M_n(t))$. Hence, $\langle M_i(t)\rangle$ is a solution of the system of n difference equations $\langle D_t(M_i(t)) = \alpha_i(M_1(t), \ldots, M_n(t))\rangle$. Conversely, suppose $\langle M_i(t)\rangle$ is a solution of the system of n difference equations $\langle D_t(M_i(t)) = \alpha_i(M_1(t), \ldots, M_n(t))\rangle$. Then, I must prove that, for some $x_1, \ldots, x_n$, $M_i(t) = M_i[x_1, \ldots, x_n](t)$. Let $\boldsymbol{x}_1, \ldots, \boldsymbol{x}_n$ satisfy $\langle M_1(0) = \boldsymbol{x}_1, \ldots, M_n(0) = \boldsymbol{x}_n\rangle$. I will prove that $M_i(t) = M_i[\boldsymbol{x}_1, \ldots, \boldsymbol{x}_n](t)$. The proof is by induction on t. Suppose $t = 0$. Then, $M_i(0) = \boldsymbol{x}_i = M_i[\boldsymbol{x}_1, \ldots, \boldsymbol{x}_n](0)$. The thesis thus holds for $t = 0$. Suppose the thesis holds for t, that is, $M_i(t) = M_i[\boldsymbol{x}_1, \ldots, \boldsymbol{x}_n](t)$. I prove that the thesis also holds for $t + 1$. $M_i(t + 1) = D_t(M_i(t)) = \alpha_i(M_1(t), \ldots, M_n(t)) = \alpha_i(M_1[\boldsymbol{x}_1, \ldots, \boldsymbol{x}_n](t), \ldots, M_n[\boldsymbol{x}_1, \ldots, \boldsymbol{x}_n](t)) = g_i(M_1[\boldsymbol{x}_1, \ldots, \boldsymbol{x}_n](t), \ldots, M_n[\boldsymbol{x}_1, \ldots, \boldsymbol{x}_n](t)) = M_i[\boldsymbol{x}_1, \ldots, \boldsymbol{x}_n](t+1)$. I have thus shown that the first two conditions of the definition of an implicit specification hold.

Finally, I must prove that $M_i[x_1, \ldots, x_n](t + w) = M_i[M_1[x_1, \ldots, x_n](t), \ldots, M_n[x_1, \ldots, x_n](t)](w)$. The proof is by induction on w. Suppose $w = 0$. Then, $M_i[x_1, \ldots, x_n](t + 0) = M_i[x_1, \ldots, x_n](t) = M_i[M_1[x_1, \ldots, x_n](t), \ldots, M_n[x_1, \ldots, x_n](t)](0)$. The thesis thus holds for $w = 0$. Suppose the thesis holds for w, that is, $M_i[x_1, \ldots, x_n](t + w) = M_i[M_1[x_1, \ldots, x_n](t), \ldots, M_n[x_1, \ldots, x_n](t)](w)$. Then, the thesis also holds for $w + 1$. In fact, $M_i[x_1, \ldots, x_n](t + w + 1) = g_i(M_1[x_1, \ldots, x_n](t + w), \ldots, M_n[x_1, \ldots, x_n](t + w)) = g_i(M_1[M_1[x_1, \ldots, x_n](t), \ldots, M_n[x_1, \ldots, x_n](t)](w), \ldots, M_n[M_1[x_1, \ldots, x_n](t), \ldots, M_n[x_1, \ldots, x_n](t)](w)) = M_i[M_1[x_1, \ldots, x_n](t), \ldots, M_n[x_1, \ldots, x_n](t)](w + 1)$. Therefore, the system of n difference equations $\langle D_t(M_i(t)) = \alpha_i(M_1(t), \ldots, M_n(t))\rangle$ of GL_1 is an implicit specification of $\{g^t\}$.

q.e.d.

THEOREM 3 *(ordinary implicit specification of the set of state transitions* $\{g^t\}$ *of a possible Galilean model of a* K-system *with discrete time)*

Assume that we want to specify the set of state transitions $\{g^t\}$ *of a possible Galilean model of a* K-system KRS, *and that the set of values* T *of the magnitude time is the set of the integers* Z, *and the sets of values of* n $(1 \le n)$ K-*magnitudes* $M_1, \ldots, M_n$ *of* KRS *are the* n *components of the state space* $M = M_1 \times \ldots \times M_n$ *of this possible model.*

Let GL_2 *be a Galilean language of* KRS *such that (1) the domain of the variable* t *is* Z; *(2) the difference operator* $D_t(\ )$ *is one of the mathematical operators of* GL_2; *for any* i $(1 \le i \le n)$, *(3)* $M_i(t)$ *is one of the function terms of* GL_2, *and (4) the parameter* x_i, *whose domain is the set of values of* K-*magnitude* M_i *of* KRS, *is one of the parameters of* GL_2.

Let $\alpha_i(x_1, \ldots, x_n)$ *be a law term of* GL_2 *such that (a) no parameter of* GL_2 *different from* $x_1, \ldots, x_n$ *occurs in it; (b) the variable* t *does not occur in it; (c) the equation* $g_i(x_1, \ldots, x_n) = \alpha_i(x_1, \ldots, x_n)$ *is satisfied by exactly one function* $g_i(x_1, \ldots, x_n)$ *whose values belong to the set of values of* K-*magnitude* M_i; *and (d) the function* $g(x_1, \ldots, x_n) = \langle g_1(x_1, \ldots, x_n), \ldots, g_n(x_1, \ldots, x_n)\rangle$ *is a bjjection on the state space* M. *Let* g^{-1} *be the inverse of* g, *and let* $f_i(x_1, \ldots, x_n) =$ *the* i-*th component of* $g^{-1}(x_1, \ldots, x_n)$.

Then, the system of n *difference equations* $\langle D_t(M_i(t)) = \alpha_i(M_1(t), \ldots, M_n(t))\rangle$ *of* GL_2 *is an implicit specification of* $\{g^t\}$. *I will show below that the three conditions of the definition of an implicit specification hold without solving this system of* n *difference equations.*

PROOF. Consider the choice of time evolution functions $\langle M_i[x_1, \ldots, x_n](t)\rangle$ such that $M_i[x_1, \ldots, x_n](0) = x_i$, $M_i[x_1, \ldots, x_n](t + 1) = g_i(M_1[x_1, \ldots, x_n](t), \ldots, M_n[x_1, \ldots, x_n](t))$, and $M_i[x_1, \ldots, x_n](t) = f_i(M_1[x_1, \ldots, x_n](t+1), \ldots, M_n[x_1, \ldots, x_n](t+1))$. Suppose that, for some $x_1, \ldots, x_n$, $M_i(t) = M_i[x_1, \ldots, x_n](t)$. Then, I must prove that $\langle M_i(t)\rangle$ is a solution of the system of n difference equations $\langle D_t(M_i(t)) = \alpha_i(M_1(t), \ldots, M_n(t))\rangle$. Let $\boldsymbol{x}_1, \ldots, \boldsymbol{x}_n$ be n values of $x_1, \ldots, x_n$ such that $M_i(t) = M_i[\boldsymbol{x}_1, \ldots, \boldsymbol{x}_n](t)$. Then, $D_t(M_i(t)) = M_i(t+1) = M_i[\boldsymbol{x}_1, \ldots, \boldsymbol{x}_n](t+1) = g_i(M_1[\boldsymbol{x}_1, \ldots, \boldsymbol{x}_n](t), \ldots, M_n[\boldsymbol{x}_1, \ldots, \boldsymbol{x}_n](t)) = g_i(M_1(t), \ldots, M_n(t)) = \alpha_i(M_1(t), \ldots, M_n(t))$. Hence, $\langle M_i(t)\rangle$ is a solution of the system of n difference equations $\langle D_t(M_i(t)) = \alpha_i(M_1(t), \ldots, M_n(t))\rangle$. Conversely, suppose $\langle M_i(t)\rangle$ is a solution of the system of n difference equations $\langle D_t(M_i(t)) = \alpha_i(M_1(t), \ldots,$

$M_n(t)\,)\rangle$. Then, I must prove that, for some $x_1, \ldots, x_n$, $M_i(t) = M_i[x_1, \ldots, x_n](t)$. Let $\boldsymbol{x}_1, \ldots, \boldsymbol{x}_n$ satisfy $\langle M_1(0) = \boldsymbol{x}_1, \ldots, M_n(0) = \boldsymbol{x}_n \rangle$. I will prove that $M_i(t) = M_i[\boldsymbol{x}_1, \ldots, \boldsymbol{x}_n](t)$. The proof is by induction on t. Suppose $t = 0$. Then, $M_i(0) = \boldsymbol{x}_i = M_i[\boldsymbol{x}_1, \ldots, \boldsymbol{x}_n](0)$. The thesis thus holds for $t = 0$. Suppose the thesis holds for t, that is, $M_i(t) = M_i[\boldsymbol{x}_1, \ldots, \boldsymbol{x}_n](t)$. I first prove that the thesis also holds for $t + 1$. $M_i(t + 1) = D_t(M_i(t)\,) = \alpha_i(M_1(t), \ldots, M_n(t)\,) = \alpha_i(M_1[\boldsymbol{x}_1, \ldots, \boldsymbol{x}_n](t), \ldots, M_n[\boldsymbol{x}_1, \ldots, \boldsymbol{x}_n](t)\,) = g_i(M_1[\boldsymbol{x}_1, \ldots, \boldsymbol{x}_n](t), \ldots, M_n[\boldsymbol{x}_1, \ldots, \boldsymbol{x}_n](t)\,) = M_i[\boldsymbol{x}_1, \ldots, \boldsymbol{x}_n](t + 1)$. Suppose the thesis holds for $t + 1$, that is, $M_i(t + 1) = M_i[\boldsymbol{x}_1, \ldots, \boldsymbol{x}_n](t + 1)$. I now prove that the thesis also holds for t. $M_i[\boldsymbol{x}_1, \ldots, \boldsymbol{x}_n](t) = f_i(M_1[\boldsymbol{x}_1, \ldots, \boldsymbol{x}_n](t + 1), \ldots, M_n[\boldsymbol{x}_1, \ldots, \boldsymbol{x}_n](t + 1)\,) = f_i(M_1(t + 1), \ldots, M_n(t + 1)\,) = f_i(D_t(M_1(t)\,), \ldots, D_t(M_n(t)\,)\,) = f_i(\alpha_1(M_1(t), \ldots, M_n(t)\,), \ldots, \alpha_n(M_1(t), \ldots, M_n(t)\,)\,) = f_i(g_1(M_1(t), \ldots, M_n(t)\,), \ldots, g_n(M_1(t), \ldots, M_n(t)\,)\,) = M_i(t)$. I have thus shown that the first two conditions of the definition of an implicit specification hold.

Finally, I must prove that $M_i[x_1, \ldots, x_n](t + w) = M_i[M_1[x_1, \ldots, x_n](t), \ldots, M_n[x_1, \ldots, x_n](t)](w)$. The proof is by induction on w. Suppose $w = 0$. Then, $M_i[x_1, \ldots, x_n](t + 0) = M_i[x_1, \ldots, x_n](t) = M_i[M_1[x_1, \ldots, x_n](t), \ldots, M_n[x_1, \ldots, x_n](t)](0)$. The thesis thus holds for $w = 0$. Suppose the thesis holds for w, that is, $M_i[x_1, \ldots, x_n](t + w) = M_i[M_1[x_1, \ldots, x_n](t), \ldots, M_n[x_1, \ldots, x_n](t)](w)$. I first prove that the thesis also holds for $w + 1$. In fact, $M_i[x_1, \ldots, x_n](t + w + 1) = g_i(M_1[x_1, \ldots, x_n](t + w), \ldots, M_n[x_1, \ldots, x_n](t + w)\,) = g_i(M_1[M_1[x_1, \ldots, x_n](t), \ldots, M_n[x_1, \ldots, x_n](t)](w), \ldots, M_n[M_1[x_1, \ldots, x_n](t), \ldots, M_n[x_1, \ldots, x_n](t)](w)\,) = M_i[M_1[x_1, \ldots, x_n](t), \ldots, M_n[x_1, \ldots, x_n](t)](w + 1)$. Suppose the thesis holds for $w + 1$, that is, $M_i[x_1, \ldots, x_n](t + w + 1) = M_i[M_1[x_1, \ldots, x_n](t), \ldots, M_n[x_1, \ldots, x_n](t)](w + 1)$. I now prove that the thesis also holds for w. In fact, $M_i[x_1, \ldots, x_n](t + w) = f_i(M_1[x_1, \ldots, x_n](t + w + 1), \ldots, M_n[x_1, \ldots, x_n](t + w + 1)\,) = f_i(M_1[M_1[x_1, \ldots, x_n](t), \ldots, M_n[x_1, \ldots, x_n](t)](w + 1), \ldots, M_n[M_1[x_1, \ldots, x_n](t), \ldots, M_n[x_1, \ldots, x_n](t)](w + 1)\,) = M_i[M_1[x_1, \ldots, x_n](t), \ldots, M_n[x_1, \ldots, x_n](t)](w)$. Therefore, the system of n difference equations $\langle D_t(M_i(t)\,) = \alpha_i(M_1(t), \ldots, M_n(t)\,)\rangle$ of GL_2 is an implicit specification of $\{g^t\}$.

q.e.d.

Notes

1. I use the terms *observable* and *theoretical* for lack of better terms. It is not my intention to suggest that the division of the K-magnitudes $M_1, \ldots, M_n$ into two groups corresponds to, or can be identified with, the usual

distiction between observable and theoretical magnitudes which still is a controversial issue in the philosophy of science.

2. The parametric time evolution function of magnitude M_i $(1 \leq i \leq n)$ determined by $MDS = \langle T, M_1 \times \ldots \times M_n, \{g^t\}\rangle$ is the parametric function $M_i[x_1, \ldots, x_n](t)$ such that $M_i[x_1, \ldots, x_n](t) =$ the i-th component of $g^t(x_1, \ldots, x_n)$. I then say that $M_i[x_1, \ldots, x_n](t)$ depends on magnitude M_j $(1 \leq j \leq n)$ if and only if there are $x_1, \ldots, x_j, y_j, \ldots, x_n$, and t such that $M_i[x_1, \ldots, x_j, \ldots, x_n](t) \neq M_i[x_1, \ldots, y_j, \ldots, x_n](t)$.

3. It is intended that each mathematical operator have its own syntax. Therefore, in general, we cannot apply a mathematical operator to *arbitrary* individual terms, function terms, or complex terms, but only to those terms which agree with its syntax. For example, if the addition sign + stands for the addition of two real numbers, we cannot apply this mathematical operator to a term that does not stand for a real number.

4. If time is discrete, the difference operator $D_t(\ )$ is defined by $D_t(M_j(t)) = M_j(t + 1)$.

FOUR

Cognitive Systems and the Scientific Explanation of Cognition

1 Introduction

A *cognitive system* is any real system that has some cognitive property. Therefore, cognitive systems are a special type of *K*-systems (see chapter 3, section 3). Note that this definition includes both natural systems such as humans and other animals, and artificial devices such as robots, implementations of AI (artificial intelligence) programs, some implementations of neural networks, etc. Focusing on what all cognitive systems have in common, we can state a very general but nonetheless interesting thesis: *All cognitive systems are dynamical systems*. Section 2 explains what this thesis means and why it is (relatively) uncontroversial. It will become clear that this thesis is a basic methodological assumption that underlies practically all current research in cognitive science.

The goal of section 3 is to contrast two styles of scientific explanation[1] of cognition: computational and dynamical. Computational explanations are characterized by the use of concepts drawn from computation theory, while dynamical explanations employ the conceptual apparatus of dynamical systems theory. Further, I will suggest that all scientific explanations of cognition might end up sharing the same dynamical style, for dynamical systems theory may well turn out to be useful in the study of all types of models currently employed in cognitive science. In particular, a dynamical viewpoint might even benefit those scientific explanations of cognition which are based on symbolic models. Computational explanations of cognition, by contrast, can only be based on symbolic models or, more generally, on any other type of computational model. In particular, those scientific explanations of cognition which are based on an important class of connectionist models cannot be computational, for this class of models falls beyond the scope of computation theory. Arguing for this negative conclusion requires the formal explication of the concept of a computational system that I gave in chapter 1 (see definition 3).

Finally, section 4 explores the possibility that scientific explanations of cognition might be based on *Galilean models* of cognitive systems (see chapter 3, section 5). Most cognitive scientists have not yet considered this possibility. The goals of this section are to contrast this proposal with the current modeling practice in cognitive science, to make clear its potential benefits, and to indicate possible ways to implement it.

2 Cognitive systems as dynamical systems

This section proposes a methodological interpretation of the thesis that *all cognitive systems are dynamical systems*, and then provides an argument which in fact shows that this thesis underlies all current research on cognition. Before doing this, however, we must recall the distinction between mathematical and real dynamical systems made in chapter 3 (see section 2). A real dynamical system is any real system that changes over time. A mathematical dynamical system, on the other hand, is an abstract mathematical structure that can be used to describe the change of the real system as an evolution through a series of states.

2.1 All cognitive systems are dynamical systems: the meaning

Let us now see what the distinction between real and mathematical dynamical systems has to do with the interpretation of the thesis that all cognitive systems are dynamical systems. First, if we interpret "dynamical system" as *real* dynamical system, the thesis turns out to be trivial. A real dynamical system is any real system that changes over time. But, since any real system can be said to change in time (in some respect), *any* real system is a real dynamical system. Furthermore, a cognitive system is a real system of a special natural kind, that is, a real system which has some cognitive property. It thus trivially follows that any cognitive system is a real dynamical system. Second, if we instead interpret "dynamical system" as *mathematical* dynamical system, the thesis affirms an absurdity, for a cognitive system, which is a *real* system, is said to be identical to a mathematical dynamical system, which, by definition, is an *abstract* mathematical structure.

It thus seems that we face here a serious difficulty: Depending on how we interpret the term *dynamical system*, the thesis that all cognitive systems are dynamical systems turns out to be either trivial or absurd. However, this is a false dilemma, for this thesis is better interpreted in a third way, which provides a definite and nontrivial meaning. When we say that a certain object is a *cognitive* system, we describe this object at a specific level, that is, the level of its cognitive properties. And when we further say that this object is a *dynamical* system, we are making a methodological claim as to how its cognitive properties can be explained. This claim is that a cognitive property of a cognitive system can be explained by studying a mathematical dynamical system that correctly describes some cognitive aspect of the cognitive system. According to this methodological interpretation, then, a cognitive system is a dynamical system if and only if its cognitive properties can be explained by studying *mathematical* dynamical systems *instantiated* by it, that is, by studying dynamical *models* of the cognitive system (see chapter 3, section 3).

Interpreted this way, the thesis that all cognitive systems are dynamical systems means, first, that any cognitive system is a *real* dynamical system and, second, that this system instantiates *mathematical* dynamical systems whose study allows us to explain the *cognitive* properties of the real system.

We have seen that the first clause of this thesis is trivial. However, the second clause gives us an interesting methodological indication: If we want to explain some *cognitive* property of a cognitive system, then we may study an appropriate mathematical dynamical system instantiated by it, that is, a *specific mathematical structure* that correctly describes some cognitive aspect of the cognitive system.

2.2 All cognitive systems are dynamical systems: the argument

In the previous section, I proposed a methodological reading of the thesis that all cognitive systems are dynamical systems. According to this interpretation, the thesis means that *the cognitive properties of an arbitrary cognitive system can be explained by studying mathematical dynamical systems instantiated by it*. How might one argue for this thesis?

First we need a crucial premise concerning the models currently employed in cognitive science (see figure 4-1). These models can be classified into three different types: symbolic processors, neural networks, and other continuous systems specified by differential or difference equations.[2] Each of these three types corresponds to a different approach to cognition. The *symbolic* or classic approach (Newell and Simon 1972; Newell 1980; Pylyshyn 1984; Johnson-Laird 1988) employs symbolic processors as models. The *connectionist* approach (Rumelhart and McClelland eds. 1986) employs neural networks; and models of the third type are typically proposed by non-connectionist researchers who nevertheless believe that cognition should be studied by means of dynamical methods and concepts. Nonconnectionist researchers favoring a dynamical perspective are active in many fields; for examples, see Port and van Gelder (1995).

Now, the crucial premise is that all systems that belong to any of these three types are mathematical dynamical systems. That a system specified by differential or difference equations is a mathematical

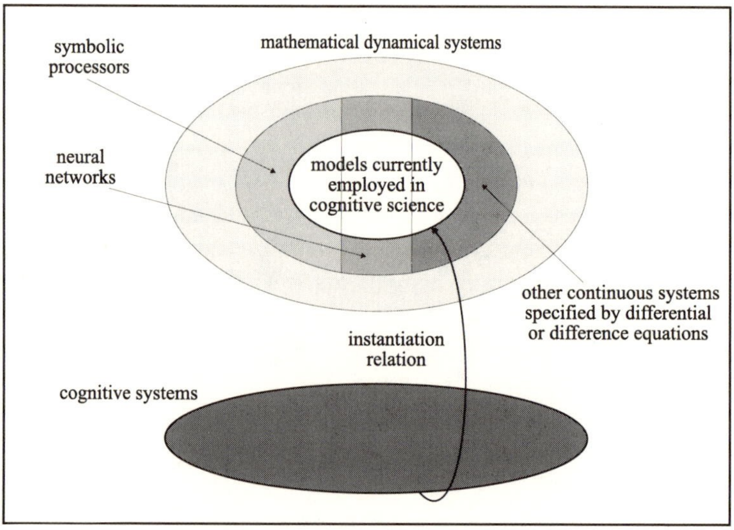

FIGURE 4-1 Types of models currently employed in cognitive science.

dynamical system is obvious, for this concept is expressly designed to describe this class of systems in abstract terms. That a neural network is a mathematical dynamical system is also not difficult to show. A complete state of the system can in fact be identified with the activation levels of all the units in the network; the set of state transitions, on the other hand, is determined by the differential (or difference) equations that specify how each unit is updated. To show that all symbolic processors are mathematical dynamical systems is a bit more complicated. The logical strategy I prefer first considers a special class of symbolic processors (such as Turing machines, monogenic production systems, etc.) and then shows that all systems of this special type are mathematical dynamical systems. Given the strong similarities between different types of symbolic processors, it is then not difficult to see how the argument given for one type could be modified to fit any other type. Here, I limit myself to show that an arbitrary Turing machine is in fact a mathematical dynamical system (see also the analogous argument given in chapter 1, example 3).

A Turing machine is an ideal mechanism that evolves in discrete time steps. This mechanism is usually pictured as having three parts: First, a *tape* divided into a countably infinite number of adjacent squares; each square contains exactly one symbol taken from a finite alphabet[3] $\{a_j\}$. Second, a *head* which is located on a square of the tape and can perform three different operations: Write a symbol on that square, move to the adjacent square to the right, or move to the adjacent square to the left. Third, a *control unit* which, at any time step, is in exactly one of a finite number of internal states $\{q_i\}$. The behavior of the machine is specified by a *set of instructions*, which are conditionals of the form: If the internal state is q_i, and the symbol on the square where the head is located is a_j, write symbol a_k (move one square to the right, move one square to the left) and change internal state to q_l. Each instruction can thus be written as a *quadruple* of one of the three types: $q_i a_j a_k q_l$, $q_i a_j R q_l$, $q_i a_j L q_l$, where R and L stand, respectively, for "move to the right" and "move to the left." The only requirement that the set of quadruples must satisfy is that it be *consistent*, in the sense that this set cannot contain any two conflicting instructions, that is, two different quadruples that begin with the same ⟨*state*, *symbol*⟩ pair.

Given this standard description of an arbitrary Turing machine, it is now not difficult to see that this ideal mechanism can in fact be identified with a *mathematical dynamical system* $\langle T, M, \{g^t\}\rangle$. Since a Turing machine evolves in discrete time steps, we may take the time set T to be the set of the nonnegative integers. Since the future behavior of the machine is determined when the content of the tape, the position of the head, and the internal state are fixed, we may take the state space M to be the set of all triples ⟨*tape content, head position, internal state*⟩. And, finally, the set of state transitions $\{g^t\}$ is determined by the set of quadruples of the machine. To see this point, first note that the set of quadruples tells us how the *complete state* of the machine changes after *one* time step. That is, the set of quadruples defines the state transition g^1. We then obtain any other state transition g^t $(t > 1)$ by iterating g^1 t times, and we simply take the state transition g^0 to be the identity function on M. We may thus conclude that any Turing machine is in fact a mathematical dynamical system $\langle T, M, \{g^t\}\rangle$ with discrete time, that is, a *cascade* (see chapter 1, section 2). A similar argument can be given for any other type of symbolic processor that we may consider, so that we can also conclude that *any* symbolic processor is a mathematical dynamical system.

Having thus established that symbolic processors, neural networks, and continuous systems specified by differential (or difference) equations are three different types of mathematical dynamical systems, we can finally provide an argument for the thesis that all cognitive systems are dynamical systems.

Typical research in cognitive science attempts to produce explanations of the cognitive properties that belong to some cognitive system, and these explanations are usually obtained by studying models that reproduce, as accurately as possible, some cognitive aspects of the cognitive system. These models can be of three types: symbolic processors, neural networks, or continuous systems specified by differential (or difference) equations. Any system of these three types is a mathematical dynamical system. Therefore, the explanations of the cognitive properties of the cognitive system are typically obtained by studying mathematical dynamical systems instantiated by it. But, according to the interpretation proposed above (see section 2.1), this precisely means that the cognitive system whose cognitive properties are explained by typical research in cognitive science is a dynamical system.

The argument I have just given shows only that any cognitive system which has already been object of typical research in cognitive science is a dynamical system. However, the conclusion of this argument also supports the unrestricted version of the thesis. For, unless the cognitive systems that have been considered so far are not representative of all cognitive systems, we may also reasonably conclude that *all* cognitive systems are dynamical systems.

3 Two conceptual repertoires for the explanation of cognition: computation theory and dynamical systems theory

In section 2 I first proposed a methodological reading of the thesis that all cognitive systems are dynamical systems, and then gave an argument to support it. According to the proposed interpretation, this thesis means that the cognitive properties of an arbitrary cognitive system can be explained by studying mathematical dynamical systems instantiated by it. If the explanations of the cognitive properties of a cognitive system can be obtained by studying mathematical dynamical systems instantiated by it (i.e., models of the real system), then it is important to pay attention to the type of theoretical framework we use when we carry out this study, for the style of the explanations we construct in general depends on the type of theoretical framework we use in the study of the models. Let me make this point clearer by means of two examples.

According to the symbolic approach, cognition essentially is a matter of the computations that a system performs in certain situations. But the very idea of a computation belongs to a specific theoretical framework, *computation theory*, which is thus presupposed by the explanatory style of this approach. In the last few years, however, both connectionists (e.g., Smolensky 1988) and dynamicists (e.g., Skarda and Freeman 1987; Busemeyer and Townsend 1993) have been developing a new style of explanation that represents a clear alternative to the computational one. Tim van Gelder (1991, 1992) has called explanations of this type *dynamical explanations*. One of the key ideas on which this style of explanation is based is that to understand cognition we must first understand the *state space evolution* of a certain system. The point I wish to stress here is that the concept of a state space evolution (as well as many other concepts employed in dynamical explanations) belongs to *dynamical systems theory*, which is thus the theoretical framework presupposed by this new explanatory style.

Let me now draw a broad picture of the state of the current research in cognitive science. If we look at the *models* employed, that is, at the mathematical dynamical systems actually used in the study of cognition, we can distinguish three different approaches: (1) the symbolic (or classic) approach, which employs symbolic processors; (2) the connectionist approach, which employs neural networks; and (3) the dynamicists' approach, whose models are neither symbolic nor connectionist, but are nonetheless continuous systems specified by differential (or difference) equations. If, instead, we look at the *explanatory styles*, they can be sorted roughly into (at least) two different types of explanation: computational and dynamical. These two explanatory styles are characterized by the use of two different sets of concepts, which respectively come from computation theory and dynamical systems theory. More precisely, computational explanations are obtained by studying symbolic models by means of concepts drawn from computation theory, while dynamical explanations are obtained by studying neural networks or models of the third type by means of concepts drawn from dynamical systems theory.

But then, if this is the current situation, two questions arise:

1. Why is it that dynamical explanations are exclusively based on neural networks or models of the third type? Or, to put it in a different way, why not use dynamical systems theory to study symbolic models too, so that, independently of the type of model employed, all scientific explanations of cognition might end up sharing the same dynamical style?
2. Is it possible to obtain an analogous conclusion for computation theory instead? That is, why not study neural networks and models of the third type by means of concepts drawn from computation theory, thus extending the scope of the computational style of explanation?

3.1 Dynamical systems theory and the explanation of cognition based on symbolic models

With regard to the first question, it is clear that symbolic models can be studied from a dynamical point of view, for these models are a special type of mathematical dynamical systems, and the most basic concepts of dynamical systems theory apply to *any* type of mathematical dynamical system. However, there is an important point to keep in mind: Only a limited part of the conceptual apparatus of dynamical systems theory applies to symbolic processors. For example, we can think of the *state space* of the processor, and of its *time evolution* as a motion along an *orbit* in this space. We may also classify different types of orbits: periodic, aperiodic, and eventually periodic. Furthermore, since most symbolic processors have merging orbits, the notions of *attractor* and *basin of attraction* also make clear sense,[4] but not much more. To mention just one example, the whole theory of *chaos* does not seem to apply, in its present form, to symbolic processors. The basic reason is that the usual definitions of chaos presuppose (at least) a topological or a metrical structure on the state space of the system. The state space of a symbolic processor, however, typically lacks a natural topology or metric.

Therefore, given that only the most basic part of dynamical systems theory applies to symbolic processors, the real question seems to be: If we study symbolic models of a cognitive system by means of this restricted dynamical apparatus, is this sufficient to explain the cognitive properties of the system? Or, instead, is a computational perspective the only way to explain these properties?

At present there is no definite answer to this question. However, I would like to suggest that, even when symbolic models are concerned, a dynamical viewpoint might turn out to be extremely useful for a deeper explanation of cognition. This conjecture is supported by the fact that some problems which are usually treated within the conceptual framework of computation theory can be better solved by applying dynamical concepts (see example 1).

EXAMPLE 1 (applying dynamical systems theory to computational systems)

It is well known that the *halting problem* for the class of *all* Turing machines is undecidable. More precisely, given an arbitrary Turing machine, there is no mechanical procedure to decide whether that machine will stop when started on an arbitrary input. However, it is obvious that the halting problem for some *specific* machine is instead decidable. For example, the machine specified by $\{q_0 00 q_0,\ q_0 11 q_0\}$ immediately stops on any input. The problem which thus arises is to find nontrivial *classes* of Turing machines for which the halting problem is decidable. The interesting result is that, by using dynamical concepts, it is possible to find one of such classes.

First, we need to think of the halting condition of a Turing machine in dynamical terms. When a Turing machine stops, its tape content, head position, and internal state no longer change. Dynamically, this means that the Turing machine enters a cycle of period one in state space. More precisely, there are two possibilities. Either the Turing machine immediately enters the cycle, or it gets to it after one or more steps. In the second case, we say that the Turing machine has an *eventually periodic orbit.*

Second, we need the concept of a *logically reversible system* (see chapter 1, section 5). Intuitively, a mathematical dynamical system $\langle T, M, \{g^t\}\rangle$ is logically reversible if, given its state x at an arbitrary time t, we can tell the state of the system at any time $w \leq t$. This is formally expressed by the requirement that *any* state transition g^t be injective, that is, for any two different states x and y, $g^t(x) \neq g^t(y)$.

Third, we must recall a basic theorem of dynamical systems theory: Any system $\langle T, M, \{g^t\}\rangle$ with eventually periodic orbits has at least one state transition g^t which is not injective. In other words, a system with eventually periodic orbits is logically irreversible (for a proof, see chapter 1, lemma 6.1).

Let us now consider the class of all logically reversible Turing machines. It is then easy to see that the halting problem for this class of machines is decidable. In fact, by the previous theorem, no such machine has eventually periodic orbits. But then, given *any input*, a logically reversible Turing machine either halts immediately or never halts. Therefore, to decide the halting problem for a logically reversible Turing machine, we may just check whether the machine halts on the first step.

The interest of example 1 is twofold. First, this result gives us a better understanding of the halting problem: We now know that the undecidability of the halting problem is limited to *logically irreversible* Turing machines. In other words, we have discovered an intriguing connection between one of the classic negative results of computation theory and the dynamical concept of logical irreversibility. Second, this result is also interesting because it shows that dynamical systems theory can improve the solution of problems which are usually treated by means of the conceptual apparatus of computation theory. Since the explanation of cognition based on symbolic models is one of these problems, this result suggests that a dynamical viewpoint might turn out to be useful in this case too.

3.2 Computation theory and the explanation of cognition based on neural networks or other continuous dynamical models

Thus far, I have argued that a dynamical approach to the study of symbolic models of cognitive systems is possible, and that it might be useful to better explain the cognitive properties of these systems. If this conjecture turned out to be true, then all scientific explanations of cognition might end up sharing the same dynamical style, independent of the type of model employed.

In this section, I will discuss the analogous question that concerns the computational style of explanation: Is it possible to study neural networks, and other continuous models specified by differential or difference equations, by means of the conceptual apparatus of computation theory, so that computational explanations of cognition might no longer be exclusively based on symbolic models?

Computation theory studies a family of abstract mechanisms which are typically used to compute or recognize numeric functions, sets of numbers, or numbers. These devices can be divided into two broad categories: (1) automata or machines (e.g., Turing machines, register machines, cellular automata, etc.), and (2) systems of rules for symbol manipulation (e.g., monogenic production systems, monogenic Post canonical systems, tag systems, etc.). I call any device studied by computation theory a *computational system* (see chapter 1, section 1). The problem we are concerned with, then, reduces to the following question: Are neural networks and continuous systems specified by differential (or difference) equations computational systems? If they are, we might be able to extend the computational style of explanation to connectionist models and models of the third type. If they are not, however, this extension is impossible, for these two types of models fall beyond the scope of computation theory.

The strategy I will use to answer this question consists of two steps. First, I will recall the *explication* of the concept of a computational system that I gave in chapter 1 (see definition 3). Second, I will deduce from this formal definition two sufficient conditions for a system not to be computational, and I will then argue that all continuous systems specified by differential (or difference) equations and an important class of neural networks satisfy at least one of these conditions. I will thus conclude that, whenever models of the third type or connectionist models that belong to this class are employed, a computational explanation of cognition based on these models is impossible.

3.2.1 A formal definition of a computational system

In chapter 1, in order to formulate a formal definition of a computational system, I first considered the mechanisms studied by computation theory, and I then asked (1) what type of system they belong to, and (2) what specific feature distinguishes these mechanisms from other systems of the same type.

As mentioned, computation theory studies many different kinds of abstract systems. A basic property that is shared by all these mechanisms is that they are mathematical dynamical systems with discrete time, that is, *cascades* (see chapter 1, section 2). I have already shown that this is true of Turing machines (see section 2.4), and it is not difficult to give a similar argument for any other type of mechanism which has been actually studied by computation theory. Therefore, on the basis of this evidence, we may reasonably conclude that all computational systems are cascades.

However, computation theory does not study all cascades. The specific feature that distinguishes computational systems from other mathematical dynamical systems with discrete time is that a computational system can always be described in an effective way. Intuitively, this means that the constitution and operations of the system are purely mechanical or that the system can always be identified with an idealized machine. However, since we want to arrive at a formal definition of a computational system, we cannot limit ourselves to this intuitive characterization. Rather, we must try to express it more precisely.

Since I have informally characterized a computational system as a cascade that can be effectively described, let us ask first what a *description* of a cascade is. If we take a structuralist viewpoint, this question has a precise answer. A description (or a representation) of a cascade consists of a second cascade isomorphic to it where, by definition, a cascade $MDS_1 = \langle T, M_1, \{h^t\}\rangle$ is isomorphic to a given cascade $MDS = \langle T, M, \{g^t\}\rangle$ if and only if there is a bijection $f: M \rightarrow M_1$ such that, for any $t \in T$ and any $x \in M$, $f(g^t(x)) = h^t(f(x))$.

Second, let us ask what an *effective* description of a cascade is. Since I have identified a description of a cascade $MDS = \langle T, M, \{g^t\}\rangle$ with a second cascade $MDS_1 = \langle T, M_1, \{h^t\}\rangle$ isomorphic to MDS, an effective description of MDS will be an *effective cascade* MDS_1 isomorphic to MDS. The problem thus reduces to an analysis of the concept of an effective cascade. Now, it is natural to analyze this concept in terms of two conditions: (1) there is an effective procedure for recognizing the states of the system or, in other words, the state space M_1 is a *decidable* set; and (2) each state transition function h^t is effective or *computable*. These two conditions can be made precise in several ways which turn out to be equivalent. The one I prefer is by means of the concept of Turing computability.[5] If we choose this approach, we will then require that an effective cascade satisfy these conditions: (1) the state space M_1 is a subset of the set $P(A)$ of all finite strings built out of some finite alphabet A, and there is a Turing machine that decides whether an arbitrary finite string is member of M_1; and (2) for any state transition function h^t, there is a Turing machine that computes h^t.

We are now in a position to formally define a computational system. This definition expresses in a precise way the informal characterization of a computational system as a cascade that can be effectively described.

DEFINITION *(computational system)*
MDS *is a computational system if and only if* MDS = ⟨T, M, $\{g^t\}$⟩ *is a cascade, and there is a second cascade* MDS_1 = ⟨T, M_1, $\{h^t\}$⟩ *such that* MDS_1 *is isomorphic to* MDS *and*

1. *If* P(A) *is the set of all finite strings built out of some finite alphabet* A, $M_1 \subseteq P(A)$ *and there is a Turing machine that decides whether an arbitrary finite string is member of* M_1*;*
2. *for any* $t \in T$*, there is a Turing machine that computes* h^t.

This definition is formally correct.[6] However, the question remains whether it is also *materially* adequate. This question will have a positive answer if we can argue that the systems specified by the definition are exactly the systems studied by computation theory. First, we can give an argument *a priori*. If a cascade satisfies this definition, then computation theory certainly applies to it, for it is always possible to find an effective description of that cascade. Conversely, if a cascade does not satisfy this definition, then there is no effective description of that cascade, so that computation theory cannot apply to it. Second, we can also give an argument *a posteriori*. In fact, it is tedious but not difficult to show that all systems that actually have been studied by computation theory (Turing machines, register machines, monogenic production systems, cellular automata, etc.) satisfy the definition.[7]

3.2.2 Two sufficient conditions for a system not to be computational

The definition allows us to deduce two sufficient conditions for a mathematical dynamical system not to be computational. Namely, a mathematical dynamical system $MDS = \langle T, M, \{g^t\}\rangle$ is not computational if it is continuous in either time or state space or, more precisely, if either (1) its time set T is the set of the (nonnegative) real numbers, or (2) its state space M is not denumerable.[8]

An immediate consequence of condition (*2*) is that *any finite neural network whose units have continuous activation levels is not a computational system*. A complete state of any such network can always be identified with a finite sequence of real numbers and, since each unit has a continuous range of possible activation levels, the set of all possible complete states of this network is not denumerable. Therefore, by condition (*2*), any finite network with continuous activation levels is not a computational system.[9] We can reach the same conclusion if we consider a continuous system specified by differential (or difference) equations. Since all these systems are continuous (in time or state space), none of them is computational (see figure 4-2).

Now, we can finally go back to the question posed at the beginning of section 3.2: Is it possible to produce computational explanations of cognition on the basis of connectionist models or other continuous models specified by differential or difference equations? For this to be possible, computation theory must apply to these two types of models. However, we have just seen that all neural networks with continuous activation levels and all continuous systems specified by differential (or difference) equations are not computational systems. Therefore, computation theory does not apply to them. We must then conclude that, whenever connectionist models with continuous activation levels or other continuous models specified by differential or difference equations are employed, a computational explanation of cognition based on these models is impossible.

A point of clarification is essential here. Let us approach it by imagining someone objecting to this claim in the following way. The operation of a standard digital computer is based on the storage and interaction of electrical currents. These electrical activities are continuous, and their behavior is specified by differential equations. Yet,

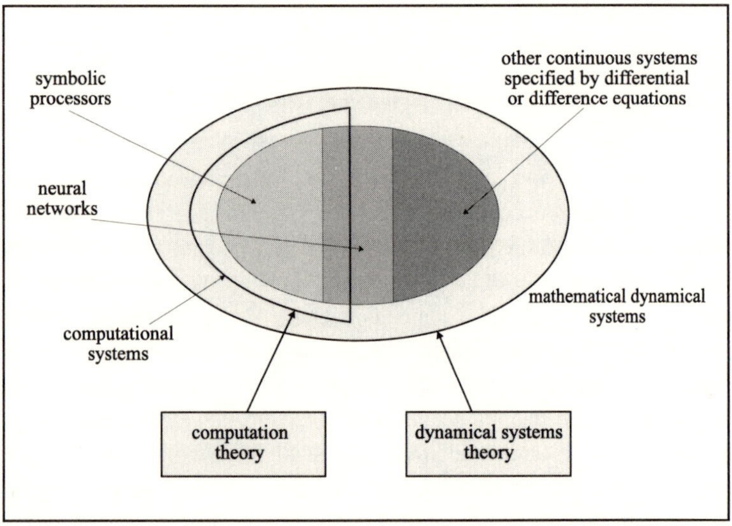

FIGURE 4-2 The domains of dynamical systems theory and computation theory.

this is a paradigm example of a system whose relevant properties are explained by using the tools and concepts of computation theory. Therefore, it is not impossible to produce computational explanations based on continuous systems specified by differential equations.

This objection is confused because it fails to keep clear the distinction between a *K*-system and the abstract mathematical structures that turn out to be models of it (see chapter 3, section 3). First, note that a digital computer is a real system that belongs to at least two different natural kinds: On the one hand, a digital computer is an *information processing* system and, on the other hand, it is also a *physical* system. Therefore, we can have two kinds of models of a digital computer: one which is a model of the *information processing system*, and another which is a model of the *physical system*. The first kind of model is a symbolic processor, so it is a special type of computational system. By contrast, the second kind of model is a continuous mathematical dynamical system, and thus it is not a computational system. The claim for which I have argued in this section is that it is impossible to base computational explanations on continuous dynamical models (though it is possible to base dynamical explanations on symbolic models). That is, it is a claim about the relation between conceptual/explanatory frameworks and mathematical models, not between conceptual/explanatory frameworks and *K*-systems. As a matter of empirical fact, it is true that there are many kinds of *K*-systems for whose *K*-properties there are no really good computational explanations (e.g., physical systems), and it may turn out that cognitive systems belong to this class. However, this can be established only by detailed empirical investigation, not by abstract argument.

4 Cognitive systems and their models

Thus far I have identified a *model* of a cognitive system with a mathematical dynamical system instantiated by it where, according to the discussion of chapter 3 (see section 3), the instantiation relation holds if and only if the mathematical dynamical system *correctly describes some cognitive aspect* of the cognitive system. However, since this clause can be interpreted in different ways, there are different types of instantiation relation. Therefore, we can distinguish different types of models of a cognitive system by looking at the specific type of instantiation relation that holds between the model and the cognitive system. More precisely, the type of instantiation relation depends on three elements: (1) what cognitive aspect of the cognitive system the mathematical dynamical system intends to describe; (2) what counts as a description of this aspect, and (3) in what sense this description is correct.

4.1 Simulation models of cognitive systems

The three types of models currently employed in cognitive science (symbolic processors, neural networks, and other continuous systems specified by differential or difference equations) are standardly characterized by a special type of instantiation relation, which is based on the fact that these models allow us to *simulate* certain aspects of the behavior of cognitive systems. For this reason, I call a model with this type of instantiation relation a *simulation model* of a cognitive system. The three elements of the instantiation relation proper of this type of model are as follows.

First, the cognitive aspect of a cognitive system that a simulation model intends to describe is a *cognitive process* involved in the completion of a given task. For example, if the cognitive system is a subject who has been asked to solve a simple logic problem, a simulation model will attempt to describe the subject's problem-solving process (see Newell and Simon 1972). If, instead, the cognitive system is a young child who is learning the past tense of English verbs, a simulation model will attempt to describe the child's past tense acquisition process (see Rumelhart and McClelland 1986).

Second, a simulation model allows us to produce a simulation of the cognitive process it intends to describe, and it is this *simulating process* that counts as a description of the real cognitive process. In general, a simulation of a cognitive process is obtained by first implementing the model (usually, by means of a computer program), and by then assigning this implemented version of the model a task similar to the one assigned to the cognitive system. In dealing with this task, the implemented model goes through a certain process: the simulating process that counts as a description of the real cognitive process.

Third, the description of a cognitive process provided by a simulation model is *correct* in the sense that we are able to empirically establish that the simulating process is similar to the cognitive process in some relevant respect. Which respects are to be considered relevant, and which empirical methods we may employ to establish the similarity, is usually clear in each specific case.

Example 2 (an example of a simulation model)

A classic example of a simulation model is Rumelhart and McClelland's (1986) Past Tense Acquisition model (PTA). This neural network intends to describe the process of past tense acquisition in a young child learning English verbs from everyday conversation.

Rumelhart and McClelland implemented PTA by means of a certain computer program, and they then assigned this implemented version of the model a task which they claim to be similar to the child's task. PTA's task is intended "to capture approximately the experience with past tenses of a young child picking up English from everyday conversation. Our conception of the nature of this experience is simply that the child learns first about the present and past tenses of the highest frequency verbs; later on, learning occurs for a much larger ensemble of verbs, including a much larger proportion of regular forms" (Rumelhart and McClelland 1986, 240–41). According to this conception of the child's experience, Rumelhart and McClelland divided PTA's task into two parts: first, learning just ten high-frequency verbs, most of which were irregular; and second, learning a greatly expanded repertoire of verbs, most of which were regular.

In dealing with this task, PTA went through a certain acquisition process. This is, in fact, the *simulating process* that counts as a description of the child's past tense acquisition process. According to Rumelhart and McClelland, this description is correct, in the sense that the data they obtained from the simulation, together with other data from previous psychological studies, would show that the simulating process is similar to the real acquisition process under many relevant respects. Such similarities include, for example, the U-shaped learning curve for high-frequency irregular verbs, and the difference in performance on different types of irregular and regular verbs.

4.2 Galilean models of cognitive systems

It is now interesting to ask whether, besides the relation of instantiation proper of simulation models, there are other ways in which a cognitive system can instantiate a mathematical dynamical system. To answer this question, we must first recall the concept of a *K*-magnitude of a *K*-system discussed in chapter 3 (see section 5). Given a natural kind *K* and a *K*-system *KRS*, a *K-magnitude of KRS* is a *K*-property that belongs to *KRS* (or, if *KRS* has more than one part, to one of its parts) and that, at different times, may assume different values.

Let us then consider an arbitrary *cognitive* system *CRS* and all its *cognitive* magnitudes. According to the discussion of chapter 3, section 5, a *possible Galilean model of CRS* is a mathematical dynamical system generated by a choice of time evolution functions of a finite number of cognitive magnitudes of *CRS*, and a *Galilean model of CRS* is a possible Galilean model of *CRS* which is instantiated by it. The three elements of the instantiation relation proper of this type of model are the following. First, the cognitive aspect of *CRS* that a Galilean model intends to describe is the simultaneous variation in time of those cognitive magnitudes of *CRS* whose sets of values are the components of the state space of the model. Second, the description of this variation is provided by the set of state transitions of the model. And, third, this description is correct in the sense that all the measurements of the observable magnitudes of the model turn out to be consistent with the values we deduce from the conjunction of (1) a specification of the set of state transitions, and (2) a specification of some initial state of the model (see chapter 3, section 6). If we now compare these three elements of the instantiation relation proper of Galilean models with those of the instantiation relation proper of simulation models, we must conclude that the two relations are quite different.

Let us then ask two further questions: Are the models employed so far in cognitive science Galilean models of cognitive systems? If they are not, what would we gain if we instead based the explanation of cognition on Galilean models?

As regards the first question, it is clear that most models employed so far in cognitive science are not Galilean models of cognitive systems. A Galilean model of a cognitive system is a mathematical dynamical system generated by a choice of time evolution functions of a finite number of cognitive magnitudes of the system. Therefore, a Galilean model of a cognitive system has a very strong interpretation, for each component of the state space of the model corresponds to a *cognitive magnitude* of the *cognitive system*. The models currently employed in cognitive science, however, lack this strong interpretation, for their components do not correspond directly to cognitive magnitudes of the cognitive system itself. The correspondence between these models and the cognitive system is at best indirect, by means of a simulation (see figure 4-3).

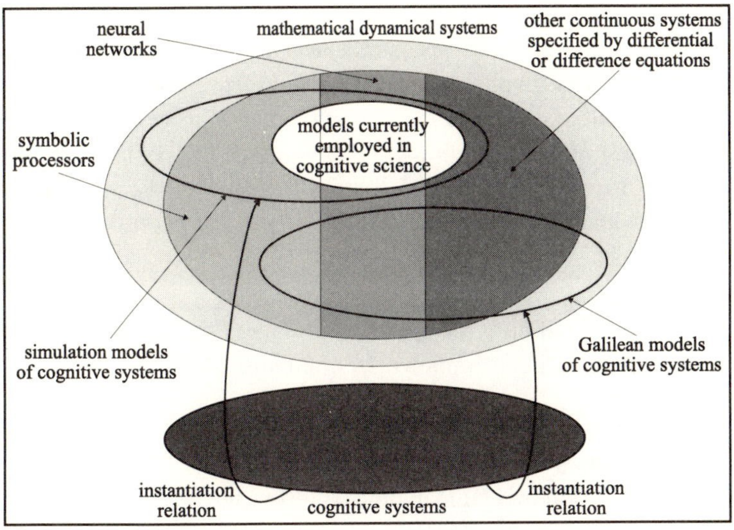

FIGURE 4-3 Simulation and Galilean models of cognitive systems.

Since most models currently employed in cognitive science are not Galilean models of cognitive systems, it is important to understand what we would gain if we changed this practice, and instead based the explanation of cognition on Galilean models. We have just seen that the first gain would be a dramatic increase in the strength of the interpretation that links our models to the cognitive systems they describe.

Besides this first gain, the use of Galilean models of cognitive systems may allow us to improve our scientific explanations of cognition. To see this point, we must briefly reconsider how a scientific explanation of cognition is usually obtained. First, we specify a model that allows us to simulate a cognitive process of a cognitive system and, second, we study this simulation model in order to explain certain cognitive properties of the cognitive system. Now, the main problem with this type of explanation is that it is based on a model that has a weak interpretation. In particular, we have seen that the components of the state space of the simulation model do not correspond directly to cognitive magnitudes of the cognitive system. Further, since the correspondence between the simulation model and the cognitive system is at best indirect, by means of the simulation, nothing ensures that *each* component of the state space of the model corresponds to a real element of the cognitive system. In other words, some, or even all, the components of the state space of the model may be fictitious. But then, an explanation based on such a model is bound to take into account also those components of the model which may not have any counterpart in the cognitive system. The strong interpretation of a Galilean model, instead, ensures that each component of the state space of the model corresponds to a cognitive magnitude of the cognitive system. Therefore, if an explanation of cognition were based on a Galilean model, it would not take into account any fictitious component.

4.3 A new possibility for cognitive science: *P*-explanatory and correct Galilean frameworks of cognitive systems

The use of Galilean models of cognitive systems may possibly yield at least two important benefits. The goal of actually basing the explanation of cognition on Galilean models is thus one which is worth pursuing. We must now consider how we could proceed to accomplish this goal.

Clearly, this question is not one that can be answered in detail without real research which aims at this goal. The general analysis of a Galilean explanation carried out in chapter 3, however, can give us some useful indications. To obtain a Galilean explanation of a cognitive property of a cognitive system, we must study a Galilean model of the system, which must first be specified or described. Therefore, the problem of costructing a Galilean explanation of a cognitive property of a cognitive system presupposes the problem of specifying a Galilean model of the system. We saw in chapter 3 (see section 6) that this second problem reduces to that of producing a correct Galilean framework of the cognitive system. This correct framework must also be *P*-explanatory, in the sense that it must specify a Galilean model of the cognitive system *CRS* whose study will then allow us to produce an explanation of the particular cognitive property *P* we want to explain (see figure 4-4). Therefore, to achieve our main goal, we must first set the subgoal of constructing a correct Galilean framework of *CRS* which is *P*-explanatory (see chapter 3, section 8).

According to the discussion of chapter 3 (see sections 8 and 9), there are at least two general procedures that allow us to construct a correct Galilean framework of *CRS* that has good a chance of being *P*-explanatory: the inductive and deductive methods. These two methods lead to the construction of two different types of Galilean frameworks, which differ only with respect to the way of specifying the set of state transitions $\{g^t\}$ of a Galilean model of *CRS*. The frameworks produced by the inductive method give an *explicit specifi-*

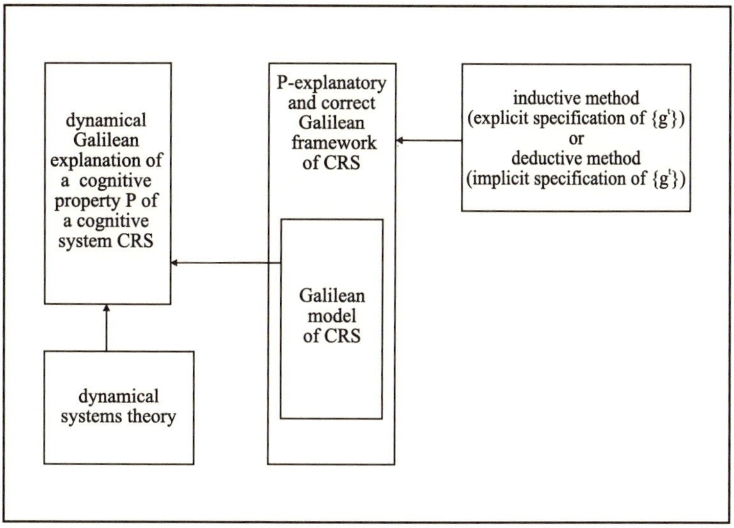

FIGURE 4-4 The Galilean approach to cognitive science.

cation of the set of state transitions $\{g^t\}$, while those produced by the deductive method give an *implicit specification* of $\{g^t\}$ (see chapter 3, section 7).

4.4 The Galilean approach to cognitive science

I began this chapter by making explicit a basic methodological assumption that underlies all current research in cognitive science, namely, that all cognitive systems are dynamical systems. According to this thesis, the cognitive properties of an arbitrary cognitive system can be explained by studying mathematical dynamical systems instantiated by it or, in other words, by studying dynamical *models* of the cognitive system. I then contrasted the computational and the dynamical style of explanation, and I argued that the dynamical style does not depend on the type of dynamical model employed, while the computational style can only be based on computational models. I also suggested that all scientific explanations of cognition might end up sharing the same dynamical style, for dynamical systems theory may well turn out to be useful in the study of *any* type of dynamical model.

Finally, I explored the possibility of basing the explanation of cognition on a type of dynamical model that cognitive scientists generally have not considered yet. This type of model is the class of all the

Galilean models of cognitive systems. The methodological thesis underlying this proposal is that the *cognitive properties of an arbitrary cognitive system can be better explained by studying Galilean models of the cognitive system.* This thesis can thus be interpreted as the basic methodological assumption of a possible research program in cognitive science. Whether we will in fact be able to produce explanations of cognition based on Galilean models is a question that can only be answered by actually starting concrete research that explicitly aims at this goal. In this chapter, I have tried to state this goal clearly, to show why we should care to pursue it, and to indicate possible ways to implement it. I don't see any reason why, in principle, this kind of dynamical approach should not turn out to be successful. This, however, does not mean that we will not encounter some serious difficulty along the way. In fact, we can already anticipate some of the problems we will have to solve.

First, we will have to radically change our way of looking at cognition. So far, in order to explain cognition, we have been focusing on the cognitive processes involved in the completion of some task, and we have then tried to produce models that *simulate* these processes. If, instead, the explanation of cognition is to be based on Galilean models of cognitive systems, we should not primarily focus on the processes involved in cognition but, rather, on how the values of the *cognitive magnitudes* of a cognitive system vary in time.

The two main problems we face are that we will have to discover what the cognitive magnitudes are, and we will then have to invent appropriate experimental techniques to measure the values of at least some of these magnitudes. If are able to solve these two basic problems, then the way to the actual production of explanations of cognition based on Galilean models of cognitive systems will be open.

Notes

1. By a scientific explanation of *cognition* I mean a scientific explanation of a *cognitive property* of a *cognitive system.*

2. By a *continuous* system specified by differential or difference equations I mean a mathematical dynamical system whose state space is not denumerable. Recall that a set is denumerable if and only if it can be put in a one-to-one correspondence with (a subset of) the natural numbers.

3. The first symbol of the alphabet a_0 is usually identified with a special symbol, the *blank*, also indicated by *b*. Only a finite number of squares may contain nonblank symbols. All the other squares must contain the blank.

4. If a mathematical dynamical system $MDS = \langle T, M, \{g^t\}\rangle$ is irreversible (see chapter 1, section 5), an *attractor* can be defined as a state x such that (*1*) there are times u and v, and two different states a and b, such that $g^u(a) = x = g^v(b)$ and, for any time w, $g^w(a) \neq b$ and $g^w(b) \neq a$; (2) for any state y, if $x \notin orb(y)$ and $y \notin orb(x)$, then, for any time t, $g^t(y) \notin orb(x)$. The *basin of attraction* of attractor x is the set of all states y such that, for some time t, $g^t(y) = x$ and, for any state $z \neq y$, for any time w, $g^w(z) \neq y$.

5. An equivalent approach is by using the concept of *recursive function*.

6. Also note that the definition I have just given is equivalent to definition 3 of chapter 1. For, since MDS_1 is a cascade, the requirement that *any* state transition function h^t be Turing computable is equivalent to the Turing computability of h^1 (or, if $T = Z$, to the Turing computability of both h^1 and h^{-1}).

7. See chapter 1, examples 5 and 6, where I proved that both Turing machines and cellular automata satisfy the definition. Similar proofs can be given for all other types of computational system.

8. A set is denumerable if and only if it can be put in a one-to-one correspondence with (a subset of) the nonnegative integers. If condition (*1*) is satisfied, then MDS is not a cascade, so that, by the definition, MDS is not a computational system. If condition (*2*) holds, then, since by the definition MDS is isomorphic to MDS_1, M_1 is not denumerable. But then, M_1 cannot be a subset of the set $P(A)$ of all finite strings built out of some finite alphabet A, for any such subset is denumerable. Therefore, condition (*1*) of the definition is not satisfied, and MDS is not a computational system.

Let me also point out that an analogous argument applies to the more general definition of computational system given in chapter 2 (see definition 2). Therefore, a mathematical dynamical system $MDS = \langle T, M, \{g^t\}\rangle$ is not a computational system on *any* pattern field F if either (1) its time set T is the set of the (nonnegative) real numbers, or (2) its state space M is not denumerable.

9. A computational system can of course be used to *approximate* the state transitions of a network of this type. Nevertheless, if the real numbers involved are not computable, we cannot conclude that this approximation can be carried out to an arbitrary degree of precision. This is exactly the same situation that we have when we use computers to approximate the behavior of dynamical models of physical systems. These models are continuous (in both time and state space) so that they can in principle handle infinite amounts of information and, in general, they cannot be described in an effective manner. Computational systems, on the other hand, are limited to a finite amount of information, and they can always be effectively described.

References

Computation theory and dynamical systems theory (chapters 1 and 2)

Arbib, Michael A. 1964. *Brains, machines, and mathematics*. New York: McGraw-Hill.

Arnold, V. I. 1977. *Ordinary differential equations*. Cambridge: The MIT Press.

Barwise, J., H. J. Keisler, and K. Kunen. 1980. *The Kleene symposium*. Amsterdam: North Holland.

Beckman, Frank S. 1980. *Mathematical foundations of programming*. Reading, MA: Addison Wesley.

Bennett, Charles H. 1973. Logical reversibility of computation. *IBM Journal of Research and Development* November: 525–32.

———. 1982. The thermodynamics of computation—a review. *International Journal of Theoretical Physics* 21, 12: 905–40.

Bennett, Charles H., and Rolf Landauer. 1985. The fundamental physical limits of computation. *Scientific American* 253, July: 48–56.

Berlekamp, E. R., J. H. Conway, and P. Y. Guy. 1982. *Winning ways for your mathematical plays*. London: Academic Press.

Blum, Lenore, Mike Shub, and Stephen Smale. 1989. On a theory of computation and complexity over the real numbers: NP-Completeness, recursive functions and universal machines. *Bulletin of the American Mathematical Society* 21, 1: 1–46.

Boolos, George S., and Richard C. Jeffrey. 1980. *Computability and logic*. Cambridge: Cambridge University Press.

Burks, Arthur W. 1970. *Essays on cellular automata*. Urbana: University of Illinois Press.

Davis, Martin. 1958. *Computability and unsolvability*. New York: McGraw-Hill.

———. 1974. *Computability*. New York: Courant Institute of Mathematical Sciences.

Davis, Martin, ed. 1965. *The undecidable*. Hewlett, NY: Raven Press.

Deutsch, D. 1985. Quantum theory, the Church-Turing principle, and the universal quantum computer. *Proceedings of the Royal Society of London* A 400:97–117.

Devaney, R. L. 1989. *An introduction to chaotic dynamical systems*. Menlo Park, CA: Benjamin Cummings.

Dewdney, A. K. 1989. Two-dimensional Turing machines and Tur-mites. *Scientific American* 261, 9:180–83.

Farmer, Doyne, Tommaso Toffoli, and Stephen Wolfram, eds. 1984. *Cellular automata*. Amsterdam: North Holland Physics Publishing.

Francois, Robert. 1986. *Discrete iterations*. Berlin: Springer Verlag.

Friedman, Harvey. 1971. Algorithmic procedures, generalized Turing algorithms, and elementary recursion theory. In *Logic colloqium '69*, 361–89. See Gandy and Yates 1971.

Gandy, R. O. 1980. Church's thesis and principles for mechanisms. In *The Kleene symposium*, 123–48. See Barwise, Keisler, and Kunen 1980.

Gandy, R. O., and C. M. E. Yates, eds. 1971. *Logic colloquium '69*. Amsterdam: North Holland.

Garey, Michael R., and David S. Johnson. 1979. *Computers and intractability*. San Francisco: W. H. Freeman and Co.

Geroch, Robert, and Hartle, James B. 1986. Computability and physical theories. *Foundations of Physics* 16, 6:533–50.

Harrington, L. A., et al., eds. 1985. *Harvey Friedman's research on the foundations of mathematics*. Amsterdam: North Holland.

Herken, Rolf, ed. 1988. *The universal Turing machine: A half century survey*. Oxford: Oxford University Press.

Heyting, A., ed. 1959. *Constructivity in mathematics*. Amsterdam: North Holland.

Hildebrand, Francis B. 1968. *Finite difference equations and simulations*. Englewood Cliffs, NJ: Prentice Hall.

Hirsh, Morris W., and Stephen Smale. 1974. *Differential equations, dynamical systems, and linear algebra*. New York: Academic Press.

Hopcroft, John E., and Jeffrey D. Ullman. 1979. *Introduction to automata theory, languages, and computation*. Reading, MA: Addison Wesley.

Hsu, C. S. 1987. *Cell-to-cell mapping*. New York: Springer Verlag.

Kalmar, Laszlo. 1959. An argument against the plausibility of Church's thesis. In *Constructivity in mathematics*, 72–80. See Heyting 1959.

Kleene, S. C. 1967. Computability. In Sidney Morgenbesser (ed.) *Philosophy of science today*, 36–45. New York: Basic Books.

Koçak, Huseyin. 1986. *Differential and difference equations through computer experiments*. New York: Springer Verlag.

Margolus, Norman. 1984. Physics-like models of computation. In *Cellular automata*, 81–95. See Farmer, Toffoli, and Wolfram 1984.

Martin, Olivier, Andrew M. Odlyzko, Stephen Wolfram. 1984. Algebraic properties of cellular automata. *Communications in Mathematical Physics* 93:210–58.

Mickens, Ronald E. 1987. *Difference equations*. New York: Van Nostrand Reinhold.

Minsky, Marvin. 1967. *Computation: Finite and infinite machines*. Englewood Cliffs, NJ: Prentice Hall.

Péter, Rózsa. 1981. *Recursive functions in computer theory*. Chichister, England: Ellis Horwood.

Pour-El, Marian B., and J. Ian Richards. 1979. A computable ordinary differential equation which possesses no computable solution. *Annals of Mathematical Logic* 17:61–90.

———. 1981. The Wave equation with computable initial data such that its unique solution is not computable. *Advances in Mathematics* 39:215–39.

———. 1982. Non-computability in models of physical phenomena. *International Journal of Theoretical Physics* 21, 6/7:553–55.

———. 1989. *Computability in analysis and physics*. Berlin: Springer Verlag.

Rogers, Hartley Jr. 1987. *Theory of recursive functions and effective computability*. Cambridge: The MIT Press.

Rose, H. E., and John C. Shepherdson, eds. 1975. *Logic colloquium '73*. Amsterdam: North Holland.

Shepherdson, John C. 1975. Computation over abstract structures: serial and parallel procedures and Friedman's effective definitional schemes. In *Logic colloquium '73*, 445–513. See Rose and Shepherdson 1975.

———. 1985. Algorithmic procedures, generalized Turing algorithms, and elementary recursion theory. In *Harvey Friedman's research on the foundations of mathematics*, 285–308. See Harrington et al. 1985.

———. 1988. Mechanisms for computing over abstract structures. In *The universal Turing machine: A half century survey*, 581–601. See Herken 1988.

Smith, Alvy Ray III. 1969. *Cellular automata theory*. Technical report n. 2. Stanford, CA: Stanford University, Digital Systems Laboratory, Stanford Electronics Laboratories.

———. 1971. Simple computation-universal cellular spaces. *Journal of the Association for Computing Machinery* 18, 3:339–53.

Szlensk, Wieslaw. 1984. *An introduction to the theory of smooth dynamical systems*. Chichister, England: John Wiley & Sons.

Turing, Alan M. 1965. On computable numbers, with an application to the Entscheidungsproblem. In *The undecidable*, 115–54. See Davis 1965.

Vichniac, Gerard Y. 1984. Simulating physics with cellular automata. In *Cellular automata*, 96–116. See Farmer, Toffoli, and Wolfram 1984.

Wagner, Klaus, and Gerd Wechsung. 1986. *Computational complexity*. Dordrecht, Netherlands: D. Reidel Publishing.

Wainwright, Robert T. 1974. Life is universal! *Winter Simulation Conference*, January 14–16:449–59.

Wolfram, Stephen. 1983a. Statistical mechanics of cellular automata. *Reviews of Modern Physics* 55, 3:601–44.

———. 1983b. Cellular automata. *Los Alamos Science* 9:2–21.

———. 1984a. Computer software in science and mathematics. *Scientific American* 56:188–203.

Wolfram, Stephen. 1984b. Cellular automata as models of complexity. *Nature* 311:419–24.

———. 1984c. Universality and complexity in cellular automata. In *Cellular automata*, 1–35. See Farmer, Toffoli, and Wolfram 1984.

———. 1984d. Computation theory of cellular automata. *Communications in Mathematical Physics* 96:15–57.

———. 1986. Random sequence generation by cellular automata. *Advances in Applied Mathematics* 7:123–69.

Wolfram, Stephen, ed. 1986. *Theory and applications of cellular automata*. Singapore: World Scientific.

Wright, Robert. 1988. *Three scientists and their gods*. New York: Times Books.

Models, theories, and explanation (chapter 3)

Agassi, Joseph. 1965. The nature of scientific problems and their roots in metaphysics. In *The critical approach to science and philosophy*, 189–211. See Bunge 1965.

Asquith, P. D., and I. Hacking, eds. 1978. *PSA 1978: Proceedings of the 1978 biennial meeting of the philosophy of science association*. East Lansing, MI: Philosophy of Science Association.

Baltzer, Wolfgang, C. Ulises Moulines, and Joseph D. Sneed. 1987. *An architectonic for science: The structuralist program*. Dordrecht, Netherlands: D. Reidel Publishing.

Belnap, Neul D. Jr., and Thomas B. Steel Jr. 1976. *The logic of questions and answers*. New Haven, CT: Yale University Press.

Braithwaite, R. B. 1964. *Scientific explanation: A study of the function of theory, probability and law in science*. Cambridge: Cambridge University Press.

Bromberger, Sylvain. 1966. Why-questions. In *Mind and Cosmos*, 86–111. See Colodny 1966.

Bunge, Mario, ed. 1965. *The critical approach to science and philosophy*. New York: Free Press.

Churchland, Paul M., and Clifford A. Hooker, eds. 1985. *Images of science*. Chicago: The University of Chicago Press.

Colodny, Robert G., ed. 1966. *Mind and Cosmos*. Pittsburgh, PA: Pittsburgh University Press.

———. 1972. *Paradigms and paradoxes: The philosophical challenge of the quantum domain*. Pittsburgh, PA: Pittsburgh University Press.

Dalla Chiara, Maria Luisa, and Giuliano Toraldo di Francia. 1981. *Le teorie fisiche: Un'analisi formale*. Torino, Italy: Boringhieri.

De Mey, Marc. 1982. *The cognitive paradigm*. Dordrecht, Netherlands: D. Reidel Publishing.

Drake, Stillman. 1989. *History of free fall*. Toronto: Wall & Thompson.

Ellis, Brian. 1985. *What science aims to do*. In *Images of Science*, 48–74. See Churchland and Hooker 1985.

Feyerabend, Paul. 1975. *Against method*. London: Verso.

Galilei, Galileo. 1914. *Dialogues concerning two new sciences*. Translated by Henry Crew and Alfonso de Salvio. Reprint. New York: Dover Publications, Inc.

———. 1953. *Dialogue concerning the two chief world systems*. Translated by Stillman Drake. Berkeley: University of California Press.

———. 1957. *Discoveries and Opinions of Galileo*. Translated by Stillman Drake. Garden City, NY: Doubleday & Company.

———. 1979. *Galileo's notes on motion*. Edited by Stillman Drake. Firenze, Italy: Istituto e Museo di Storia della Scienza.

Giere, Ronald N. 1984. *Understanding scientific reasoning*. Second edition. New York: Holt, Rinehart and Winston.

———. 1985. Constructive realism. In *Images of science*, 75–98. See Churchland and Hooker 1985.

———. 1988. *Explaining science: A cognitive approach*. Chicago: The University of Chicago Press.

Giere, Ronald N., and P. D. Asquith, eds. 1980. *PSA 1980: Proceedings of the 1980 biennial meeting of the philosophy of science association*. East Lansing, MI: Philosophy of Science Association.

Giunti, Marco. 1988. Hattiangadi's theory of scientific problems and the structure of standard epistemologies. *The British Journal for the Philosophy of Science* 39:421–39.

Hattiangadi, J. N. 1978. The structure of problems (part I). *Philosophy of the Social Sciences* 8:345–65.

———. 1979. The structure of problems (part II). *Philosophy of the Social Sciences* 9:49–76.

Hempel, Carl G. 1965. *Aspects of scientific explanation and other essays in the philosophy of science*. New York: The Free Press.

Hooker, C. A., A. C. Micholos, and R. S. Cohen, eds. 1976. *PSA 1974: Proceedings of the 1974 biennial meeting of the philosophy of science association*. Dordrecht: Reidel.

Kitcher, Philip, and Wesley C. Salmon, eds. 1989. *Scientific explanation*. Vol. XIII of *Minnesota studies in the philosophy of science*. Minneapolis: University of Minnesota Press.

Koertge, Noretta. 1982. Explaining scientific discovery. In *PSA 1982*, vol. 1, 14–28. See Nickles and Asquith 1982.

Kuhn, Thomas S. 1970. *The structure of scientific revolutions*. Second edition. Chicago: The University of Chicago Press.

Lakatos, Imre. 1970. Falsification and the methodology of scientific research programmes. In *Criticism and the growth of knowledge*. See Lakatos and Musgrave 1970.

———. 1976. *Proofs and refutations*. Cambridge: Cambridge University Press.

Lakatos, Imre, and Musgrave, Alan, eds. 1970. *Criticism and the growth of knowledge*. Cambridge: Cambridge University Press.

Langley, Pat, Herbert A. Simon, Gary L. Bradshaw, and Jan M. Zytkkow. 1987. *Scientific discovery: Computational explorations of the creative process*. Cambridge: The MIT Press.

Laudan, Larry. 1977. *Progress and its problems: Towards a theory of scientific growth*. Berkeley: University of California Press.

Morgenbesser, Sidney, ed. 1967. *Philosophy of science today*. New York: Basic Books.

Nagel, Ernest. 1961. *The structure of science: Problems in the logic of scientific explanation*. New York: Harcourt, Brace & World.

Nickles, Thomas. 1978. Scientific problems and constraints. In *PSA 1978*, vol. 1, 134–48. See Asquith and Hacking 1978.

———. 1980. Scientific problems: Three empiricist models. In *PSA 1980*, vol. 1, 3–19. See Giere and Asquith 1980.

———. 1981. What is a problem that we may solve it? *Synthese* 47:85–118.

Nickles, Thomas, and P. D. Asquith, eds. 1982. *PSA 1982: Proceedings of the 1982 biennial meeting of the philosophy of science association*. East Lansing, MI: Philosophy of Science Association.

Polyia, G. 1945. *How to solve it: A new aspect of mathematical method*. Princeton, NJ: Princeton University Press.

———. 1962. *Mathematical discovery*. Vol. 1. New York: John Wiley & Sons.

———. 1965. *Mathematical discovery*. Vol. 2. New York: John Wiley & Sons.

Popper, Karl Raimund. 1963. *Conjectures and refutations*. London: Routledge & Kegan Paul.

———. 1972. *Objective knowledge: An evolutionary approach*. Oxford: Clarendon Press.

Przelecki, Marian. 1969. *The logic of empirical theories*. London: Routledge & Kegan Paul.

Salmon, Wesley C. 1984. *Scientific explanation and the causal structure of the world*. Princeton, NJ: Princeton University Press.

———. 1990. *Four decades of scientific explanation*. Minneapolis: University of Minnesota Press.

Sneed, Joseph D. 1971. *The logical structure of mathematical physics*. Dordrecht, Netherlands: D. Reidel Publishing.

Stegmüller, Wolfgang. 1976. *The structure and dynamics of theories*. New York: Springer-Verlag.

———. 1979. *The structuralist view of theories*. Berlin: Springer-Verlag.

Suppe, Frederick. 1989. *The semantic conception of theories and scientific realism*. Urbana: University of Illinois Press.

Suppe, Frederick, ed. 1974. *The structure of scientific theories*. Urbana: University of Illinois Press.

Suppes, Patrick. 1957. *Introduction to logic*. Princeton, NJ: D. Van Nostrand Company.

———. 1967. What is a scientific theory? In *Philosophy of science today*, 55–67. See Morgenbesser 1967.

———. 1969. *Studies in the methodology and foundations of science: Selected papers from 1951 to 1969*. Dordrecht, Netherlands: D. Reidel Publishing.

van Fraassen, Bas C. 1967. Meaning relations among predicates. *Nous* 1:161–79.

———. 1969. Meaning relations and modalities. *Nous* 3:155–67.

———. 1970. On the extension of Beth's semantics of physical theories. *Philosophy of Science* 37:325–39.

———. 1972. A formal approach to the philosophy of science. In *Paradigms and paradoxes*, 303–66. See Colodny 1972.

———. 1980. *The scientific image*. Oxford: Clarendon Press.

———. 1985. Empiricism in philosophy of science. In *Images of science*, 245–308. See Churchland and Hooker 1985.

———. 1989. *Laws and symmetry*. Oxford: Clarendon Press.
Veloso, Paulo A. S. 1984. Aspectos de uma teoria geral de problemas. *Cadernos de Historia e Filosofia da Ciência* 7:21–42.
Wessels, Linda. 1974. Laws and meaning postulates. In *PSA 1974*, 215–34. See Hooker and Micholos 1976.
Westfall, Richard S. 1977. *The construction of modern science: Mechanisms and mechanics*. Cambridge: Cambridge University Press.

Cognition and philosophy of mind (chapter 4)

Anderson, John R. 1990. *Cognitive psychology and its implications*. New York: W. H. Freeman.
Bechtel, William, and Adele Abrahamsen. 1991. *Connectionism and the mind*. Cambridge, MA: Basil Blackwell.
Benacerraff, Paul. 1967. God, the devil, and Gödel. *The Monist* 51:9–32.
Boden, Margareth A. 1988. *Computer models of mind*. Cambridge: Cambridge University Press.
Brown, R. 1973. *A first language*. Cambridge: Harvard University Press.
Busemeyer, J. R., and J. T. Townsend. 1993. Decision field theory: A dynamical-cognitive approach to decision making in an uncertain environment. *Psychological Review* 100:432–59.
Bybee, J. L., and D. I. Slobin. 1982. Rules and schemas in the development and use of the English past tense. *Language* 58:265–89.
Churchland, Paul M. 1979. *Scientific realism and the plasticity of mind*. Cambridge: Cambridge University Press.
———. 1988. *Matter and consciousness.* Revised edition. Cambridge: The MIT Press.
———. 1989. *A neurocomputational perspective*. Cambridge: The MIT Press.
Churchland, Paul M., and Patricia Smith Churchland. 1990. Could a machine think? *Scientific American* 262, 1:32–37.
Clark, Andy. 1989. *Microcognition: Philosophy, cognitive science, and parallel distributed processing*. Cambridge: The MIT Press.
Colombo, J., and J. W. Fagen, eds. 1990. *Individual differences in infancy: Reliability, stability and prediction*. Hillsdale, NJ: L. Erlbaum Associates.
Davis, Steven, ed. 1992. *Connectionism: Theory and practice*. New York: Oxford University Press.
Dewdney, A. K. 1991. Insectoids invade a field of robots. *Scientific American* July:118–21.
Dreyfus, Hubert L., and Stuart E. Dreyfus. 1986. *Mind over machine*. New York: The Free Press.
Ervin, S. 1964. Imitation and structural change in children's language. In *New directions in the study of language*. See Lennenberg 1964.
Feigenbaum, Edward A. 1959. *An information processing theory of verbal learning*. P-1817. Santa Monica, CA: The Rand Corporation Mathematics Division.
———. 1963. The simulation of verbal learning behavior. In *Computers and thought*. See Feigenbaum and Feldman 1963.

Feigenbaum, Edward A., and Herbert A. Simon. 1962. A theory of the serial position effect. *British Journal of Psychology* 53, 3:307–20.

Feigenbaum, Edward A., and Julian Feldman, eds. 1963. *Computers and thought*. New York: Mc-Graw Hill.

Fetzer, J., ed. 1988. *Aspects of artificial intelligence*. Dordrecht, Netherlands: Kluwer Academic Publishers.

Fodor, Jerry A. 1975. *The language of thought*. New York: Thomas Y. Crowell.

———. 1979. *The modularity of mind*. Cambridge: The MIT Press.

Fodor, Jerry A., and Zenon W. Pylyshyn. 1988. Connectionism and cognitive architecture: A critical analysis. *Cognition* 28:3–71.

Freeman, W. J. 1991. The physiology of perception. *Scientific American* 264:78–85.

Giunti, Marco. 1992. *Computers, dynamical systems, phenomena, and the mind*. Doctoral dissertation. Bloomington: Indiana University, Department of History and Philosophy of Science.

———. 1995. Dynamical models of cognition. In *Mind as motion: Explorations in the dynamics of cognition*, 549–77. See Port and van Gelder (eds.) 1995.

Good, I. J. 1967. Human and machine logic. *The British Journal for the Philosophy of Science* 18:144–47.

———. 1969. Gödel theorem is a red herring. *The British Journal for the Philosophy of Science* 19:357–58.

Harnad, Stevan. 1987. Category induction and representation. In *Categorical perception: The groundwork of cognition*. See Harnad (ed.) 1987.

———. 1989. Minds, machines, and Searle. *Journal of Experimental and Theoretical Artificial Intelligence* 1:5–25.

———. 1990. The Symbol Grounding Problem. *Physica D* 42:335–46.

Harnad, Stevan, ed. 1987. *Categorical perception: The groundwork of cognition*. New York: Cambridge University Press.

Haugeland, John, ed. 1987. *Mind design*. Cambridge: The MIT Press.

Hofstadter, Douglas R. 1979. *Gödel, Escher, Bach*. New York: Basic Books.

Hofstadter, Douglas R., and Daniel C. Dennett, eds. 1981. *The mind's I*. New York: Basic Books.

Izawa, Hizuko, ed. 1989. *Current issues in cognitive processes*. Hillsdale, NJ: L. Erlbaum Associates.

Johnson-Laird, Philip N. 1988. *The computer and the mind*. Cambridge: Harvard University Press.

Judson, Webb. 1968. Metamathematics and the philosophy of the mind. *Philosophy of Science* 35:156–78.

Korb, Kevin. 1991. Searle's AI program. *Journal of Theoretical and Experimental Artificial Intelligence* 2:283–96.

Kuzcaj, S. A. 1977. The acquisition of regular and irregular past tense forms. *Journal of Verbal Learning and Verbal Behavior* 16:589–600.

Lee Bowie, G. 1982. Luca's number is finally up. *Journal of Philosophical Logic* 1982:279–85.

Lennenberg, E., ed. 1964. *New directions in the study of language*. Cambridge, MA: the MIT Press.

Lewis, David. 1979. Lucas against mechanism II. *Canadian Journal of Philosophy* IX, 3:373–76.

Lucas, J. R. 1961. Minds, machines and Gödel. *Philosophy* 36:112–27.
———. 1968a. Satan stultified: A rejoinder to Paul Benacerraff. *The Monist* 52:145–58.
———. 1968b. Human and machine logic: A rejoinder. *British Journal for the Philosophy of Science* 19:155–56.
Maudlin, Tim. 1989. Computation and consciousness. *The Journal of Philosophy* LXXXVI, 8:407–32.
McClelland, James L. 1981. Retrieving general and specific information from stored knowledge of specifics. In *Proceedings of the Third Annual Meeting of the Cognitive Science Society*, 170–72.
McClelland, James L., and David E. Rumelhart. 1988. *Explorations in parallel distributed processing: A handbook of models, programs, and exercises*. Cambridge: The MIT Press.
Minsky, M., and S. Papert. 1969. *Perceptrons*. Cambridge: The MIT Press.
Nagel, Thomas. 1981. What is it like to be a bat? In *The mind's I*, 391–403. See Hofstadter and Dennett 1981.
Newell, Allen. 1980. Physical symbol systems. *Cognitive Science* 4:135–83.
Newell, Allen, and Herbert Simon. 1972. *Human problem solving*. Englewood Cliffs, NJ: Prentice Hall.
Penrose, Roger. 1989. *The emperor's new mind*. Oxford: Oxford University Press.
Port, Robert F., and Timothy van Gelder, eds. 1995. *Mind as motion: Explorations in the dynamics of cognition*. Cambridge: The MIT Press.
Putnam, Hilary. 1960. Review of Nagel E. and Newman R. Gödel's Proof. *Philosophy of Science* 27:205–7.
Pylyshyn, Zenon W. 1980. Computation and cognition: Issues in the foundations of cognitive science. *The Behavioral and Brain Sciences* 3:111–69.
———. 1984. *Computation and cognition*. Cambridge: The Mit Press.
Pylyshyn, Zenon W., and Liam J. Bannon, eds. 1989. *Perspectives on the computer revolution*. Norwood, NJ: Ablex Publishing.
Pylyshyn, Zenon W., and William Demopoulos, eds. 1986. *Meaning and cognitive structure*. Norwood, NJ: Ablex Publishing.
Rapaport, W. 1988. Syntactic semantics. In *Aspects of artificial intelligence*. See Fetzer 1988.
Rumelhart, D. E., and J. L. McClelland. 1986. On learning the past tenses of English verbs. In *Parallel distributed processing*, vol. 2, 216–71. See Rumelhart and McClelland (eds.) 1986.
Rumelhart, David E., and James L. McClelland, eds. 1986. *Parallel distributed processing*. 2 vols. Cambridge: The MIT Press.
Saltzman, E., and J. A. S. Kelso. 1987. Skilled actions: A task dynamic approach. *Psychological Review* 94:84–106.
Skarda, C. A., and W. J. Freeman. 1987. Brain makes chaos to make sense of the world. *Behavioral and Brain Sciences* 10:161–95.
Searle, John. 1980. Minds, brains, and programs. *The Behavioral and Brain Sciences* 3:417–24.
———. 1984. *Minds, brains and science*. Cambridge: Harvard University Press.
———. 1990a. Is the brain's mind a computer program? *Scientific American* 262, 1:26–31.

Searle, John. 1990b. Is the brain a digital computer? *Proceedings and Addresses of the American Philosophical Association* 64, 3:21–37.

Shank, Roger C., and Kenneth Mark Colby, eds. 1973. *Computer models of thought and language*. San Francisco: W. H. Freeman.

Smart, J. J. C. 1961. Gödel's theorem, Church's theorem, and mechanism. *Synthese* 13, 1961:105–10.

Smith, Linda B., and Esther Thelen, eds. 1993. *A dynamic systems approach to development: Applications*. Cambridge: The MIT Press.

Smolensky, P. 1988. On the proper treatment of connectionism. *The Behavioral and Brain Sciences* 11:1–74.

Thelen, Esther. 1990. Dynamical systems and the generation of individual differences. In *Individual differences in infancy: Reliability, stability and prediction*. See Colombo and Fagen 1990.

Townsend, J. T., and J. R. Busemeyer. 1989. Approach-avoidance: Return to dynamic decision behavior. In *Current issues in cognitive processes*. See Izawa 1989.

Turing, Alan M. 1956. Computing machinery and thinking. *Mind* LIX, 236:433–60.

Turvey, M. T. 1990. Coordination. *American Psychologist* 45:938–53.

Tye, Michael. 1989. *The metaphysics of mind*. Cambridge: Cambridge University Press.

van Geert, P. 1991. A dynamic systems model of cognitive and language growth. *Psychological Review* 98:3–53.

van Gelder, Tim. 1991. Connectionism and dynamical explanation. In *Proceedings of the 13th Annual Conference of the Cognitive Science Society*, 499–503. Hillsdale, NJ: L. Erlbaum Associates.

———. 1992. The proper treatment of cognition. In *Proceedings of the 14th Annual Conference of the Cognitive Science Society*. Hillsdale, NJ: L. Erlbaum Associates.

Winograd, Terry. 1983. *Language as a cognitive process*. Vol. I, *Syntax*. Reading, MA: Addison-Wesley.

Index